THE BRAVE REMEMBERED

Battle Men at War 1914–1919

THE BRAVE REMEMBERED

Battle Men at War 1914–19

George Kiloh

The Battle and District Historical Society

ISBN: 978-1-903099-01-8

First published in the UK by
The Battle and District Historical Society
c/o 16 Upper Lake, BATTLE, East Sussex TN33 0AN
Tel: 01424 775590 / 07836 522257
E-mail: neil@clephane-cameron.com
Contact: Neil Clephane-Cameron, Honorary Secretary
www.battlehistorysociety.btck.co.uk

Typeset in Garamond by Helm Information
amandahelm@helm-information.co.uk

Printed and bound in Great Britain by
Berforts Information Press Ltd

Contents

Illustrations

Maps

**see colour section between pp. 90 and 91*

Preface

"Show me a hero and I will write you a tragedy."
F. Scott Fitzgerald, *The Crack-Up*, ed. Edmund Wilson, 1945

Every November we observe a minute's silence in memory of those who have died in war. The precise moment is eleven in the morning of 11 November, the point at which the guns fell silent in 1918. Though many have died in war since then, that moment remains our guide. The shadow of 1914–18 hangs over us.

The parades preceding the silence usually make for the local war memorial. In almost every town and village there are monuments that try to list those who went from there and never returned. Even more than in later wars, in 1914–18 almost every family in the land was touched by death, let alone by the less immediate effects on their loved ones by way of wounds and mental disorder. But the memorials are just lists. And very few show the names of those who went out and were lucky enough to come back.

What we do not know is who those men really were: what they did for a living, where they lived and what their families were like; or how and where they died. We know even less of those who returned, even when they had been wounded, physically or mentally or sometimes both. Yet whether a man was killed or survived was by chance – where his battalion was sent, what actions were required of him, whether a shell or a bullet or a microbe put an end to him – and so death was wholly unpredictable. Some men served unscathed throughout the war. Others died on their first appearance at the front. Very many were wounded, gassed or suffered mental trauma. We praise those who died as heroes, while failing to give the same honour to the survivors.

So this account attempts to identify all of the men of Battle who played a naval or military role in the Great War of 1914–18. It is also an attempt to provide more than the bare lists that one can already find inadequately and sometimes inaccurately given on the various memorials: it tries to give some background to those who fought and in particular to those who died or were wounded, and to give some context for the actions in which they took part. It is certain that over 393 men went to the war from Battle and returned alive, though identifying them all would almost certainly be too hard to achieve at this distance of time. The list of those who survived is here relegated to an appendix, though the main account includes them if they are known to have been wounded or to have made themselves noticeable in some other way.

Battle is a small town, and it was even smaller a century ago. But men of Battle fought in almost every theatre of the war: on the sea and in the air, and on land not only on the western front but also in Mesopotamia, Palestine, Salonica, Gallipoli, east Africa and Italy. They also served in India, Egypt, Russia and even the United States. Very few of them would have left British shores before and so, at least at the beginning, to join up must have been to take part in a great adventure.

There is no need here to rehearse the stories of all the botched offensives that cost so many lives at the gain of so little ground, though some background information is inevitable: why, and rather how, we went to war, how the men were recruited, what the conflicts were in which the men of Battle engaged. The wider view is for the many historians who have tried to establish why the war began and why it continued for so long.

When a man has been identified as dying or wounded or mentioned in the text for some other special reason I have tried to fill in rather more about him without naming descendants or near-relatives likely to be still alive. This has meant recourse not only to the surviving military records but also to the public records on births, marriages and deaths and the census returns available up to and including 1911. In some cases this has been very difficult. Some names are more common than others. People move away or arrive at points inconvenient to the researcher: for example those who arrived in Battle between the 1911 census and the end of the war are very hard to pin down. In later years some moved elsewhere and some would have emigrated, and census data are not yet available for 1921 and later. Some worked at Battle but lived elsewhere, and they can be traced only with great difficulty.

By 'Battle' is meant the town of Battle, including Netherfield and Telham. Extending the definition would be possible, for example by including Whatlington – and indeed the boundary between Battle and Whatlington has changed since that war – but where does one stop? The ancient Hundred of Battle comprised Battle and Whatlington; the Battle Union (for the poor law) and the original Battle Rural District went much further, as did the Petty Session area. But in 1914–18 Battle was well-defined as a single civil parish and urban district, so I have confined the study to that one area. In doing so one must include Netherfield, which was ecclesiastically and physically separate but a place then and now with very strong connections to the main town of Battle, indeed being officially part of the town. The changes to the boundaries, although minor, are rather more worrying: Battle has shrunk a little along its eastern side. But these changes were made only after the second world war, so I have included in the records one man who lived in the area later lost to Sedlescombe.

There is also the question of the kind of connection with Battle that places a man on the local record. Certainly being born here (though some moved away at a very young age) would qualify; so would marrying someone from Battle. But simply working in the town is less convincing, although inconsistently applied in the memorial record: it includes a postman from Hastings but not one from Pevensey or a policeman from Brighton. Being at school here suggests that the parents lived here, but not necessarily and if so for how long? And did the schoolchildren actually live in Battle? I have tried not to discriminate too finely, and have added several names to the lists. In some cases the men concerned might never have even visited the town but they are still listed because of their family connections, following the logic apparently adopted by the then Dean in drawing up the names for the churchyard memorial, so there is an element of fairness at work here. I have, however, omitted those who came to Battle later.

At least 500 men joined the ranks who qualify for inclusion in this record; there were almost certainly many more. As in every part of Britain, they came from all walks of life, from the humblest road-man and farm labourer to the family that provided the lords of the manor. In appendix A there is a crude analysis of where the men (or their families) lived who were killed, and it will be seen that no part at all of Battle was spared the fear that their fathers, brothers and sons, their daughters' husbands and even their grandsons, would be mutilated or killed. The same kind of analysis is made for the survivors at the end of appendix B.

Similarly the later effects of the war have not been considered. Of course its effects in general have been the subject of many works even if, as Chou En-lai is reported to have said when asked of the effects of the French Revolution of 1789, 'it is too early to say'. Not much has been done on local effects, and this is a possible further area of research, though a difficult one given that it would be difficult to associate known changes with the war itself rather than with wider social, economic and cultural factors. On the wider issues of international effects one can say only that the war created the conditions for the Bolshevik coup of 1917 and that the peace settlements after the war led almost directly to the second. Taken together one can with some confidence say that this was the point at which Europe committed collective suicide, not only in human terms but as the leader of the world.

This is not another history of the war. There must be thousands already. In general I do not try to argue in detail the case for or against any particular action or inaction, to describe conditions in detail or to try to explain why warfare began, or continued for so long, or ended when it did; ideally the men must do that. It is a record of what the people of a small Sussex town did: how they answered the call to arms and fought the enemy, and how, in over a hundred cases, they lost their lives.

I am aware that there may be mistakes in any study of this kind. There will also inevitably be omissions. It would be good to have them pointed out.

Sources

Other than the names on the memorials the only collected local record is the Netherfield List held by the East Sussex Records Office. This has ninety entries, though two appear to be for the same man; it originally had a photograph for each of them, though a very few have now been lost. In almost every case the official records substantiate the claim that the man concerned 'belonged' to Netherfield, and the presence of the tiny handful of others has been taken in this account as proof that that was so of them too. The List also contains (very few) press cuttings, though they are undated and unattributed. The List does in fact omit at least some men, but it remains a much more comprehensive statement than anything from the centre of Battle, and for men from the main town we must look elsewhere once we have examined the names on the two memorials.

The first national resource is by those responsible for the 'rolls of honour' website. It has two lists, one for Battle itself and one for Netherfield, both based on the churchyard lists. (There is also a scroll in Netherfield church.) There are others by the same organisation, for example for Ashburnham, Bexhill and Crowhurst that contain Battle names not listed in the town itself. In this account these records are referred to simply as the Roll of Honour.

The second national resource is by Hugh Miller: *We wunt be druv* (Reveille Press, 2010), a very detailed history of the involvement of The Royal Sussex Regiment on the western front – it was active also in India, the Near East and in Italy – charting each battalion's experiences and listing all those killed, matching their deaths with the actions on the days concerned. Unless otherwise noted, details of the regiment's actions are from this work. One of Miller's great-uncles, though a Pevensey man, is listed here among Battle's dead.

Behind those works is the massive database organised by www.ancestry.co.uk which carries (not without problems) data on all births, marriages and deaths at least since 1837 and is host to the military records of the war. Those who served can be difficult to identify from this source because most of those military records were lost through enemy action in the second world war. Nevertheless much information survives, and it happens that much more is available than for 1939–45 because official records for the later war have not yet been released. (Because of its sheer volume, information obtained from www.ancestry.co.uk is not referenced in the footnotes.)

Newspapers of the time are vital because they contain news of individuals that would otherwise be lost, both of the dead and of the survivors. In Battle library there is a useful list of the burials in Battle cemetery, usually giving ages and dates of death, by which some family connections can be established. Regimental histories and records and a variety of other sources have been used. However, as set out in Appendix A, in one case it has been impossible even to identify the dead man beyond his name, number and regiment, let alone his relatives. Of lesser importance is the record held by the National Archives for the Royal Navy: http://discovery. nationalarchives.gov. uk/, for few Battle men served in the Navy.

A few other sources have proved valuable and are similarly unreferenced: in particular the records of the Commonwealth War Graves Commission and of the Australian and Canadian armed forces. There are also the Royal Navy records at the National Archives. The sources of further information are mentioned below, under Acknowledgements.

It may be helpful to point out the present names of particular yards: Carriers Yard and Cruttendens Yard have not been identified, but they ran off the High Street. Kenwards Yard is the entry next to 5 High Street, off the Abbey Green. The Abbey Green itself was then known as the Market Green, though referred to here by its present name. Parks Yard is behind the Bull, off the High Street. The sites of Thorpe's Plot and Newbery's Cottages are now beneath the Mount Street car park. A list of abbreviations appears on the next page.

References to Sterling are in the original values. All references to weights and measures are in Imperial values as used at the time.

The names of counties are as difficult here as they are in present life, so much have they been tampered with over the years for specific purposes quite unrelated to the historic loyalties of the people. I have tried to keep to the original, pre-1888 position still respected by most of the 1911 census entrants (and in ordinary life by this author) but have failed to some extent to do so with London. References to Kingston and Richmond are always to Kingston and Richmond in

Surrey unless otherwise stated. Other place-names may baffle those unfamiliar with some areas of the country but space always to add county names to the appendices is very limited.

All the forces of the Crown are described in general as British, though distinguished by dominion where individuals are concerned. Such a description would have been proper at the time and so it is proper here. 1st/5th (and similar constructions) are to be interpreted as meaning the first reserve section of 5th Battalion, i e not at this point front-line troops. References greater than 1 were to sections even further back from the front.

Reference works of the time specify that the term Middle East is reserved to the area between Persia (sic) and India, inclusively. Near East was used for the Palestine–Iran area but I have followed modern usage. Mesopotamia is of course present-day Iraq.

Acknowledgements

This account owes much to a number of people, among them:

Neil Clephane-Cameron, Keith Foord and Sarah and Adrian Hall of Battle; Ian Cheveralls and Kevin Regan of Battle, the latter in particular for correcting some of my assumptions about the men and their backgrounds; Charlotte Moore of Whatlington for my being able to read the diaries of her family, text from which is reproduced with kind permission; The Estate of Edmund Blunden for its kind permission to reproduce his poem 'Pillbox'; Pan Macmillan for their permission to reprint from *The Imperial War Museum Book of the Somme* by Malcolm Brown, copyright © Malcolm Brown, 2002; The Penguin Group and Lyn Macdonald for permission to quote from *Somme* by Lyn Macdonald (Penguin Books 1993) © Lyn Macdonald and from *To The Last Man: Spring 1918* by Lyn Macdonald (Penguin Books 1999) Copyright © Lyn Macdonald and from *They Called it Passchendaele* (Penguin Books 1993) © Lyn Macdonald: all reproduced with permission by Penguin Books Ltd; David W. Hughes for his kind permission to reprint from 'The HMS Hythe Disaster' at http://www.kentfallen.com/PDF%20reports/HMS%20HYTHE.pdf; The

Imperial War Museum for their permission to reprint the maps that appear in the colour section © IWM; Councillor Sylvie Pry of Battle; Mr A Morrison, Mrs J Macvicker, Ms Sue Blackman, Ralfe Whistler, Ruth Carter, Georgina Doherty and Colin and Kathy Kiley of Battle for family information; Mike Payne of Bexhill; Battle Library for their exhibition of names and for many publications; Saxonwood House in Battle for help in trying to obtain family memories, amoung them those of Eric Holliman; the East Sussex Records Office at Falmer (in particular Ms Jenny Geering) for access to correspondence and other records and for photographs; Brigadier Hugh Willing of Battle for advice on military terminology; and finally Amanda Helm of St Leonards for her expertise in publishing.

George Kiloh
Battle, 2015

Abbreviations Used

2 Lt	Second Lieutenant
A/	Acting
AB	Able Seaman
ASC	Army Service Corps*
AVC	Army Veterinary Corps*
att	Attached
Aust	Australian
Bde	Brigade
Bn	Battalion
Capt	Captain
CB	Confined to barracks
CEF	Canadian Expeditionary Force
CMG	Commander of the Order of St Michael and St George
Coy	Company
Cpl	Corporal
CQSM	Company Quarter Master Sergeant
CSM	Company Sergeant Major
CWGC	Commonwealth War Graves Commission
DCM	Distinguished Conduct Medal
DSO	Distinguished Service Order
Gnr	Gunner
HE	High explosive
HLI	Highland Light Infantry
HMAT	His Majesty's Australian Transport
KRRC	Kings Royal Rifle Corps
L/	Lance-
L/C	Lance Corporal
Lt	Lieutenant
Maj	Major
MC	Military Cross
MM	Military Medal
NCO	Non-Commissioned Officer
NZ	New Zealand
NZEF	New Zealand Expeditionary Force
NZMGC	New Zealand Machine Gun Corps
OTC	Officer Training Corps
Pte	Private
RAF	Royal Air Force
RAMC	Royal Army Medical Corps
RE	Royal Engineers
Regt	Regiment
RFA	Royal Field Artillery
RFC	Royal Flying Corps
RGA	Royal Garrison Artillery
RHA	Royal Horse Artillery
RN	Royal Navy
RNAS	Royal Naval Air Service
RSM	Regimental Sergeant Major
RSR	The Royal Sussex Regiment
Sgt	Sergeant
Temp	Temporary
VAD	Voluntary Aid Detachment
WA	Western Australia

*Prefixed Royal from 27.11.18

Introduction

Any account of the men of Battle who went to war must start with what is already known, and that must direct us to those memorials that list the local dead. In the town itself the war memorials contain 41 and 42 names respectively (that in the churchyard being short by one compared with that in the Memorial Halls), and Netherfield adds a further 17.

The Netherfield memorial presents us with few problems. One further death was disclosed in the Roll of Honour and one has come to light since. The real difficulty is that the identity of one man on the memorial, and on the scroll in the church there, is very difficult to establish, and his likely origin are discussed elsewhere in this account. Whoever compiled the list – probably the vicar – took a fairly wide view of who should qualify for it and included at least one man who had left Netherfield at a very young age. But then, that man's father had been the vicar too, some thirty years before. The Netherfield memorial was unveiled by Brigadier General Charles George Lewes CMG DSO on 2 November 1919.[1]

But commemorating the dead of Battle itself did give rise to much greater problems, and to some extent still does. The Memorial Halls version dates from the 1930s and is quite obviously based on that in the churchyard. Therefore the original test, as it were, is of the churchyard version of 41 names. It is clearly inadequate. That memorial was the work of the Dean, the Very Rev Edward Reid Currie (Dean since 1882). The Dean cast his net very wide, including some people with very little connection with the town, but he missed a much larger number of men who had either the same degree of connection or even a much higher degree.

The origins of the memorial are known. In March 1919 a local solicitor and the great panjandrum of the town William Raper chaired a meeting to discuss how the dead might be commemorated. It appears that by the end of the month it had been agreed that a memorial should be built where it now stands, at a slight eminence towards the front of St Mary's churchyard, easily seen from the road.[2]

In fact there must have been some disagreement. There was in fact no clear resolution that the churchyard should be the site. A report from the next year reviewed the history, starting with the Raper meeting:

> Several suggestions were made at that meeting, including the erection of a maternity and nursing home, or, as an alternative, the erection of a monument in a prominent position in the town, and that any surplus funds be handed over to the Hastings Hospitals. It was decided that the Nursing Home proposal be carried forward, and a new Committee was appointed to go on with it. In this matter Mr. G. Kendall was a leading light, and worked strenuously to bring it to a successful issue. He was ably backed up by Mrs. Smithe, CBE, and other prominent residents. After circularising the town, it was feared that the scheme was not a popular one and the founders reluctantly had to drop it.
>
> A movement was put on foot to erect a copy of the London Cenotaph on a plot of ground at the cross-roads opposite the Police Station. Meanwhile the handsome memorial cross which the Dean and Mrs. Currie had provided was placed in the churchyard and dedicated at a service which will be memorable in the history of the town. In view of this, the erection of a second monument did not find popular support.
>
> The ex-Service men then came on the scene with a very worthy proposal – that of suitable club premises for their use. With the scheme – a most laudable one – came the suggestion of adding a town building, including a suitable hall, which was sadly needed for the social well-being of the town, and the inhabitants duly appointed a representative committee to carry out the details. Now this Committee have failed in their endeavour.[3]

(The reference to Kendall is to Dr George Kendall, who had proposed the home in the first place, and who is discussed later in this account. The reference to Mrs Smithe must be to Ida Elizabeth Smithe of

Campfield House (later Burnt Wood), Powdermill Lane. Her CBE in 1918 was in recognition of her work for the VAD.)

In retrospect it seems clear and understandable that the Dean wanted a memorial in his churchyard, whatever the town might conclude, if indeed it were to reach any conclusion at all. As he and his wife were bearing its costs he could proceed without delay. First, however, he had to find the names to be inscribed on the memorial, and one wonders how he managed to construct the first list of 36 of them, published, with an appeal for more, in the *Hastings Observer*.[4] It seems probable that he must have begun with the names of his parishioners whose deaths he had had to record on too many Sundays throughout the war. Five more names appeared in time, though as will now be evident there were many others that did not appear. In fact three weeks *before* his appeal the *Hastings Observer* had published a report from the Battle school showing eleven names that never reached the churchyard list, and it is a mystery why they were excluded. It is unlikely that the Dean would have ruled out any proposals, given the very broad criteria that he evidently adopted, and there could be many reasons for these further names being missed. Some families might not wish to remember; some might object to an Anglican net being cast; some might have hoped still that their sons, brothers or husbands would in time return, especially when no body had been recovered; some might have thought that their connection with Battle was too slim; others probably never knew of the appeal, especially in the many cases where the family had moved away. The search may not have been helped by the condition of the Dean and his wife Frances: she was to die early in 1920 and he a year later.

By the end of 1919 the final list of 41 names was complete, and the memorial was unveiled on 15 February 1920 in a ceremony in which the main speech was given by the Rev Prebendary Thomas William Cook, Rural Dean of Hastings and later Bishop of Lewes.[5]

The British Legion, however, wanted its own memorial, in its own club. In 1932 it ordered from Hastings Municipal School of Art the memorial that now has pride of place in the entrance to the Memorial Halls. The list of names it supplied to be included were those already on the churchyard memorial and one named *?Neeves*. This last man turned out to be Samuel Neeves, who is indeed commemorated on this board but not in the churchyard.[6] The list supplied gave accurate information on all 42 men concerned, which means that the one mistake on it must be the responsibility of the School of Art: the board lists E C instead of F C Blackman. The board was transferred to the Memorial Halls when they opened in 1960, with a further panel for 1939–45. There was no opportunity taken for a further search for names from 1914–18.

So for more than the last ninety years these 58 or 59 names have represented Battle's dead. But in the course of investigation many more have come to light, some from neighbouring memorials, some from newspaper accounts, some from internet searches and some from two pieces of research that have been very valuable. (It may be noted that the Netherfield Memorial lists two sets of brothers who died, but that the Battle memorials make no mention of brothers who died – two in each case – in the Eldridge, Ling, Meppem and Vitler families. They are included in this account.) The combined total of the names on the memorials is 59, but the total so far uncovered is 112. To these 112, Netherfield contributed 20 and Battle at least 90, in the latter case more than twice the number found by the Dean.

In one important respect this account closely follows the Dean in adopting a wide interpretation of what connection with Battle entitles a man to be remembered. Not to do so would suggest that some of his list should not be honoured on the memorials, and that must be unthinkable. It also takes account of the logic of the Netherfield Memorial, which lists some who had been born there but who had already left. But it means that some rather distant men are now newly on the list of those who died, as well as some who would qualify under any criteria.

One must be only too aware that a military study is only a part of the story. Only men could go on active service but the vital role of women in the war has been frequently discussed. Many women went as close to the front as they were allowed, mainly as nurses (who were allowed in the front lines from 1915) and some of them were killed, though none from Battle. There were also the non-combatant Women's Royal Naval Service (1917), the Women's Royal Air Force (1918) and the Women's Auxiliary Army Corps (1918), but their records have so far yielded no Battle member. One woman of the

WRNS is recorded as having been born at Battle, but further enquiry shows that the birth was actually in Ewhurst or possibly in Hastings. The one known participant was not at that stage from Battle but from Vinehall, in the parish of Mountfield: Margaret Ashton, who married into the Whistler family in 1925. (Her role is described in the chapter on 1917.)

At home the contribution of women to nursing the injured was obvious, in Battle itself but also at the hospital by the tennis courts at Normanhurst. That VAD hospital received its first convoy of wounded in June 1915, and in all it treated 1536 men during the war and lost only two of them. Writing in 1919 the Commandant (Countess Brassey, Viscountess Hythe until 1918) wrote of the staff

> performing an operation, giving an anaesthetic, doing a dressing, making a bed, giving out stores and kits, looking after the linen, cooking the food, dusting the rooms, laying the table, cleaning silver and knives, washing up greasy plates, mending endless holes in worn out linen and socks, making curtains, covering lockers, painting, or, last but not least, giving a weekly address or keeping the records and accounts; there was work for all, and very loyally and cheerfully it was done ...[7]

Many Battle names that were associated with that hospital appear later in this account – not only the mothers, wives and sisters who were the great majority of staff but also men who had been soldiers or would be later.

Women kept households going in the absence of the men, they provided 'comforts' for the men such as supplementary clothing, they looked after soldiers and refugees billeted in the town and, less identifiably, they took up work that had previously been done by the men who had left. They worked in almost every occupation that did not require specific qualifications and did not bar women on traditional grounds (working underground at the gypsum mines being the obvious local example). One could have found more women than before behind shop counters, in the tannery, in the jam factory, in Dannreuther's fruit farm and on some of the other farms. This expansion was barely organised, there being no Land Army as in the second world war. It may have begun slowly but must have accelerated with the advent of conscription in 1916. Norman Moore, a frequent visitor to London, noted on 19 June 1916 that "nearly all the omnibus conductors I now see are girls".[8] Many women elsewhere worked in munitions factories, without which the war effort would have stuttered to a halt. The local experience needs further study.

There must also have been men of the right age who did not join up. Some were exempted on grounds of disability, some on grounds of conscience, and some for their reserved occupations, which at Battle could understandably include providing foodstuffs for the forces and for the country at large. Their histories have melted away. Of the refusers we know only the stories of the famous – and none of them were from Battle. There was one man from Battle who was exempted from combatant service and was conscripted into the Non Combatant Corps: Basil Abbotts Warren. He had been born at Wooburn near Marlow in Buckinghamshire and was 35 when he was called up in 1916. In 1911 he was recorded as a bank clerk living at 9 St Mary's Villas. He never married and died at Heathfield in 1936. In addition, those who were too old or too young must have contributed to the war effort in ways that have never been explored.

Notes

1 *Hastings Observer,* 1 November 1919.
2 *Hastings Observer,* 29 March 1919.
3 *Hastings Observer,* 19 June 1920.
4 *Hastings Observer*, 14 June 1919.
5 *Hastings Observer,* 21 February 1920.
6 Correspondence held by East Sussex Records Office.
7 Normanhurst VAD Hospital (Martin & Sturt, printers, Farnham), 1919
8 Norman Moore diary.

1

The Beginning of the War

In 1939 the British had long expected involvement in a European war, but in 1914, right up to the very last few days of peace, they did not. The country had other serious problems, Ireland (then of course part of the United Kingdom), labour troubles and women's suffrage being among the most pressing. But within a few days Britain was to be involved in its first western European war for very nearly a century. Unlike previous wars, it would involve almost every family and every settlement down to the smallest hamlet.

Battle had then rather less than half the population it has now. The 1911 census reported 2,924 inhabitants in the civil parish. This area was almost exactly the same as that now covered by Battle Town Council, including Netherfield and Telham. The town itself had 2,503 people. From 1894 it had had an elected urban district council with duties to provide clean water and to rid the town of nuisances such as overflowing sewage. It had recently obtained planning powers and the power to build houses. Since 1889 main roads and education had been responsibilities of the new council for the eastern half of the county.

In 1914 there was not only substantial self-government but also substantial commercial autonomy. Though even in those days there was one (almost) chain shop – International Stores at 61 High Street – all ordinary supplies were available from a number of competing traders. Those in the High Street alone included, among others, five bakers/confectioners, two butchers, three grocers, a fishmonger, two general stores, three shoe shops and six clothing shops. Telephones were for the privileged few, and in 1914/15 only 12 of the 85 properties in the High Street (excluding the telephone exchange itself) published numbers for themselves.[1] And of course there were no broadcasts, let alone any electronic communication. Urgent messages went by bicycle or by telegram, though the postal service was so efficient that in many circumstances one could receive a reply to a letter on the same day that it had been sent. A motor bus service had begun but the normal mode of transport was by train or horse cart or bicycle or foot. Motor cars were known but confined to the wealthy.

Such electricity as there was came from a few private generators and batteries – for example on the Abbey estate, which had its own electrician, and at the workhouse from 1915 – and not until 1918 was there serious discussion of obtaining a mains supply for the whole town. The turn of Netherfield would come later. Almost every property relied instead on gas or oil lamps or candles, as did the streets. As to visitors, one guidebook recommended the accommodation available at the George and the Star Hotels (rooms at 2/6d per night);[2] perhaps the Railway Hotel was cheaper. It was common practice for hotels to employ coachmen to meet the trains, and a son of the Railway Hotel coachman appears in this account.

On all sides the town was pressed in by large estates and farms. The greatest estate was of course the Abbey, owned again since 1902 by the Webster family and including Powdermill, but south of that there were Telham Court and Beauport Park. There were no housing estates except for the very recent creation of six council houses on Netherfield Hill;[3] new developments came only in the 1920s.

Except for those on the farms and the large estates, almost all Battle residents lived along the main roads and lanes, an ancient feature of the town that is still obvious. They lived in Lower and Upper Lake, the High Street, Mount Street and the St Mary's area of Battle Hill, though there were small settlements at Watch Oak and Virgins Croft, in detached houses along North Trade Road and on the north side of Hastings Road to just after the Blacksmith's Arms. What is now the entry road to Glen Gorse was then the private lane through woods to Telham Court with a large field where the houses now stand; the gate lodge remains at the corner of Battle Hill. What is now Frederick Thatcher Place at the edge of town on North Trade Road was a large workhouse. In 1911 it had 14 officers and their families and 122 inmates. It was run by the Battle Union, a grouping of parishes created in 1835 under the 1834 Poor Law Act.

As to industry, there were some substantial employers apart from the farmers and the estates. The Newbery jam factory was a major concern, reported as employing 60 people in 1916,[4] though the tannery on Battle Hill (where Tesco now stands) was smaller. The brewery was still in its yard, as it remains, and though it had produced no beer since 1911 it was a depot for Ballards of Lewes. The shops, inns and hotels provided more work. There was a constant demand for grooms and gardeners. The railway was busy and a substantial employer. Today there are only the two through tracks but earlier there were sidings on either side of them and a large goods yard on what is now the lower part of the station car park, with a building and a crane, with further lines into what is now Foster's Motors. In addition more staff were needed simply to keep the railway moving, including porters, platelayers and the signalman at Marley Lane. The gas works was in Lower Lake, where Picardy Close now stands, a position that required coal to be carted the short distance from the station just as it was, much further, to the work-house far along North Trade Road and to almost every house.

Netherfield was conveniently placed for the Mountfield gypsum mine, opened in 1876 and subsequently greatly expanded, which was the source of employment for many of its men in this account. Even in 1878 it was employing 60–70 men to produce about 300 tons each week,[5] and at least 47 Battle men at the 1911 census. The mine was less than a mile from Netherfield church.

Many of the unmarried women were 'in service', that is, they were domestic servants in better-off households. Very few married women were in employment though a few had incomes as laundresses or dressmakers or helped their husbands in their businesses, a situation that lasted until after the next world war. Many women helped in the fields at harvest-time. More of them would have done so after the formation of the Women's Land Army in response to the food crisis of 1917.

The occupations of those who fought, or of their fathers if they were very young when the information was given, show how greatly Battle has changed. Netherfield had a very flat social structure, dominated by farm workers and those connected with the gypsum works; Battle itself was more mixed but the middle classes were much weaker than now. One can pick out of group of gentry, very small indeed, followed by an only slightly larger group of professionals – doctors, hotel managers, bank managers and lawyers. Then there were the traders and manufacturers, mostly self-employed. There was also a small group who occupied some of the offices in the town, the most notable being the Ticehursts who had been postmasters and stationers but were later registrars and clerks to several of the public bodies. And then there was the great mass of carters, carmen, general labourers, builders' labourers, railway porters, jam boilers, tannery workers, farm workers, shop assistants and so on.

In 1914 the thought of war can hardly have been in the minds of the people of Battle, let alone of a major and bloody conflict that would last more than four years and that would lead to another, longer, war within a generation. Over the previous fifteen years it was Germany that had become the perceived threat rather than France, the traditional enemy against whom coastal fortifications had been renewed as recently as at the turn of the century, but that such a threat should lead to war was barely thinkable. People were living in what appears in retrospect to have been a stable and peaceable part of a great empire with which any kind of contest was barely conceivable, albeit a part with very great differences among its people in wealth and status. If there were tensions on the Continent, there usually were; no doubt many Britons thought that that was how foreigners always behaved. The murders of the heir to the throne of Austria–Hungary and of his wife increased those tensions, but not until later was there a suspicion that within a very short time Britain would be engaged in war. Even in the last week of July the general view was that Britain could and should stand aside from any more general conflict.

The murders were on 28 June. It took until 23 July for the Austrians to send a Note to Serbia that amounted to an ultimatum, with 48 hours in which to reply, and war between them followed on 28 July. Thereafter the system of European alliances and the strategic requirements of the German armed forces led to the German declaration against Russia on 1 August and to the invasion of Belgium the next day, a country that had long held a guarantee of neutrality and protection from Germany, Britain and France. There then followed the German declaration against France on 3 August. On the same day Britain mobilised its forces and gave Germany an ultimatium; it expired in the last hour of the day. The British declaration against Austria waited a few days. Within weeks Turkey and Bulgaria came in on the side of Germany; Portugal joined the Allies late in 1914, Italy in the spring of 1915 and Romania in 1916.

Early August was the height of the holiday season, and 3 August had been a bank holiday. Hastings was a centre of the holiday trade, and for some time there seems to have been little change to its habits. The hotels were full and concerts went on. At first there were no efforts to expel the numerous enemy aliens in the town. Indeed, on 15 August there was a report of an enthusiastic response to a concert given by the Blue Hungarian Band at the Hastings Pier Pavilion, conducted by Herr Bernhard Nussbaum.[6] The cricket season was in full swing, and at first there was no thought of cancelling matches. Nor, until 1915, were there controls placed on showing lights at night; and not until the summer of 1916 did petrol begin to be rationed. Some foods were rationed from 1917. In other words, this was nothing like the total war that was to arrive so rapidly in 1939.

That journal of the upper and middle classes, *Punch*, summed it up well for August 1914:

> Four weeks ago we stood on the verge of the great upheaval and knew it not. We were thinking of holidays; of cricket and golf and bathing, and then we were suddenly plunged in the deep waters of the greatest of all Wars. It has been a month of rude awakening, of revelation, of discovery – of many moods varying from confidence to deep misgiving, yet dominated by a sense of relief that England has chosen the right course.[7]

It is hard now to accept that the war was actually popular. One diarist reported crowds in Trafalgar Square on 3 August that were very enthusiastic (but rather irresponsible, he added).[8] There was similar enthusiasm for war elsewhere. One can see the change of mood from about 1916, as poetry took on a sombre tone, leading to the expression of a kind of dark despair. But at the beginning and at least early in 1915 things were different, even as the death rolls and the lines of wounded lengthened.

Some informed observers, including those in government, failed to share *Punch*'s reported confidence in continued peace. Already the German economy had overtaken that of Britain, the home of the industrial revolution. To prevent one country from dominating Europe had been a principal foreign policy objective of Britain for a very long time, and the preservation of the balance of power was regarded as essential. The German army was regarded as highly effective, and not only for its swift defeat of France in 1870–71. Some believed that if war broke out it would be in Paris in about a week and certainly in less than a fortnight.[9] There can have been little confidence in the ability of the French to repel it without outside support.

The general and optimistic view was that, if Britain had to fight, it would be unassailable and would certainly win in a short time too. However, the British naval and military commands had seen things without complacency. The mobilisation of British forces was one of the very few things about the war of which the high command could justly be proud. They and the government moved fast. In fact the first British officers landed in France as early as 7 August, and first fighting units on 13 August. The high command did have some difficulties and there were confusions. For example the Grenadier Guards were sent up to the Cromarty Firth by mistake and after a day were called back,[10] and depots had great difficulty handling the unheralded arrival of large numbers of new recruits. The Whatlington man who was the first local man to die in the war recorded that he and his men arrived at Le Havre on 28 August but were then shunted about France, reaching Amiens only in mid-October. In the meantime they had visited Le Mans, St Nazaire, Angers, Nantes and Versailles.[11]

The King and the Prime Minister issued proclamations on 4 August. Of those issued by the King, the first called out the Army Reserve – those men who had left the forces but were still of an age to serve and those in the various local territorial forces. The second required those men who were about to be transferred to the Reserve to remain in the forces. The Prime Minister, Asquith, issued two more, with more general effect. The first authorised requisitioning:

> requiring Justices of the Peace to issue warrants for the provision, for the purposes mentioned in the Requisition, of carriages, animals, vessels, and aircraft, ...
>
> ... His Majesty's Order may authorise ... Officers to extend such Requisitions to the provision of carriages, animals, vessels, and aircraft for the purpose of being purchased, as well as of being hired, on His Majesty's behalf ...

The second extended the concept of requisitioning to the billeting of servicemen:

> ... His Majesty ... is pleased to order and authorise any General or Field Officer Commanding any part of His Majesty's Forces in any military district or place in the United Kingdom to issue Billeting Requisitions under the said Act.

Already there was a comprehensive and detailed War Book defining the action to be taken in case of war. It was a set of documents covering everything needed for mobilisation, and relevant instructions were already in the safes of every authority, whether governmental, naval, military or commercial. It dealt not only with actual mobilisation but with overseas travel and communications, with international financial transactions and insurance. It needed only the insertion of the enemy's name. In Battle as in every other town in the country the authorities were therefore on full alert from 3 August.

There was another sense in which every town was prepared. Everywhere there was a Territorial Army unit that trained volunteers in preparation for war. In Battle this was B Company of 5th Battalion, the Royal Sussex Regiment: the Cinque Ports Battalion. Many of those who were to serve had been trained in it or were active volunteers when the war began. The availability of the Territorial Army must have been of enormous benefit to a country whose small army was no match in numbers for those of the continental Powers and where conscription did not appear until 1916.

On the declaration of war the service commands immediately sent telegrams to all regulars on leave and to all territorial forces and reservists, requiring them to report for service. At the same time control of the railways passed from the companies concerned to the

War Office, under the Regulation of the Forces Act 1871. This meant that the railway companies still owned and operated the lines but that military and naval demands were to be given absolute priority. As the railways also owned the cross-channel ferries the operation of those services was affected, and the government also had powers to commandeer other vessels. The war did not stop the holiday season, of course: the railways put on augmented services that month between London and the south coast for holiday traffic and continued to do so for some summers. It was thought, for example, that at the August bank holiday of 1915 Battle had the largest number of visitors in its history,[12] and the great majority must have come by train.

Requisitions began during the very first days of the war, beginning with horses, which were needed in very large numbers. On 7 August there was a sharp indication of the new state of things. The fortnightly meeting in Battle of the Battle Guardians (who ran the poor law Union), took place as usual, and most members would have come to it by horse or horse-drawn vehicles – understandably so given the few motor cars available and the deeply rural nature of the area. But the meeting was interrupted by an army officer who informed the members that he was requisitioning their horses. The members then had to find their own way home to Brightling, Penhurst and elsewhere.[13] A few days later George Dann, a Whatlington farmer, complained that his horse had gone, and how was he now to get his produce to Hastings? He might have to buy a motor.[14] The same was happening across the country.

The famous Defence of the Realm Act was passed on 8 August. In its original form it was brief but firm. However it became rapidly clear that rather more drastic powers were necessary if disaffection were to be kept in check and the war pursued under military control, and it was amended on various occasions, the last being on 27 November. In its final form it read:

> (1) His Majesty in Council has power during the continuance of the present war to issue regulations for securing the public safety and the defence of the realm, and as to the powers and duties for that purpose of the Admiralty and Army Council and of the members of His Majesty's forces and other persons acting in his behalf; and may by such regulations authorise the trial by courts-martial, or in

> the case of minor offences by courts of summary jurisdiction, and punishment of persons committing offences against the regulations and in particular against any of the provisions of such regulations designed:
>
> (a) to prevent persons communicating with the enemy or obtaining information for that purpose or any purpose calculated to jeopardise the success of the operations of any of His Majesty's forces or the forces of his allies or to assist the enemy; or
>
> (b) to secure the safety of His Majesty's forces and ships and the safety of any means of communication and of railways, ports, and harbours; or
>
> (c) to prevent the spread of false reports or reports likely to cause disaffection to His Majesty or to interfere with the success of His Majesty's forces by land or sea or to prejudice His Majesty's relations with foreign powers; or
>
> (d) to secure the navigation of vessels in accordance with directions given by or under the authority of the Admiralty; or
>
> (e) otherwise to prevent assistance being given to the enemy or the successful prosecution of the war being endangered.
>
> (3) It shall be lawful for the Admiralty or Army Council:
>
> (a) to require that there shall be placed at their disposal the whole or any part of the output of any factory or workshop in which arms, ammunition, or warlike stores and equipment, or any articles required for the production thereof, are manufactured;
>
> (b) to take possession of, and use for the purpose of, His Majesty's naval or military service any such factory or workshop or any plant thereof.

It was under this Act that postal censorship was instituted, with large buildings being commandeered for the purpose, that objectors to the war were sometimes imprisoned and a whole host of other actions taken, some of which were not easily or promptly reversed after peace came.

Despite the local popularity of individual 'enemy aliens' there was much resentment at their continued presence in Sussex, and a great fear of their spying. Almost immediately after the declaration of war there was compulsory registration of all aliens, and there were fines for any landlord, lodging-house keeper or anyone offering accommodation who failed to obtain and report a visitor's nationality. Germans were prohibited from some areas close to the coast. In eastern Sussex that meant the coastal areas themselves and a swathe of parishes north of Eastbourne; as other enemies joined Germany the rules were applied to their nationals too.[15] Naturally it took some time for the police to process the names and for the individuals to come under scrutiny, be collected and sent away. In Brighton it was as late as mid-October before the Chief Constable started to round them up and move them away from the restricted area. Those who were allowed to remain were subject to restrictions: for example, in August 1914 three Germans and an Austrian were bound over for travelling more than five miles from their place of registration.[16] The landlord of the Ostrich Inn at Robertsbridge was thought to be an Austrian and was taken away; he was later determined to be a Prussian and was interned.[17] Ordinary ferries arriving from mainland Europe were stopped and searched and could be diverted to ports other than their usual destinations.[18]

The attitude to enemy aliens soon became fierce and was a good example of the panic that overtook much of Britain in the early months of the war. Even the most unlikely places were thought to harbour German spies or supplies (a disused tube tunnel in London was one example), and anyone not able to account for himself might be thought a spy. In May 1915, for example, a man of no fixed abode was picked up in Westfield on suspicion of spying when he was simply a beggar (he drew two weeks' hard labour)[19] and all over the country people of German extraction were thinking of changing their names to something more British; some of them did, though after 10 October 1914 this was illegal without special permission. Some politicians known to have German connections had to be sidelined, though this did not apply to the royal family.[20] Traffic on roads was liable to be stopped and people questioned, even if this sometimes got out of hand. As early as August 1914 strategic bridges were being guarded. In September 1915 official notices were to be sent to warn the population that in the case of enemy raids or invasion all women and children were to be evacuated to north of the Burwash–Heathfield ridge, able-bodied men to remain behind to assist the military.[21] As in the second world war, invasion was to be signalled by the ringing of church bells, but by jangling, not by the usual sound.[22]

Very soon the German Kaiser was being violently abused in the press and the Germans were being accused of horrible atrocities, most of them wholly false. White feathers began to appear for those apparently fit men who had not volunteered for service.

Sussex was far from immune to these pressures. Indeed, Lord Hythe (heir to Earl Brassey, whose Normanhurst estate was shortly to house the VAD hospital) wrote to his head gardener on 21 August:

> I am arranging for the luggage car to take into Battle, on every practice night, the men who have joined the Rifle Club at Battle. Every able-bodied man should join the Rifle Club either at Battle or Ninfield. I shall not keep on in my employment any man of the age to go on active service.[23]

No doubt other employers were of the same mind.

Appeals were soon made for assistance from the women left behind. The Red Cross began to organise in Battle from 5 August,[24] and started its first sewing circle in Hastings before 15 August,[25] and the role of women in supporting the troops cannot be overemphasised. They made enormous efforts throughout the war. The army was simply undersupplied for a long war in the trenches and men had to rely on voluntary supplies from home known as 'comforts', quite apart from family support for their morale. As early as November the first large consignment left Hastings for 2nd Battalion, The Royal Sussex Regiment: it included, inter alia, 882 pairs of socks, 64 pairs of gloves and 27 of mittens, 183 handkerchiefs, 106 woollen scarves, 109 cakes of soap, 11 vests, 461 shirts and five housewives. This last was not human cargo, though the troops might have preferred that. A 'housewife' was a kind of universal sewing and mending kit.

The Red Cross was active in other ways too. Their earliest concern was for wounded Belgian refugees, some of whom were treated in a temporary hospital in the old Church Hall. Only one Belgian was left there by the end of 1914.[26] Wounded soldiers also arrived. There were three VAD detachments involved, one of men and two of women. The men's one was commanded by George Thorpe and the two women's by Ida Smithe of Powdermill Lane and Millicent Moore of Whatlington. Regular publication of Mrs Smithe's name alongside that of the volunteer recruiter Joshua Mathis gave the existence of the Red Cross continuing publicity and meant that no-one could be unaware of its work or of the need to assist. Several of the men who later went to the front or had returned from it were in the men's detachment.[27]

There was one other comfort for the troops that today sounds strange. The medical reasons for insidious death from the weed were to be broadly established only in the 1950s. So it was to great applause that Thomas Clark, the tobacconist at 66 High Street, appealed for people to give cigarettes for the troops by means of placing them in a donation box in his shop. Clark's initiative is useful to us too, because he continued to receive letters of thanks from the front and it is from them that we can identify some of the men concerned. Starting in October 1914, by December he was sending 700 cigarettes a week to the Royal Sussex Regiment in France.[28] He continued to send them throughout the war. By August 1915 he estimated that he had sent just under 30000 [29] and by the end of the war he estimated that he had sent out 38850,[30] a figure that suggests a certain slowing down of the supply. A similar group was established in Hastings, and many others elsewhere. Men at Normanhurst hospital received gifts of cigarettes too.[31] The cigarettes were much appreciated, as frequent letters from the front showed. In October 1915 Major R G Raper of Battle wrote to him a letter of thanks, including this passage:

> As long as the men are kept well supplied with cigarettes they don't worry much about the hardships which they have to put up with out here.[32]

So desperate were men for tobacco that they sometimes had to resort to substitutes: in Mesopotamia in 1917 it appears that some of them were trying to achieve the same effect with dried tea leaves.[33] And of course it is possible that – as in prisons – tobacco could have formed a kind of currency between the men. It may be noted that similar appeals for reading matter, for example old magazines, do not appear to have attracted the same support or gratitude, despite the crushing boredom of most soldiers' time at the front as they waited for action. The only press mention of such an appeal was of one from Lance-Corporal William Saunders in 1915.[34] (He was later wounded, and his family details are given in connection with his brother Alfred who was killed in 1917.) Just before Christmas 1914 Clark sent a football in response to a request from the front. Unfortunately there is no record of the Royal Sussex having taken part in the football matches with the Germans between the lines.[35]

The promptness of the military authorities is shown by the fact that the volunteers of 1/5 Battalion, The Royal Sussex Regiment, left Hastings for Dover as early as 5 August, to the music of a band and the accompaniment of cheering crowds.[36] They were to take up garrison duties at Dover and would not be sent to France until the next year. 2nd Battalion, The Royal Sussex Regiment was among the first arrivals in France, on 13 August.[37] When the battalion reached Rouen the men were greeted with cheering crowds and flowers, a reception that quickly turned sour when it became known that their cap badge, the Roussillon plume, celebrated the French defeat at Québec and the loss of very nearly all the then French possessions north of what became the United States.[38]

The British army was tiny by comparison with the armies of Germany and France. It had been used to fighting colonial wars, the most recent major conflict being in South Africa in 1899–1902, and the bulk of defence expenditure went to the Royal Navy on the principle that it had to be at least as large as the next two largest navies in the world. Nevertheless the training of the men of the regular army was so good that their rapid and accurate rifle fire was to mislead some German units into believing that they were facing machine guns.*

Army recruitment started almost at once after 4 August. The Hastings recruitment office was in operation at 33 Brook Street before 8 August. That in Battle was reported to be in operation before 22 August and was run by Joshua Mathis, watchmaker and jeweller of 57 High Street; he was also Colour Sergeant and Instructor of the Battle and District Rifle Club which met at the long-established Drill Hall.[39] (The Drill Hall site is now occupied by the BT building and telephone exchange, opposite the Police Station.) Mathis himself did not serve in the war but was destined not to survive it, dying at home in 1917 at the age of 53.[40] In December 1914 there was a

*Developed at Hythe in response to defence cuts in 1905–06.

major recruitment event at the George Hotel, with speeches, songs and the Battle Town Band, but its effect on recruitment levels is not recorded.[421]The response to the appeal for recruits appears to have been poor in Hastings but good in the rural areas.[41] Within a few days of the declaration the reserves had been called up, and when the Battle Rural District Council met early in August it was without its Surveyor and Inspector of Nuisances who wrote to say that as an existing volunteer he was already in uniform. His role was taken over by the Highways Surveyor.[43] Already in August the Battle football team had decided to suspend activities because so many of its members had joined up, and the annual flower show had been cancelled.[44] By early October it was evident to the Battel Bonfire Boyes that they must cancel their annual bonfire because, out of a membership of 80, 28 had already gone for military service.[45] It was beginning to be not 'business as usual' after all. The Boyes were not able to revive themselves until the autumn of 1919.[46]

Meanwhile, the war had begun with the French suffering enormous casualties in an attempt to invade the heavily fortified German province of Alsace Lorraine and with the Germans forcing their way through Belgium towards the northern border of France. The British came up through the Channel ports to man the lines that they would hold, with varying degrees of success, until 1918. To their left was the small Belgian army and some French, and to their right was the main force of French; later some Portuguese were to arrive. Between the major battles the sniping and shelling continued to pick off men at an alarming rate. Immediately after the war the casualties were added up. It was estimated that Germany had lost 1.7 million men, and France 1.4 million; Britain (without the empire) lost some 700 000 or about 1.5 per cent of the population.[47] While the western front remains the greatest focus for remembrance, we should not forget the other theatres. Battle lost at least 19 of its 112 dead elsewhere. And this account tries to remember also those who served and had the good fortune to survive.

Notes

1 *Pike's Directory,* 1915.
2 *Michelin Guide to the British Isles* for 1912.
3 *Jubilee Review of the Rural District of Battle 1894–1954* (Battle Rural District Council)
4 *Hastings Observer*, 13 May 1916.
5 *Post Office Guide,* 1878.
6 *Hastings Observer*, 15 August 1914
7 *Mr Punch's history of the Great War* (Cassell, London, 1919), p 1
8 Gillachrist Moore diary.
9 Opinion reported in the Norman Moore diary, 31 July 1914.
10 Alan Moore diary, September 1914.
11 Gillachrist Moore diary.
12 *Hastings Observer,* 7 August 1915.
13 *Hastings Observer,* 8 August 1914.
14 Norman Moore diary 21 August 1914.
15 *Sussex Expess,* 13 August 1914.
16 *Hastings Observer*, 22 August 1914.
17 Norman Moore diary 15 August 1914.
18 Alan Moore diary.
19 *Hastings Observer*, 8 May 1915.
20 Several near relatives of the King, including two members of the House of Lords, joined the German forces and the pair concerned were deprived of their peerages in 1920.
21 Norman Moore diary, 1915.
22 *Sussex Express,* 15 January 1915.
23 Keith Grieves: *Sussex in the First World War* (Sussex Record Society, 2004)
24 Norman Moore diary 5 August 1914.
25 *Hastings Observer*, 15 August 1914.
26 *Hastings Observer*, 26 December 1914
27 *Sussex Express,* 2 October 1914.
28 *Hastings Observer*, 12 December 1914.
29 *Hastings Observer*, 7 August 1915.
30 *Hastings Observer*, 15 February 1919.
31 Normanhurst, as above.
32 *Hastings Observer*, 16 October 1915.
33 *Hastings Observer*, 23 June 1917.
34 *Hastings Observer* 4 September 1915.
35 http://www.1914–1918.net/truce.htm
36 *Hastings Observer* 8 August 1914
37 Unless otherwise stated, all Royal Sussex movements in this account are from Keith Grieves: *Sussex in the First World War* (Sussex Record Office, 2004) or Miller: *We wunt be druv* ((Reveille Press, 2010)

38 Lyn Macdonald: *1914 Days of Hope* (Michael Joseph 1987)
39 *Hastings Observer*, 22 and 29 August 1914.
40 *Hastings Observer*, 22 September 1917.
41 *Sussex Express,* 18 December 1914.
42 *Hastings Observer*, 29 August 1914.
43 *Hastings Observer*, 8 August 1914.
44 *Hastings Observer*, 22 August 1914.
45 *Hastings Observer*, 17 October 1914
46 *Hastings Observer*, 18 October 1919.
47 *Whitaker's Almanack*, 1920.

2

The First Months: 1914

For Britain, the European campaign of 1914 was limited to stemming the German advance. German strategy was to force its army through Belgium and then, in France, to surround the French capital and as many French troops as possible. Speed was of the essence because France's ally Russia would be slow to mobilise, so France had to be quickly neutralised to avoid a war being fought simultaneously on both eastern and western fronts. The strategy failed almost at once. Russia mobilised quickly and efficiently, needing a prompt and heavy response by the Germans to drive them out of east Prussia; the German advance through Belgium took longer than expected; and the British arrived in sufficient numbers to stop the Germans moving west of Paris. By late October the war of movement would cease and be succeeded by the immovable trenches.

After a long and tiring journey 2nd Battalion, The Royal Sussex Regiment, reached Givry, near Mons, on 23 August. It was just in time for the famous retreat. Very shortly news of casualties began to make its appearance at home. The first local casualties were two men wounded in September. One was on 10 September: Corporal Richard Saunders of Netherfield (*see over*), a professional soldier since 1905 and now serving in 2nd Battalion, The Royal Sussex Regiment. The records are unclear but it appears that it was from a shell that he received wounds to his thigh and foot. Uniquely in this account, he was wounded at the battle of the Marne, where his regiment was then assisting the French in keeping the Germans away from Paris; they were finally stopped just over 20 miles from the centre of the city. Richard was the brother of Frederick, to be wounded later in the year, and of Alfred and Nelson, who were to die in the war.

Richard would be wounded again before the end. He had already seen service in Malta and Crete (during that curious period when the British were securing a form of peace between the Greek majority and the Turks to whom the island still technically belonged). He had been put on the reserve in February 1914 but was remobilised on 6 August, going to France with 2nd Battalion. He had been a Corporal in his first service but moved up the ranks to Acting CQMS – but unfortunately lost this position and reverted to Sergeant in 1916 when an incorrect return was noticed.

The second wounded man was not from the Royal Sussex but from the Highland Light Infantry: Second Lt Ralfe Whistler was wounded on 12 September in the advance to the Aisne, about four miles east of Braisne. He was allowed to recuperate at his home on Caldbec Hill. He was to be wounded three times more, the last wound being fatal.

The first local death from the army ranks was from 2nd Battalion, The Royal Sussex Regiment: Second Lt Gillachrist Moore of Whatlington, who had left for France on 24 September and who was killed by a sniper on 7 November.[1] His father (later Sir) Norman Moore had a distinguished medical practice in London and had moved to Whatlington only seven years before. His great-niece records that a sniper killed him in the woods some two miles south-east of Ypres.[2] Gillachrist was a worshipper at the Catholic Church at Battle. He kept his diary up to date, the last entry being for the day before his death. His brother Alan, a doctor, served in the Royal Navy throughout the war and was later the local medical officer of health.

It is understandable that public attention focussed on the army. After all, the Royal Navy was thought to be invincible. But it was not so to be shown in November), and the events of 22 September seriously disturbed the Admiralty. Up to then the naval command had tended to discount submarine activity, perhaps as a hangover from the time when they thought the use of submarines ungentlemanly and therefore unthinkable. In fact they had already carried out a successful submarine attack against the German cruiser *Hela* near Heligoland on 15 September, so they should have anticipated the disaster that took place only a week later and in more or less the same waters. Moreover HMS *Pathfinder* had been sunk by a submarine torpedo late in August.

Three armed cruisers – the *Aboukir*, the *Cressy* and the *Hogue* – were on patrol about twenty miles off the Dutch coast. Their task was to guard against incursions by the German navy into the Channel. Unknown to them the German submarine U9 under Captain Otto Weddigen was in the area and at that stage of the war its presence could not be detected, let alone seen, until too late.

A seaman on board the *Aboukir* said later:

> On Tuesday morning, September 22nd, at about 6.30 a.m., I heard an explosion, which shook the ship .... I rushed on deck and found the ship heeling over to port.

It appears that the *Aboukir* was struck by a single torpedo and that its captain believed that the ship had hit a mine. It capsized after some 25 minutes, sinking about 5 minutes later. The crew had been able to launch only one lifeboat. The *Hogue* came to assist, but was itself torpedoed; after receiving two hits, it capsized and sank within 15 minutes. Finally the *Cressy* received one torpedo. *Cressy* had already seen the submarine and fired on it without success. It capsized and then sank at about 7.55 am.

This was a disaster of major proportions. The seaman quoted above was one of the lucky ones; 839 men were lost, among them one man commemorated on the Battle war memorials: Able Seaman Albert Edward Beaney, aged 37. But another Battle man, not on the memorials, was on the *Aboukir* that day and he too was lost. These two were the first deaths deserving commemoration in the town.

Beaney and his wife Mary (Poole) lived at 6 Chapel Cottages. He was a postman in Battle and Westfield.[4] As a postman he would have been very widely known, in those days perhaps more so than postmen are now, given the small size of the communities in question and the greater number of daily deliveries. Beaney is commemorated not only in Battle but also in Chatham and in the head post office at Hastings.

His family was doubly unfortunate, but as we shall see in this account it was far from the only one to be so affected, in that his brother was lost a month later.[5]

The name of Albert Beaney is on at least three memorials, but the other Battle death that day is not commemorated locally: AB John Weller, who was on HMS *Aboukir* and, as with Beaney, whose body was never recovered. He had left Battle early to join the Navy and by 1911 he had left it, albeit temporarily, and was living at Ilfracombe with his wife Emma (Linton), who had been born in Ireland, and his baby child Jack. We do not know when or where he rejoined, but it was early enough for him to be able to serve in September 1914. The 1911 census has him as a retired officer but he rejoined as an Able Seaman. His name is also on the Chatham Memorial.

Weller's father, who had died in 1899, was a gamekeeper from Horsham and his mother Harriet (Moore) was from Dorking; in 1881 they were recorded as living at Coarse Barn Farm at the eastern end of Uckham Lane. Harriet moved to Ilfracombe and died there early in 1917. Jack married in 1936 and died at Southwark in 1979. No reliable records can be found for Weller's sisters Eveline and Annie; his widow did not remarry and died at Hendon in 1965.

By the time that the autumn drew to a close the Germans held almost all of Belgium, missing only the extreme western corner that was protected by a large area deliberately flooded to keep them away from the major British supply ports of Calais and Boulogne; north of that, Antwerp had fallen to them on 10 October and Ostend five days later. The stubbornly-resistant town of Ypres was the other blockage inside Belgium and it remained so throughout the whole war. In France the Germans had made great advances, and the front line settled down into very roughly the shape it was to hold until the spring of 1918: unremitting trench warfare, with the occasional grand assault that led nowhere strategically and was the cause of most of the casualties for which the war became notorious.

There were no more deaths from the area around Battle for the rest of 1914 except for one from Sedlescombe (Captain Boyce Combe, aged 24, of Oaklands, who died late in November), but there were at least two more wounded soldiers.

One was Private Louis Keable of the East Kent Regiment (The Buffs). He was aged 33 and recently married. A confectioner's carman from 9 Mount Street, he suffered a shrapnel wound to the thigh reported when he returned home to recuperate in December.[6] He later served in the Labour Corps. The 1911 census gives his wife's name as Lilian (Playford). They had one known child, Patrick. Mount Street was to suffer badly from losses but Keable survived and came home at the end of the war, resuming his job with the jam factory. He had been born at Ticehurst and was to die in London late in 1964. Patrick died at Portsmouth in 1982.

The other was Frederick Saunders of Netherfield. He was a son of Henry and Mary (Selmes). A Private in 2nd Battalion, The Royal Sussex Regiment, he was in the fighting in front of Ypres when he was wounded on 30 October (the records are ambiguous: another reference is to 27 November). His right elbow had been shattered by a bullet.[7] He was never fit for front line service again, and in February 1917 he was transferred to the new Labour Corps. He lived in one of the new council houses on Netherfield Hill. Like so many, both he and his father were agricultural labourers before the war began. Two of his brothers were to be killed. We do not know precisely where Saunders was injured but it was probably near Zandfoorte, close to the French border, south-east of Ypres.

At the end of 1914, therefore, the German advance in France and Belgium had been stemmed. As one observer succinctly put it:

> On land the position seems to be little changed from the state assumed weeks ago. Both sides are solidly entrenched and it appears that neither can dislodge the other.[8]

Elsewhere, troops from India had taken the Mesopotamian port of Basra to secure the Persian Gulf. The importance of Egypt, with the Suez Canal, is obvious but that of the Gulf less so. The cheapness of oil had allowed the Royal Navy to begin to adopt it in place of coal, and its loss would have been catastrophic. The oil came almost exclusively from southern Persia through ports at the mouth of the

Tigris. These theatres of war were to give considerable trouble to the forces later.

By the end of 1914 the German surface navy had been effectively confined to home waters, to be confirmed in 1915 in the South Atlantic and east Asia but in the North Sea only in 1916. German submarines were to cause major problems in the Atlantic and the Mediterranean up to the end of the war, though much less so after the convoy system was introduced, against the opposition of the admirals, in 1917. The same observer as above, a naval man, wrote that although the Germans were a weaker force at sea they were of equal fighting value to the British, and

> In reality the lesson we have learnt is that the Germans can fight as well or almost as well as we can.[9]

At home there had been a decisive shift away from the happy thought that a quick victory would bring all the men back by Christmas to the knowledge that the country was in for a longer haul. Casualties had been great by the standards of the day. Few people can have thought that very much worse was to come on the military front.

Notes

1 *Hastings Observer*, 14 November 1914.
2 Charlotte Moore: *Hancox* (Viking, 2010), p 385.
3 *Hastings Observer*, 3 October 1914.
4 *Hastings Observer*, 14 November 1914.
5 *Hastings Observer*, 31 October 1914.
6 *Hastings Observer*, 5 December 1914.
7 *Hastings Observer*, 3 April 1915.
8 Alan Moore diary.
9 Alan Moore diary.

3

The New Year: 1915

By the end of 1914 there was a stalemate in Belgium and France, but British troops were hard at work trying to relieve the Germans of their African colonies (in which they were not wholly successful, the last German surrender being destined to take place two weeks after the armistice of 1918). A major Turkish attack on Egypt was repelled early in the year but the main campaigns in Palestine and Mesopotamia were still in the future, and there were no major naval engagements.

At home the town was now fully engaged in the war. In January 220 billets were found for men of 9th Battalion, North Staffordshire Regiment on their way to the front, something with which the locals were beginning to be familiar. Battle being near the embarkation points on the coast, it was an obvious source of billets.

South-eastern Europe and the Mediterranean

With one exception the British war in Europe was confined to attempts to break the German lines in France and Belgium. That exception was the Anglo-French campaign to force the Dardanelles, capture Constantinople and push Turkey out of the war, thereby opening up a fresh front in the Balkans to which the Austrians in particular would have had to divert more troops, stretching the Germans still further and incidentally improving Italian prospects – Italy joined the Allies in May 1915. It would also allow the Russians to join with their allies in the Mediterranean and greatly improve supplies to them from the west. Gallipoli has gone down in history as a disaster but the concept was brilliant and had it been better conducted it would have shortened the war, with incalculable results.

In March a naval expedition entered the narrow Dardanelles Straits guarding the way to Constantinople, but it ran into difficulties and was quickly deemed unlikely to succeed; a few weeks later the army landed on the northern side of the Gallipoli peninsula with the intention of securing the whole of it, thereby nullifying the Turkish defences. After the naval attack the Turks were well-warned and well-prepared. The invasion was a catastrophe that yielded nothing but graves but lasted until the very end of the year.

Four of Battle's casualties were in that campaign, which began with landings on 25 April. On 7 May Philip Fuller of Netherfield died of wounds.[1] He was a Private in 1st Battalion, The Royal Munster Fusiliers and a soldier by profession; he had previously been a waiter. His father William was a stoker and there were six siblings, all of them impossible to trace with any certainty. This death is not recorded on the otherwise admirable roll of honour in St John the Baptist Church at Netherfield, possibly because the family had moved away: in 1901 they were at St Leonards, and in 1911 Fuller was in a barracks in India. His name is on the Helles Memorial but his grave is not recorded, which is odd if he died of wounds.

The other Gallipoli deaths were the last of the year. The first man concerned was also from Netherfield: Sapper Charles Lewis

Goodsell (*left*) of 1st/3rd Kent Fortress Company, Royal Engineers. He enlisted at Gillingham on 17 May 1915 and was sent eastwards on 12 October; but he died at sea on 28 October and is commemorated on the Helles Memorial at the Dardanelles. One record states that he was on his way to Salonica, which seems unlikely.[2] The incident is known as the Hythe disaster from the vessel in which he was being taken towards the Dardanelles. Two ships collided just off Cape Helles. One was the *Hythe*, a converted cross-channel cargo ferry of 509 tons, carrying 248 men, and the other was HMS *Sarnia*, a larger vessel leaving the area after landing its own complement of men. It was dark and because of the threat of Turkish gunnery neither ship was properly lit.

> [The *Hythe*] immediately began to sink and would go down in ten minutes flat. On the deck some managed to step onto the Sarnia as she remained alongside for several minutes.... [The Captain of the *Hythe* and] A further 128 members of 1/3rd Company were lost plus 15 other Army personnel and 11 crew from the *Hythe*. Only 103 members of the 1/3rd Company survived. The disaster was compounded by the lack of life jackets/emergency lifeboats/poor organisation and could have been avoided by shipping following a set route inward and outward bound from Cape Helles.[3]

Goodsell came from a large family. The 1911 census lists him as a general labourer. His father Samuel (a farmer and wood merchant) and mother Lucy (Foster) had eleven children. Charles married Caroline Selmes at Netherfield Parish Church in 1900, and the army records list four children, one of whom died in infancy. All three surviving children married and had children of their own, all born in Sussex and some in Battle. In turn there are fresh generations, with grandchildren still living. His brothers and sisters appear to have remained in the area too. At least one brother also served.

Another Battle man died in the same incident: Richard Thomas Pook (*left*), a Driver in the RE. He had been born at Battle in 1885 and in 1891 was listed as living at Beanford (then inside the parish of Battle.) Pook was a contractor carman living at

Tunbridge Wells. He had married Florence Edith Benge in 1907 and had one child, Frances, who died unmarried in 2002. His mother Ruth (Muggridge) died at Hastings in 1930 and his father James at Wadhurst in 1931. A brother James cannot be traced, and neither can his sister Marjorie.

Shortly afterwards, on 19 November John Sharp, a stoker on HMS *Scourge*, was killed in the Aegean. The *Scourge* was a Beagle class destroyer launched on the Tyne in 1910. It had played a notable part in the Gallipoli landings of April 1915, and in 1916 was to be the first ship to rescue survivors from the hospital ship *Britannic* that had struck a mine in the Aegean. Sharp died in a boiler explosion that killed five men and seriously injured another two. At the time *Scourge* was in action bombarding Turkish positions, and presumably was hit by return fire.[4]

Sharp had been a sailor for some time and in 1911 is recorded as living in Portsmouth with his wife Emily (Hutchings) and son Frederick, born in 1909. The records are unclear as to their futures.

Later in the year, at Alexandria, William Eldridge was injured in an accident while a ship was being coaled: he suffered serious rib injuries, followed by pneumonia, and was declared unfit for further duty shortly afterwards. He was a brother of Basil Eldridge, who was to die in the battles on the western front in September 1918. William had already been married and widowed; he enlisted at Hastings in July 1915 and was sent eastwards in October. He was back shortly before Christmas. In civilian life he was a stableman, which was appropriate to his service with the Army Veterinary Corps. He came back to Sussex and died at Hastings in 1958.

And in December Frank Ling (whose details are given in connection with his death in 1916) suffered a severe gunshot wound to his shoulder at Gallipoli, and was sent to Egypt; by the time of his recovery the Allies had abandoned their efforts at Gallipoli.

The Western Front

The western front remained very active and the fighting was bitter, much worse than in the previous year as both sides tried to break the stalemate. There were major battles at Neuve Chapelle, Ypres, Aubers Ridge and Loos, though not on the scale of those to come in 1916. Between these there was continuous trench warfare, characterised mainly by shelling and sniping, and by the use of poison gas by both sides: the first use, by the Germans, was in April in the second battle of Ypres.

The trouble with the new situation was that no-one had ever fought a war like this. All previous wars had been wars of movement, of bodies of troops outmanoeuvring or overwhelming other bodies of troops or bottling them up in a siege. But now the defences erected between the two sides meant that outmanoeuvring was more or less out of the question. To the west was the sea, and to the east the frontier of neutral Switzerland.

These were siege conditions without either side being surrounded by the other. Huge banks of barbed wire and the use of machine guns checked any infantry advance, and as the war went on the shell-marked ground between the two lines became difficult to cross even in good conditions, let alone after heavy rain. Air power was in its infancy, and aeroplanes were so unusual that when one was heard at home people used to leave their houses and wave at it. The tank did not make a successful appearance until late in the war. Gas and flamethrowers were other technical innovations, both with questionable results. Before 1918 then there were only two moments when manoeuvre might have been restored, both at Ypres. In 1914 the Germans, badly battered, ceased their attack. Unknown to them, in front of their men was the last thin and damaged line of British that could easily have been broken; behind that line were only Corps Headquarters and then the Channel ports.[5] In the following year, after the first use of poison gas in warfare, the Allied line was wide open but it closed before the Germans were able to take advantage of the gap.

If manoeuvre was effectively impossible then the alternative had to be to attempt to overwhelm the enemy. But the two sides were fairly equally balanced and, even more important, they were much better at defence than attack. When threatened they could quickly bring up reinforcements, while their advancing opponents were necessarily required to tread slowly across a difficult terrain disturbed by shelling and well-guarded by barbed wire and machine gun posts. Not until 1918 was an answer to this situation found, and then only because the Germans broke the Allied lines so badly that manoeuvre was again possible. A variation of overwhelming was 'attrition' – the deliberate killing of so many of the enemy that it could not continue to fight. Attempts to do this were invariably unsuccessful, casualties never being limited to the enemy's forces. When the Germans applied it to the French at Verdun in 1916, for example, their losses approached those of their enemy.[6]

It is not that the generals of 1914 were unintelligent or inexperienced in both the reality and the study of warfare, but they had no way of finding the answers. They tried everything. Certainly they were used to, and used, diversions, but mainly they tried throwing more and more forces into action, with the effect that this war became the bloodiest by then recorded among the European peoples. Each side shelled the other in a vain attempt to break its lines. Whole Divisions attacked and secured very little ground or had to retreat with enormous losses. The generals continued their policy in the face of evidence, sometimes concealed from them, that their attacks would not succeed. The death toll mounted steeply. Back home, on both sides, there were some peace initiatives after 1916 but they failed. It would have been easy to agree conditions for a cease fire but, again on both sides, there was not only the problem of Alsace Lorraine (then part of Germany but its recovery was the main war aim of the French) but also the strongest of feelings that anything short of victory would betray those who had already died.

It is certain that both armies were at first inadequately equipped for a long war, though the Germans usually managed to provide better trenches than did the Allies. For example, the bitter winter of 1914–15 was of course miserable – the first to be spent in the trenches and under fire. It was in winter that the volunteers' supplies from home were most needed, but they did not always get through. In January William Oliver, a Lance Corporal in 2nd Battalion, The Royal Sussex Regiment was invalided out with frostbite. He did not long survive the war, dying at Battle in 1923. He was not the only one, for Walter Robert Jenner of the RFA was in hospital from the effects of the cold as late as 22 February. (But he lived until 1969.)

And it had first been experienced as early as November 1914 when Charles Buss of Netherfield, in 1st Battalion, The Rifle Brigade suffered from frostbite; his details are given in connection with his wounding in 1917.

Despite the cold the fighting continued. On 27 January Lance Corporal Frank Green of 2nd Battalion, The Royal Sussex Regiment, was seriously wounded in his right arm and left elbow at Cuinchy and found himself at No 11 General Hospital at Boulogne. He was reported to be the nephew of Mrs Highwood of St Mary's Terrace,[7] who supplied a photograph of him to the newspaper, and therefore the first cousin of William Highwood who was to die in 1918. He had been born at Guildford in 1894 and had enlisted at Battle on 31 August 1914. His attestation was witnessed by Major Fuller Whistler and carried also the name of Joshua Mathis. That the newspaper reported that prayers were said for him by name at St Mary's suggests that casualties were then still unusual.

Green reached England a month later and stayed there until March 1916 when he was discharged as physically unfit. He lived to 1971, when he died in Middlesex.

The first to go, Gunner Thomas John Jesson of the RHA/RFA, actually died at home in Brighton on 24 March. In a sense he was born into the army, for his father Frederick had been the drill instructor at Battle and the large family contained five children born there, all living at the drill hall itself. The birthplaces of the others bear witness to a life involving a lot of different postings on military service: Portsmouth, Shorncliffe, Silverhill and St Leonards. Thomas had married Mary Fry in 1898 but they had no children. The family did not return to Battle. Frederick died at Eastbourne in 1910; his wife Elizabeth had died at Hastings in 1889.

Neuve Chapelle

Across the Channel the short but bitter battle of Neuve Chapelle took place in mid-March (*see Map 1*). The army was running short of shells and therefore decided not to have a preliminary bombardment of the German lines. By surprise, therefore, they overran them; but then German resistance stiffened, as always, and the huge butchers' bill turned out to be for the gain of a ruined and insignificant village and no more.

It is likely that it was at Neuve Chapelle that a young Netherfield man died. This was William George Fuller, a Rifleman in 2nd Battalion, The Rifle Brigade. He died on 14 March, the last day of the battle, and is commemorated on the Le Touret memorial. Fuller had had a difficult youth. He had been born in Netherfield to Thomas and Esther Fuller, in 1893; Thomas was an agricultural labourer according to the 1891 census and young William was a cowman on a farm in 1911. The family moved to Penhurst later but Thomas died late in 1910. The 1911 census has Esther living with her three younger children at the Battle workhouse but she evidently escaped that because when William died her address was given as 15 Havelock Road, Bexhill. The name Fuller is so common in the area that it is impossible reliably to track down his brothers Samuel, Henry and Charles or his sister Edith. It appears that his mother remarried in Battle in 1924.

The newly-promoted Corporal Arnold Thompson of 5th Battalion, The Royal Sussex Regiment, wrote to say that he had been relieved on 13 April after five days in the trenches. He and his men had marched back about four miles, then next day more than fourteen:

> No-one had his boots off for more than six days ... The point I didn't like was stepping over the dead Germans. There were a lot outside our trenches.[8]

Very few men would have previously seen any dead human; they had quickly to adjust to the sight. And one had to be fit for this kind of work, which in general meant to be young. The oldest soldier from Battle so far identified as seeing active service was 56 when the war began, and he lasted two years before being discharged, to die within a few months.

Thompson went on to write, accurately or otherwise, that the Germans were issued with dum dum bullets. (These had cuts across the top of the bullet to allow explosion within the body of the man receiving them, and had been outlawed under the Geneva Convention of 1899. The Germans had already accused the Belgians of using them.) Thompson was 21, formerly a gardener at the Deanery and by one account an adopted son of the Smale family of Market Green. He moved away after the war.

Early in April Private Jesse Kenward of 5th Battalion, The Royal Sussex Regiment suffered another trench problem – influenza – and had to come home briefly. (His background is described later in connection with his being wounded in October 1917.) Military records are full of reports of disease: asthma and bronchitis in the west, malaria in the east.

In 1915 something of the real life of the trenches began to become widely known, not only through private correspondence but through published accounts. To his father at the end of March, Private Frederick Blackman, 5th Battalion, The Royal Sussex Regiment wrote:

> We have been in the trenches. We are out for a few days rest now, and we are glad of it too. It is very rough out here, but we stick to it very well, you see. We have got through the first round safe and well. It is a terrible sight out here; you would never believe it. Villages and churches smashed to atoms. We have to be careful in the trenches. One shell dropped about twenty yards behind the trench, in a muddy river. We had some of the mud, but we didn't get hit. I thought it was all up. Our chaps are in very good spirits, and full of fight. I had two days and two nights without a wink of sleep. When we came out we had a six miles' march with about eighty pounds on our backs. We were absolutely done up … I will never grumble again after this lot.[9]

Sgt Bernard Anderson, 1st/5th Battalion, The Royal Sussex Regiment, wrote to his mother (he was a regular, usually weekly correspondent):

> We are two days in the trenches and got off with no-one in 'B' Company hit. I never saw one German all the time we were there but plenty of our chaps saw them. Harry Crouch [of Netherfield] went to fetch water, and on the way back a shell came so close that the wind from it knocked him down.[10]

Both Blackman and Anderson were wounded early in May, Blackman on 1 May by a shell fragment in the ankle in the line in front of Aubers Ridge, and Anderson in the upper arm. Anderson wrote:

> We had to try to take some trenches, but couldn't get forward or back, so after I was hit I lay in a shell hole from 5.30 in the morning to 5.30 in the evening in two feet of water.[11]

They returned to the war but would not survive it, and their histories are explored later in this account. That a shell could knock someone down without wounding or killing him would have been surprising to those at home, but not those at the front: men could even be killed by one of them passing. The poet Edward Thomas would die in just this way in 1917.

The Second Ypres

The First Battle of Ypres had been fought in 1914 for possession of this strategic city through which the northerly French Channel ports would have been accessible to the Germans. The second battle began with a British assault on 17 February 1915, followed by the German response. The Second Ypres is notorious for a German innovation: it was on the northern flank of the Ypres salient on 22 April that poison gas was first used in warfare, and again later in the month. It proved itself. The attack was on the French sector of the front, which broke at once and the line fell back two miles in disarray. This was a major movement for the time, and occurred despite plentiful prior indications that gas was among the German weapons.

On this occasion it was the Germans who failed to make best use of their advantage – no doubt caution prevailed as their men faced large remaining pockets of gas before them. Shortly the line reformed fully and the attack was stayed. But when the fighting tailed off towards the end of May the salient was much smaller. The Allies had lost land but Ypres itself, or what was left of it, remained in their hands.

The Second Ypres was a horrible killing field. Lt Col F G Langham of the Royal Sussex wrote of the Second Ypres that he had seen men on fire who had chosen to kill themselves rather than be burned to death.[12] (This article must have caused more alarm than anything else to those at home already worried about their families, but it was sensible to let this kind of thing out gently and authoritatively at what was proving to be an early stage of a long and savage war.) Langham was already 52 in 1914. He appears to have had what was known as a 'good war', being mentioned in despatches in 1915 and awarded the CMG in the same year; he also had the Volunteer Decoration. He was a member of the general court-martial of 1914 that sentenced the German spy Karl Lody to death by shooting at the Tower of London.* Nevertheless Langham's family also suffered: one of his sons was killed at Ypres in 1917. Langham appears to have been a very able and straight-talking solicitor.** He was in partnership as a solicitor at Hastings but later lived at Battle, moving to 17 Upper Lake in 1932. He died at Half Acre, Starrs Green, in 1946.[13]

All letters from the front were censored. Routinely any place-names were removed, on security grounds, but also anything likely to spread alarm and despondency. This had begun immediately the war started: Gillachrist Moore, the first local man to die, had written in October 1914 that

> One is not allowed to say anything at all about what is going on and I don't think one knows very much here except one's own bit.[14]

A Bexhill man later wrote about these letters:

> The officer on duty would read every one and destroy it if it revealed a military secret, or black out any indiscreet or non-permissible information, e.g. *where* you were, what was happening, etc.[15]

It is small wonder that reports of the more unpleasant sides of trench life could only be made privately and to families when

*Lody was the first of several such men to be executed during the war.

** His firm has the dubious distinction of having employed Charles Dawson, the Piltdown (and other) forger; but there was never any doubt that Dawson was a competent solicitor. He appears to have taken over the Langhams' Uckfield practice in 1900 and the firm survives there today as Dawson Hart.

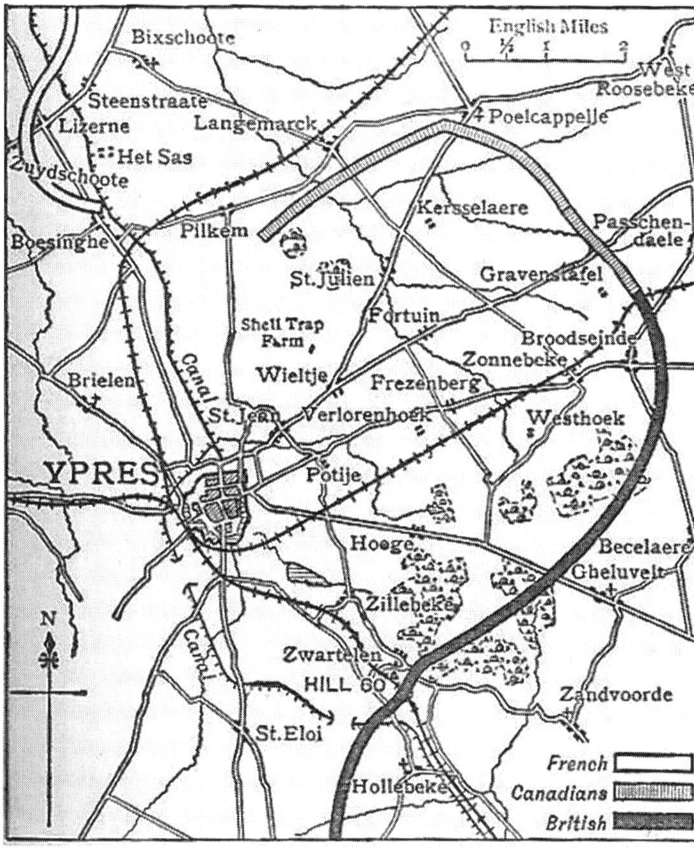

Map 2: the Second Ypres – the line broken by the German attack. This map shows where a significant gap was opened up, north of Ypres.

the soldiers were on leave, and then circulated by word of mouth: dampness and flooding, cold, trench foot, rats, the elementary sanitation, the disposal of bodies and parts of bodies, the incessant noise, the orders to go forward into what was clearly instant and unnecessary death. The stories may even have gained in the telling.

At some point in April Frank Raymond Curry was buried by a shell and when dug out had to be evacuated to the UK. (His family is discussed in connection with the death of his brother William in 1916.) Curry was a Lieutenant with 2nd Battalion, The Royal Dublin Fusiliers and after his 1915 experience was posted to India with 1st (Garrison) Battalion, The Bedfordshire Regiment. A Major on his retirement, he became a PT instructor.[16] Curry had two children by

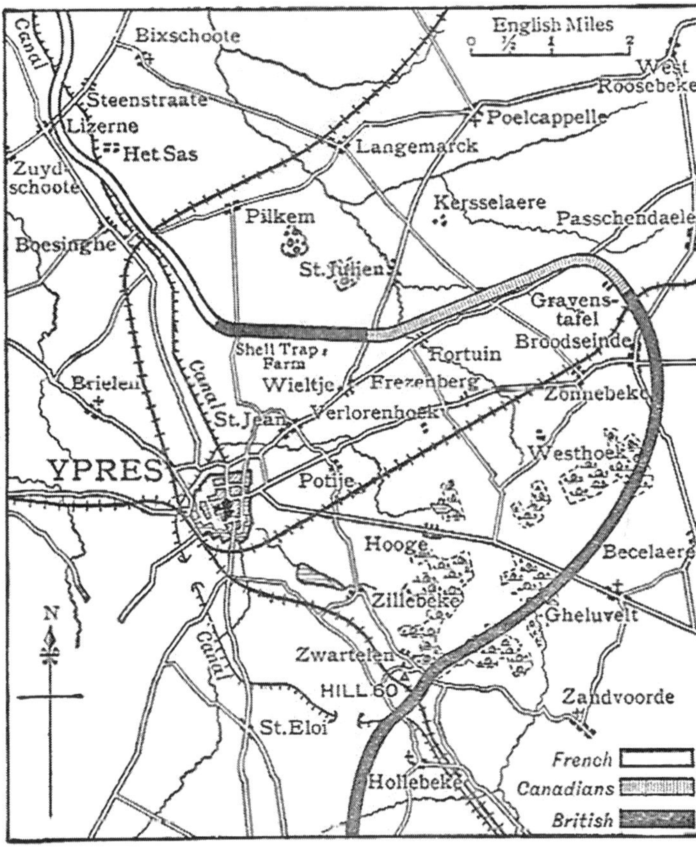

Map 3: The Second Ypres: the Allied line stabilised.

his wife Sybil (Woods) and died at Fordingbridge in 1955.

May 1915 saw more Battle deaths on the western front.

William Charles Morley, who died of wounds and is buried at Boulogne, had been born at Battle in 1878. His father was Frederick, a farm labourer, and William's own job is recorded as being a grocer's porter. William enlisted at St Leonards as a Sapper in the Royal Engineers. He had married Louisa Burns at Battle in 1901 but there were no children. By then the family had moved to Bexhill. Both his parents were Battle-born and had died before the war began: Mary Ann (Avann) in 1902 and Frederick in 1913. He had one sister.

The other was Jabez Juina Parks, who is commemorated on the Menin Gate. He came of a family that was clearly of a religious bent. Among his siblings were Esther, Job, Joseph and Ruth, and their histories are hard to trace. That is also true of his father Robert, an agricultural labourer, but we know that his mother Sarah (Muggridge) died in Sussex in 1950. In 1901 the family were at Virgin's Croft and in 1911 Jabez is recorded as being a mineral water carman aged thirty. There is no trace of a marriage for him.

The next Battle man to die was Private Charles Newbery of 3rd Battalion, The Royal Fusiliers. His was a name very well-known in the town until very recently, and the Newbery arch spans the passage where the family business was concentrated. Charles had been born in Battle in 1888, the fourth son of Joseph Newbery and his wife Kezia (formerly Long). In the 1911 census Joseph is described as confectionery maker, and in this role he provided substantial employment in the town, following his confectioner father Henry who had moved into jam making in the middle of the previous century. We shall meet some of the employees of his concern later in this account. Joseph and Kezia lived at Forest View, Mount Street, and they had a large family: eleven children.

The 1901 and 1911 censuses allow us to reconstruct the family: apart from the two parents and along with servants, there were five daughters and six sons living at Forest View at one time or another, born between 1880 and 1899. The sixth son, John, was to marry in 1922 and produce a son Peter; Peter died in action in the RAF in the second world war and is commemorated in St Mary's Church. In 1911 Charles was living away from home and working as an architectural assistant.

Charles died on 8 May 1915. In Britain his death was not known for some time. The army reported that he had been wounded and was probably a prisoner.[17] The first knowledge at home of his death was by a letter to his father from the Red Cross in Geneva. He had been shot in the stomach at Zonnebeke on 3 May and, with the German advance moving forward, had been taken by the Germans and transferred to Reserve Field Lazarett 87 in Oostniewkerke, between Ypres and Roeselare.[18] Zonnebeke was a village – or rather the site of a village – on the road leading to Passchendaele and just short of the original British front line, but some two miles behind it when the battle ground to a halt at the end of May. A historian of the Fusiliers wrote of Newbery's battalion:

> At noon on the 8th they were ordered to support an attack made by East Surreys and the 3rd Middlesex between Verlorenhoek road and Railway to regain some trenches lost in that vicinity. The battalion took no more active participation on this occasion than that of being the victim of perpetual sniping from their front and right.[19]

Newbery is buried in Tyne Cot Cemetery.

Charles's father Joseph died in Lewes on 12 January 1927, aged 74. Kezia followed, in Hastings on 24 October 1936. Of their sons George died in 1933, leaving John in charge. John died in 1966.

Also on 8 May there died Frederick Joseph White, a native of Hastings aged 27. He was a Driver with the ASC. His one surviving military record states that he committed suicide by hanging. He is buried in Samer Communal Cemetery a short distance from Boulogne, one of only four war graves there, and one of only two from 1914–18. He had only just been married when he died – to Elizabeth Kate Fuller of Netherfield, sister of several men who went to the war including Thomas who was to die in 1917.

Although some doubts exist as to his background, White's father was almost certainly Henry, a Hastings butcher born at Chiswick, who married Emily Horton from Earlswood in Warwickshire. In 1891 they were recorded as living in Western Road, Hastings, with seven sons. By 1911 Frederick was a tramcar conductor. There were no children, and Elizabeth remarried in 1923. She died in 1961. Henry died in 1901 and Emily probably in 1928.

On the day after these two deaths, in the main attack on Aubers Ridge, near Richebourg l'Avoue, there was another wounding: Stanley Whiteman, a farmer's son from Netherfield and one of three brothers who went to the war (James being killed on the Somme in 1916). Stanley was a Private in 5th Battalion, The Royal Sussex Regiment but we do not know where he was wounded. He also served in Italy. After the war, in 1945 he married Marguerite Dench at Battle but no family is recorded. He died in Surrey in 1966, and Marguerite (born in 1914) died at Battle in 1982.

In the same month Private Frank Kane was wounded at St Julien. His details are given in connection with a letter he wrote in 1916.

There was to be another death at Ypres before the two sides

decided to disengage on 25 May. This was from another well-known local family: he was Henry McLaren Lambert of Telham Court. He died only five days after Charles Newbery.

Telham Court never had the size or status of Battle Abbey or Normanhurst but it was (and remains) a substantial property with good views over the town. Originally part of the Abbey estate, it was formerly known as Quarry Hill and was occupied for some years by Samuel Carter, a lawyer and one-time MP. The estate was large: to the north it touched Blackfriars farmhouse and to the south it ran along Telham Lane. It included both sides of Hastings Road up to the Telham Lane junction as well as Telham and Loose farms. In the 1871 census it is described as a property of 553 acres employing 15 labourers and 16 boys.

Edward Tiley Lambert bought it from Carter in 1875 and at once began to assume the customary duties of a landowner of the period, including a magistracy. The family had made substantial money from engineering. They were "hydraulic and gas engineers, patentees and manufacturers of high pressure valve cocks, closets, pumps, sluice valves, wrought iron tubes and fillings" at their works in Lambeth and Walsall.[20] Edward, born at Lambeth in 1844, died at Telham in 1908 and in Henry's absence Edward's second son Reginald took over the family home; by then Henry, born in July 1879, was already embarked on a military career after school at Harrow and university at Trinity College, Cambridge. He was commissioned Second Lieutenant in 1st (Royal) Dragoons,[***] in December 1899 and went to serve in the second South African war between the British and the non-British European settlers. He was in the Orange Free State from June to November 1900, the Transvaal from January to August 1901, the Free State again from August to 1901 to March 1902, back to the Transvaal from March to May 1902 and then in Cape Colony. He was promoted Lieutenant in October 1900, and was awarded the King's and the Queen's South Africa Medals. After the South African war finished in 1902 he was posted to India and became ADC to three successive viceroys: Lord Ampthill (acting, during a vacancy) in 1904, then Lord Curzon and then the Earl of Minto,

*** It may be noted here that, as with several regiments, the German emperor had been Colonel-in-Chief of the Royal Dragoons.

and later the Commander-in-Chief Sir O'Moore Creagh. In 1907 he was promoted Captain but retired from the army in the next year, presumably after his father died.

Henry Lambert had been left Telham Court by his father but was in no position to manage it because after he left the army he spent most of his time in East Africa, where he must have mixed with the cream of the colonials of Kenya described in many places, for example (mainly in a later war) by James Fox in *White mischief.* Lambert's name is on the war memorial of the Muthaiga Country Club at Nairobi. This was opened on New Year's Eve 1913, so he must have been a very early member. He came back to the colours in August 1914.

Lambert was a temporary Captain and in charge of regimental machine guns at the time of his death on 13 May 1915.[21] He is buried in the Hop Store Cemetery, Vlamertinghe, west of Ypres. A memorial service was held at St Mary's on 2 July 1915, attended by a great multitude of titled folk and gentry,[22] and there is a memorial to him in the church. The press report of the memorial service suggests that he had been awarded the DSO, which has not been verified. His estate was later in the year valued at £26085; this can at best have included only an estimate of the value of his art collection, which went under the hammer at Christie's two years later and appears to have done rather well.[23] Lambert was unmarried.

Telham Court did not long remain in the Lambert family. Reginald (who for a short time had been a gentleman cricketer for Sussex and who himself had served in the war) sold it in 1928, but by that time the property was down to little more than 120 acres thanks to earlier disposals, and Reginald and his wife had moved to Wiltshire. He died at Shaftesbury in Dorset early in 1968.[24] The property was used as Glengorse Preparatory School for some years and is now owned by the Holmes Property Group. Lambert had three sisters. One died young, but the other two married the same man, one after the other: Sir John Gilmour, a baronet and a prominent Scottish Conservative politician.

Also in May, 2nd Lieutenant Ralfe Whistler sustained his second injury, at Festubert. (His family and his own details are outlined below in connection with his death in 1917.)

Aubers Ridge

The British attempt to take Aubers Ridge was a complete failure.

The ridge is about eleven miles west and slightly south of Lille, and only a mile or so from Neuve Chapelle (*see Map 4*). To us the idea of a ridge might conjure up a view of a steep incline perhaps somewhat short of the South Downs, but today this one would be hardly noticeable, a minor upward bulge in otherwise flat country. To the men in the trenches, however, it was a problem and a challenge because even a tiny difference in altitude gave an army the opportunity to dominate the ground and approaches. The attempt to take it was launched on 9 May.

For 2nd Battalion, The Royal Sussex Regiment which was in the first wave of the attack, it was far and away the bloodiest day of the war, so far; it lost 14 officers and 551 men. The last Battle man to die in that month fell there on that day,[25] Ernest John Rooke, an unmarried Brighton man of 29, had enlisted in the 2nd Battalion at Chichester a month after the war started. His link with Battle was that he was a policeman there from 1911 to 1913 (when he transferred to Ashburnham), during which time he joined the Reserve. He was clearly a well-regarded member of the East Sussex police, for he won his Good Conduct Badge in 1914.[26] Rooke has no known grave, and is also commemorated on the police memorial at Lewes and at the Le Touret memorial in France. He is not commemorated on either of the Battle war memorials, but his name is on that at Ashburnham. 'A noble death' said the newspapers, though no further details were given.

Further casualties

There was one more Battle death in May, though far from the front.

Percival Turner, whose father Arthur was a saddler in Cruttenden's Yard, died of scarlet fever on 19 May at the age of 30. Percival was listed in the 1901 census as a whitesmith in Battle, and in 1911 as an electrical fitter in an ironmongery, living in Shrewsbury. By 1915 he was a plumber living in Duke Street, Lower Broughton, Manchester, and unmarried. Only on 27 March had he enlisted at Manchester in 18 Battalion, the Manchester Regiment and was in training at the great Heaton Park encampment. He died at Monsall Fever Hospital and was buried with military honours at Philips Park cemetery in Manchester. He never saw active service. The family lived at Mount View Cottage on Caldbec Hill. His mother died at Battle in 1927 and his father in 1932; his only sibling, Sophie, had died there in 1918.

On 15 June Private Harry Holland of Netherfield died at Givenchy. According to army records his real name was George Herbert Holland, and he was in 2nd Battalion, The Wiltshire Regiment. A notice in the press states that he was George Harry, the eldest son of Walter and Harriet Holland of Stoneywood Cottage, Netherfield;[27] it quotes the right regiment and date and was presumably originated by the family. (CWGC assigns this parentage to another George, who was to die at Richebourg in 1916, and is silent on the background of the 1915 man. He may have been a half-brother.)

George/Harry has no known grave and is commemorated on the Le Touret memorial. His regiment was involved in the battle known as the Second Battle of Givenchy that began on 15 June, and it is probable that this is where he died. He had been in the Reserve before the war and had been called up at once, shortly being involved in the retreat from Mons; in January 1915 he was invalided home with pleurisy and pneumonia, and again after Easter. It was during this second period that he married Florence Martin of Catsfield at Battle on 15 May 1915, exactly a month before he died. In 1919, when she received his war medals, she was living at Belle Hill, Bexhill. She married a survivor, Percy Jenner, had two children and died at Maidstone in 1973.

George's half-brother Albert was to die in 1918. Their father Walter was to die early in 1919 and their mother Harriet in 1930, both at Battle.

Shortly after the death of George Herbert (Harry) a Battle man was wounded by gunshot to the right foot: Charles Elijah Eldridge. He had been born at Battle in 1885 but within a few years the whole family (which included his brother Ernest, who would die at Ypres in 1917) moved to Sidley. Charles enlisted at Hastings in October

1914 as a Sapper in the RE, and was promoted to Lance Corporal in April 1915 while another man was away; he reverted to Sapper in November 1916. In civilian life Charles was a plumber. He had married to Sarah Louise Bristow in November 1915 but (presumably unknown to his family) suffered badly from syphilis in the late summer of 1916. He was to have four children at Battle and to die there in in 1944.

Loos

The other major engagement on the western front was at Loos in the autumn – another sacrifice of lives to very little purpose in which the Germans lost almost no-one (*see Map 5*). Although many infantry regiments were engaged in this battle, the town came off relatively well but there was the death of someone once acquainted with Battle: Private Lancelot Edwin Orford, who served with 2nd Battalion, The Royal Sussex Regiment. He had been born at Little Eaton in Derbyshire but his family (his father was a teacher) had lived in Battle in the 1880s, where Lancelot's younger brother Charles had been born. Lancelot appears in the list of old boys of Battle Boys School who had joined up.[28] He died on 13 October, near Loos.[29] He has no known grave and his name appears on the Loos memorial. His parents died between the wars. The family had no further connection with Battle after they left the town, being by then in Norfolk and to some extent in Yorkshire.

And there was one known wounded soldier. This was Henry Spray, aged 25, a Private in the 4th Battalion, The Middlesex Regiment and in peace time a night-duty baker in Battle. He was the son of William Spray, a farm labourer who had been living in Whatlington Road, and was wounded at Loos.[30] Henry appears to have married in Middlesex and died there in 1962. His brothers and sisters have no readily identifiable descendants, and the family is further explored in connection with the wounding of his brother Charles in 1918.

Possibly Loos was also responsible for the loss of Harry Duke, a Private in 2nd Battalion, the Gordon Highlanders, who died in Germany on 1 October while a prisoner of war. He had been born at Battle in 1892, the son of James Duke, a domestic gardener and his wife Elizabeth (Thompsett): James lived to 1945 and Elizabeth to 1959. Harry had a brother and a sister, both of whom married and had children, one of them at Battle. In due course Harry's body was returned, and he is buried in the Valenciennes (St Roch) Communal Cemetery.

The End of the Year

As this unsuccessful year drew to its expensive close, there were two more wounded men. One was the teacher Cecil Blackhurst, who was at that point a Lance-Sergeant in 7th Battalion, The Royal Sussex Regiment. He was wounded on Christmas Eve but rejoined his regiment on 6 January 1916. He was to die later that year, and more information can be found about him at that point. The action in which he was wounded was the detonation of a German mine that buried several men but killed none.[31]

The other was Harry Archer, formerly a resident of a Upper Lake and a bootmaker like his father. Born at Battle in 1889, he died at Weston super Mare in 1977. Archer had enlisted in 7th Battalion, The Royal Sussex Regiment at Hastings in August 1914 and had achieved rapid promotion. He was Lance Corporal within weeks and Corporal by early December 1914. Sent to France the following May, he was promoted Lance-Sergeant and then Sergeant at the beginning of 1916. On 29 December he was wounded by gunfire in his left arm and left foot and was later sent to the Royal West Surrey Regiment shortly before his discharge as being no longer physically fit.

Notes

1 Ireland, Casualties of World War I, 1914–1918
2 De Ruvigny's Roll of Honour, vol 1.
3 David W Hughes: *The HMS Hythe Disaster* (June 2008) at http://www.kentfallen.com/PDF%20reports/HMS%20HYTHE.pdf
4 http://www.roll-of-honour.com/Ships/HMSScourge.html
5 Lyn Macdonald: *1914, the Days of Hope* (Michael Joseph, 1987).

6 For a review of the various estimates see Alistair Horne: *The Price of Glory* (Macmillan, 1962).
7 *Hastings Observer*, 6 March 1915.
8 *Hastings Observer*, 24 April 1915.
9 *Hastings Observer*, 3 April 1915
10 *Hastings Observer*, 3 April 1915.
11 *Sussex Express*, 14 May 1915.
12 *Hastings Observer*, 22 May 1915.
13 www.squaretoes.co.uk
14 Norman Moore diary 15 October 1914.
15 Ronald Skirth: *The Reluctant Tommy* (Macmillan, 2001)
16 Sussex *Who's Who, 1935*.
17 *Hastings Observer*, 15 May 1915.
18 *Hastings Observer*, 24 July 1915.
19 H C O'Neill: *The Royal Fusiliers in the Great War* (Heinemann)
20 Post Office Directory for London, 1882
21 http://www.foxfamilyhistory.com/Assoc_Families/Lamberts.htm, accessed 20 February 2013
22 *Hastings Observer*, 3 July 1915.
23 *Hastings Observer*, 21 April 1917.
24 http://www.espncricinfo.com/england/content/player/16438.html accessed 26 February 2013
25 *Hastings Observer*, 5 June 1915.
26 Register of police, held by East Sussex Records Office.
27 *Sussex Express*, 2 July 1915.
28 *Hastings Observer*, 25 December 1915.
29 Miller: *We wunt be druv*
30 In school list, *Hastings Observer* 25 December 1915.
31 Miller: *We wunt be druv*

4

Mass Killing: 1916

Neither side had made any substantial military progress in western Europe in 1915. All attempts to make significant territorial gains had failed, and as the year ended not only was the front line more or less where it had been at the beginning but also an alarming number of lives had been lost.

The attempt at Gallipoli at the other end of the continent would have been hailed as a masterpiece of strategy had it not been a botched and bloody failure from which Allied troops were lucky to complete an unhindered withdrawal early in January 1916. On the eastern front the Russians were being rapidly pressed back by the combined German and Austrian armies. In the south the Italians, were facing Austrian forces above them in the Alps and had made little progress below. It was clear to the Allies that something more needed to be done.

1915 had seen two major crises for Britain's role in the war, quite apart from the difficulties caused by German attacks on merchant shipping that were to lead to serious food shortages. First, there was a shell shortage, which became a factor in the fall of Britain's last Liberal government and its replacement by a coalition. It was promptly addressed by government and industry so that supplies were made at first adequate and then good by the late summer. Secondly, and much less easy to remedy, there was the beginning of a manpower shortage. It was evident that the rate at which casualties and captures were occurring was higher than the arrival of new recruits in the numbers needed for major attacks to succeed. The decision was therefore taken to impose conscription. This required legislation.

The Military Service Act of 27 January 1916 transferred to the

Reserve all unmarried British men between the ages of 19 and 41 (including widowers without dependent children). It came into force on 2 March and was extended to married men on 25 May. There were of course some exceptions – priests, temporary residents in Britain, those already rejected when they had volunteered, for example. Exemption was possible on certain limited grounds, for example for agricultural labourers and others deemed to have reserved occupations. The Act did not apply to Ireland which, given the later events there in 1916–18, may have been a sensible decision. Transfer to the Reserve meant that the men were to be treated exactly as if they were former soldiers eligible for recall to the colours.

The Act was applied by local tribunals. They met weekly to consider cases put by men (or their employers) who considered that there was a good case for them not being called up. There were two tribunals in the Battle area, one for the Urban District and one for the Rural, and there was a mechanism for appeal against their decisions. Some cases might be heard *in camera*, and though none seemed to have been so treated in Battle this was not so in Hastings. In Battle the cases put were mainly on the grounds of keeping the farms going, though there were others too. At its first meeting, for example, on 1 March 1916, the urban tribunal made decisions on twelve cases, while deferring some others. Two were refused: one farm worker whose employment was thought to be merely temporary, and a sub-carter whose services were thought to be dispensable. Of the ten approved, nine were agricultural (though two were given deferment for a limited period: they could then apply again) and one was a leather merchant working on his own.[1] The tribunals had to consider, among other things, whether the war effort would be adversely affected by men being called up, given that the services depended on work continuing at home. This was the case, for example, when George Newbery applied, citing his importance in an organisation that made jam for the troops among others and whose four brothers were already serving.[2]

Tribunals were not without their humour. Late in 1917, when food supply was particularly short and rationing biting hard, one shopkeeper applicant at Battle who was anxious to avoid conscription pleaded that he had to dispose of rather a large stock of goods brought in for Christmas, at which the Battle solicitor Frederic Sheppard (son of Charles, who had arrived as a solicitor in the town in 1872) asked in a stage whisper: *Has he any sugar or tea*? Sheppard was an applicant at the same hearing, and in due course he lost his case and went to serve.[3] In January 1918 Sheppard joined the RNAS as a Lieutenant, and a year later was to return and resume his work, which included being Clerk to the Magistrates and to the urban district council, of which his father was a member. [4] In 1917 Sheppard was 35 and lived at 1 St Mary's Villas. He had married Edith Dickins of Weymouth, in Warwick in 1906; he died in 1960 and she three years later. They appear to have no descendants. The firm is still there, busy, on the Abbey Green, now as Wykeham-Hurford Sheppard and Son, and the Sheppard brass plate is still at its door.

As with those who volunteered, every conscript had to have a medical examination to show their fitness for service. Men were examined locally to the point of enlistment and, possibly because of the pressing need for recruits, medical doubts might sometimes be resolved in favour of acceptance. A good example of failure to identify defects was in the case of Henry James Hawkins, who enlisted at Brighton in April 1918, aged 18. He already had tuberculosis in one hip and had spent five months in hospital in Hastings a few years earlier; he had recently contracted it in the other hip. He could not even march properly. In his examination for discharge in July that year the doctor reported bluntly: "This man should never have been conscripted." As the medical examination included a test in which the examinee had to hop across a room it is hard to see how the doctor responsible could have behaved honestly. Hawkins was a groom/gardener living on Battle Hill. He served as a Private in 5th Battalion, The Royal Fusiliers and fortunately did not see overseas service. Another example was John William Relfe, who had enlisted at Hastings in 1915 and had been passed fit for service. Two months later, when problems had been observed, another medic wrote:

> Mentally deficient. A case of congenital idiocy. He has been most of his life in the workhouse at Battle, and is totally unfit for a soldier.

He was immediately discharged. He died at Battle in 1936.

Similarly a third man was medically approved who was quite clearly incapable. He was William Whibley of Netherfield, who enlisted and was approved in February 1916. In June he was examined again, by a different doctor and described as mentally deficient and blind. He was immediately discharged. His later life is unclear. No doubt there were others who should not have been allowed to serve but nevertheless had to do so.

Of course the flow of new recruits was not immediately noticeable in the front lines from March 1916, because men had to be examined and trained. Nevertheless when they arrived they constituted an enormous extra resource. The result was that 1916 was the worst killing year in the history of the British army. Now the high command had enough men to throw at the enemy, and more to come if – and when – they lost them.

The first major confrontation of the war affected the British only indirectly. This was the German assault on the French-held fortresses north of Verdun, begun on 22 February. The Germans had two objectives. They wanted to take Verdun, which was blocking their way to an advance southwards east of Paris (which was what they had done in 1870); but equally clearly they planned a war of attrition. Brutally, the idea was to take out of the war as many French soldiers as possible, thereby rendering the continued resistance of the French army less effective. The efforts made to the north of Verdun, where the battle raged on until August and was not finally over until the autumn, meant some relief for the British further west. In fact the Germans lost almost as many men as the French at Verdun, which is as damning a comment as one might find on the strategy of almost all the top brass on both sides.

The new British Commander in Chief, Sir Douglas Haig, had taken over from Sir John French in December 1915. He gave great attention to a major offensive in the area assigned to the British, given that shell supply would now be good and that more troops would be available to him. Originally he wanted it to go forward in the late summer but the attack was brought forward to early July to relieve the French further east.

This year was to see a large number of deaths from Battle: 31 of those recorded, at least 23 of whom fell on the western front. Of those 23, four died in fighting before the fruitless assault began on

Richebourg on 30 June and three at Richebourg itself; two more fell on the first day of the Somme and at least 16 in the remainder of the battle. There were also deaths in the Adriatic, in Mesopotamia, in Tanganyika and in India.

Early Casualties on the Western front

The first casualty in the west was Charles John Crouch of Netherfield, a Private in 8th Battalion, The Royal Sussex Regiment. He was wounded near Givenchy on 3 March. Crouch was fairly old for the war, being then 43; he was the son of Stephen, a quarryman of Brightling and his wife Elizabeth; by 1911 he had moved to Windy Cottage, Netherfield, and with his wife Sarah Elizabeth (Jennings) had produced seven children, all born at Netherfield. One of them – Henry – also served in the war and was wounded, though we do not know where or when.[5] Another, William Cyril, born in 1907, was to be killed in the second world war. Henry went on to marry (name currently unknown) and to have five children, all born locally. He died in 1966. His mother Elizabeth was to die at Battle in 1952 and his father Charles in 1956, also at Battle.

Another early casualty was Albert Thomas Abrey, a Private in 1st Battalion, Australian Infantry Force. A son of the butler at Beauport Park, he had enlisted at Rosehill, near Sydney, in September 1914 and had left Australia in December. By the spring of 1915 he was at Gallipoli (where he suffered both diarrhoea and dysentery), leaving it on the first day of 1916. He left for France at the end of March and was seriously wounded by gunshot to his right thigh on 25 April in the Armentières sector; he was evacuated to hospital in Birmingham. The wound was serious enough to keep him from rejoining his unit until just before Christmas. He was to be killed in the following April. His two brothers also served.

At some point in April Driver William Herbert Eldridge was wounded. He was to be killed in 1918, and his details are given there.

There were four deaths before the Richebourg and Somme disasters, which began on 30 June.

The first was of Alfred Foster, a Private in 7th Battalion, The Royal

Sussex Regiment on 9 April. He died in that ever-lasting killing field between Béthune, Lens and La Bassée and is buried there, at Vermelles British Cemetery (*see Map 6*). It is likely that he and others were killed by a trench mortar. He was 32 and a general labourer living at Ore. His father and all but the last of his seven siblings had been born at Battle, but the family had moved to Hollington in the late 1880s. Henry (his father) was to die in 1931 and his mother Martha (Lower) in 1932. His other relatives cannot be reliably traced. Alfred had married Elizabeth Puxty in Battle in 1909, and she brought with her a young daughter from an earlier marriage but Alfred himself had no children.

Then there was William Buckle, aged 26 and a Private in 13th Battalion, The Suffolk Regiment. He died at home in Norfolk on 30 April, so it remains unclear where he contracted the wounds or illness that killed him. Neither do we know how long he had lived in Battle, but the 1911 census records him as a gamekeeper at Netherfield Place, and unmarried. There is no record of any of his family (parents and three siblings) having a connection with Battle. His father died in 1928 and his mother in 1939, both in Norfolk.

The next death was of Private Percy Oliver of 11th Battalion, The Royal Sussex Regiment on 21 May. From the beginning of May the battalion was just north of Béthune, preparing for the major attack on 30 June. It experienced the usual machine gun fire and shelling, and it must have been on one of these 'ordinary' days that Oliver was wounded. He is buried in Béthune Town Cemetery.

Oliver's widowed mother Emily (Nichols) was a baker and confectioner at 49 High Street and Percy was in the same business; he had been born in Erith in Kent in 1893. His immediate family was small. His father Henry Joseph, born in about 1870, was a railway official at the time of his death at Tonbridge in 1908; his mother Emily seems to have lived on to die at Hastings in 1953. His younger brother Stanley, who served in 14 Battalion, The Royal Sussex, married at Battle in 1922 but no children are recorded for him; he died there in 1970.

Shortly afterwards, on 24 June, Archibald Murdock was wounded. He was to die in 1917 and personal details are recorded in connection with his death.

The fourth death of the period before Richebourg was of Edward Ling, born at Buckland in Berkshire and a Lance Corporal in the Royal Berkshire Regiment. He was killed on 26 June and is buried in the Cabaret Rouge British Cemetery at Souchez; Souchez itself is north of Arras towards Béthune. He was 18. In 1911 his father George was manager of the Star Hotel (which in due course became the 1066 and later still Costa Coffee), and by the time of his son's death he was managing the Abbey Hotel;[6] There were 14 children of the parental marriage, three of whom died before 1911. It has been impossible to trace their histories. George himself was born in Camberwell and in his career moved around considerably: children were born in London, Oxford, Cambridgeshire, Oxfordshire and Berkshire. By 1916 he and his wife Rose were living at Downside Farm near Cobham in Surrey.[7] He died at Edenbridge in 1934, and his wife Rose at Hastings in 1939. Another son, Frank, was to die in service within two months.

On the same day Rifleman George Henry Ponsford suffered shell-shock. He was in 16th Battalion, The King's Royal Rifle Corps and had enlisted at Hastings in August 1915. Originally a Brighton man, he was a small child when his father died and he moved to live with his aunt at Blackfriars Cottage, Marley Lane (and later at 3 Prospect Cottages, Caldbec Hill). He was to be wounded again three times: at first almost at once, on 17 July (gunshot wounds), then on 14 April 1917 and on 1 December 1917 (gunshot wounds and shell-shock). By then he was a Lance-Corporal. Later in the war he was assigned to military police duties but was discharged as physically unfit in February 1919. He married Bertha Spray in 1922 and they had two children born at Battle. He died at Hastings in 1953.

Last to die before the big push was Charles Douglas Lamborn, on 30 June. No front line was ever wholly quiet, and action continued around Ypres. He had been born at Battle in 1886, son of William and Fanny who jointly ran the grammar school standing on the site of the present fire station. It was a large family, and it seems that Douglas (the name that appears on his military record) went to Canada in 1904; others may have done so too. He settled in Victoria, British Columbia, where he enlisted in 1st Battalion, West Ontario Regiment in 1915; by 1916 he was a Lance Corporal.

The Somme

We then come to the major offensive known as the battle of the Somme. So much has been written about it that it would be futile to do more. Suffice to say only that it lasted from I July to late November; that the forces under British command suffered 54470 casualties on the first day, including 19,240 who died then (or later of wounds received that day), more than on any other day in British history before or since; that the ground gained between July and the end of November was about ten miles in depth and was recaptured by the Germans later in the war. (*See Map 6*)

For the men of Battle the tally for the period 30 June to November 1916 was high, though not as high as it would be in early 1918. At least 16 of them died on the Somme itself, and the number of wounded is unknown but must be as high. On 30 June, the day before the main offensive, three men died and at least one was wounded.

Richebourg l'Avoue (The Boar's Head)

In fact the Somme offensive had really begun with diversionary attacks on 30 June, the figures for which are not included in the official casualties for the main battle. Those outside Sussex have to be thoroughly familiar with the war even to notice this date. The attack by the Royal Sussex at Richebourg is not even mentioned in the British Official History of the war, which is no doubt more concerned with the much greater events taking place on the Somme on the next day and thereafter. The South Downs battalions lost 360 killed and more than 1100 wounded in this fruitless action, the intention of which was to distract the enemy from the Somme, pin down his reserves and improve the local tactical situation.[8] Richebourg became known as 'the day that Sussex died' – the local version of the more famous killing of the 'Pals' in the main battle. It had been the site of a serious but rather less bloody battle in May 1915 *(see Map 7)*.

Richebourg lies well to the north of the Somme battlefield, slightly north-west of Béthune and part of the Aubers Ridge battlefield of 1915. It was not a quiet sector (but few sectors were quiet), and Robert Graves describes the fighting immediately south of Richebourg in late June.[9] The strategic purpose of the action was to provide a diversion, and similar attacks were carried out at Gommecourt, Plogsteert and Loos.

The Boar's Head was a German outpost, so there was some point in attacking it in addition to providing a diversion to make the enemy think that the main assault would come there rather than on the Somme, but the decision to do so was profoundly contested by the local British command. Battle suffered three deaths in this farrago.

> The Battle of the Boar's Head, Richebourg l'Avoue, was planned as a diversionary action to make the German Command believe that this area of the Pas de Calais was the one chosen for the major offensive of 1916. The intention was to prevent the Germans from moving troops to the Somme area, some fifty kilometres to the south …
>
> On the 11th of June, the three Battalions* went to the Divisional Reserve, being billeted around Locon, and commenced training for an attack (though this was still only a rumour). On June 16th they returned to the front line trenches in the Ferme du Bois area near Richebourg, holding the line until June 23rd, when news was received that the 39th Division were to make an attack on the Boar's Head, a salient of the German lines, and that the 116th Brigade, the Southdowners, had been chosen to lead the attack ... A replica of the battlefield had been built behind the lines, but the battalions had only days, not weeks, to consider it.
>
> Initial plans had been that the 11th Battalion should lead the attack, with the 12th on their right, and the 13th in reserve. At the time that these orders were received, Lieutenant Colonel Harman Grisewood, was the Commanding Officer of the 11th (1st Southdowns). Grisewood had lost his brother George, the Adjutant of the 11th Battalion until March 1916, who died of illness… on March 27th 1916. His death had deeply affected Colonel Grisewood, who, it is said, on seeing the plans, was concerned that if his untried troops attacked over unfamiliar ground a disaster might result, and is said to have informed his brigade commander: "I am not sacrificing my men as cannon-fodder!" **

* These were the 11th, 12th and 13th Battalions.

**Grisewood's second son Francis was to become a casualty of the Boar's Head, in addition to the son who had died earlier in the year. Grisewood was later posted

Needless to say the attack had to go in, but the Divisional Commander, Major General R. Dawson, aware of Grisewood's comments, was concerned that this might be passed down to the men of the 11th Battalion, and so the roles of the 11th and 13th Battalions were reversed.

According to a letter from Col. Grisewood to Captain Neville Lytton, Grisewood was told to "clear off at once...."

In consequence it was the 12th and 13th Battalions, with half the 11th supplying carrying parties, who made final preparations on 29th June, then assembled in the trenches of the Richebourg sector in the early hours of 30th June for the forthcoming attack, which was designed to "bite off the German position known as the Boar's Head", making the Germans believe that the real offensive was here, not the Somme.

At 2.50 am the preliminary bombardment commenced, final preparations were made, and scaling ladders were placed against the trench sides to allow the men to go "over the top".

In his history of the regiment Martineau writes:

.... the 11th Battalion, while supplying carrying-parties for the 12th and 13th on the day of the Richebourg and Ferme du Bois assault, sustained 116 casualties in this service alone. The 12th Battalion, assembling in the front line at Ferme du Bois, while the artillery bombarded the enemy trenches, attacked at 3.05 am., on June 30th, seized the front line, which they held for four hours against considerably superior German forces, and even broke through to the support line, which they held for half an hour.

Naturally it could not last. The Germans were ready. There is even a story that one man brought back a notice in English, announcing: "Come on, Sussex boys. We've been waiting for you for three days!"

A heavy barrage on the front line and communication trenches prevented reinforcements from being sent forward, the supply of bombs and ammunition gave out, and the valiant survivors were compelled to withdraw. The Battalion's 429 casualties included 17 officers.[10]

Grisewood was right about the likelihood of useless slaughter. Richebourg was only the precursor of what was to follow on the next day, the day after that and so on. Battle had at least five unlucky men

---

to the Manchester Regiment and was severely gassed in 1917.

in this disaster, which cost the Royal Sussex the lives of 18 officers, 76 NCOs and 267 privates.[11]

Three Battle men were killed on that day.

One was Private Fred Catton, one of those who had written to the tobacconist to thank him for his efforts, in his case only a month before.[12] He was in 12th Battalion, The Royal Sussex Regiment. Born at Battle in 1893, Catton lived with his father and sister at Great Wood in 1901 and then in Level Road, which is not officially so named now: it is part of Whatlington Road. His father was a gamekeeper, and at the age of 17 the son was an under-gamekeeper. The report of his death stated that he came from Petley Wood. His body was never identified or perhaps even found, and his name is on the Loos memorial. Catton's siblings almost all married and remained in Battle. His mother Harriet (Rush) had died at Battle in 1893 and his father there in 1919.

The second was George Holland of Netherfield (*left*), about whom we know nothing other than his regiment – the Royal Sussex. Like Catton and so many others, the 1916 George Holland is remembered at the Loos Memorial. CWGC states that he was a son of Walter and Harriet Holland of Stoney Wood Cottage, Netherfield, and may thereby confuse him with the George (Harry) Holland who died in 1915. George was almost certainly George David, whose birth was registered at Battle in the second quarter of 1881. It is possible that he was an elder half-brother of the George who died in 1915, but this seems unlikely. Walter and Ann (Walter's first wife) were diligent in having their children christened, and there is no such record for George at Netherfield. So whose child was he?

Walter and Ann had a child, Albert, born at Netherfield on 15 July 1881,[13] though a late registration of George cannot be ruled out. Walter did not marry Harriet until 1884. It is possible that this is the George who was to die in 1916 and that CWGC have confused the two.

The third was Charles Stapley Jempson, born at Netherfield in 1894 and in civilian life a general labourer. He was with 13th Battalion, The Royal Sussex Regiment and is buried at the Cabaret Rouge British Cemetery at Souchez. He had enlisted as a Private but had been promoted Lance Corporal by the time of his death. He had six siblings, none of whom can be traced at present. His father Charles Vidion Jempson was a sawyer who died at Hastings in 1939 and his mother Flora (Stapley) lived to 1956. The family moved to Hastings shortly after Charles's birth.

On the same day Walter James Hollands was wounded in the left arm and buttock, wounds that effectively put him out of the war. He was transferred to the Labour Corps in July 1917 and discharged as medically unfit in November of that year. Hollands was also from Netherfield and was a footman; he enlisted as a Private in 11th Battalion, The Royal Sussex Regiment in 1915. His father Tom was a gypsum miner, and his brother (also Tom) served in the same battalion. The elder Tom died at Hastings in 1932 and his widow Sarah (Farley) at Battle in 1940. The younger Tom seems not to have left a record of his death.

Walter married Ellen Draper at Battle in 1921, but no children of the marriage are recorded. He died at Bromley in 1972.

The second Battle man to be wounded was sent home: the postman Arthur Miller, who was wounded twice and was to reappear in France later. He was a Private in 7th Battalion, The Royal Sussex Regiment and one of those who would be killed in August 1918.

The Somme Offensive

The day after Richebourg, 1 July, saw the launch of the main offensive, following a week of heavy bombardment of the German lines. Throughout the long conflict the artillery could be heard at and near Battle (*see Map 8*).

An officer not from Battle who was involved in the attack on Mametz had written that morning:

> 1.7.16. 5–45 a m.
>
> It is a glorious morning and is now broad daylight. We go over in two hours time. It seems a long time to wait and I think, whatever happens, we shall all feel relieved once the line is launched. No Man's Land is a tangled desert. Unless one could see it one cannot imagine what a terrible state of disorder it is in. Our gunnery has wrecked that and his front-line trenches all right. But we do not yet seem to have stopped his machine guns. These are pooping off all along our parapet as I write. I trust they will not claim too many of our lads before the day is over.[14]

Private Frank Leslie Kane of 6th Battalion, the Buffs (the East Kent Regiment) described his part in a letter to his mother from hospital after he had been wounded for the third time in the war, this time in the La Boisselle sector:

> We went into the firing line overnight, and over the top at 7.30. What excitement, racing through a hail of bullets and bursting shrapnel. Luckily we had out steel helmets, which saved many a man's life. We got into the first line and bombed the Germans in their dug-outs, and polished off what few there were about. Of course we lost a lot going over, but what vim it gave us for killing them. I fixed a German officer on a bit of steel called a bayonet. He, like the rest, put up his hands and cried for mercy, but he got none from me.[15]

Almost a century later we can rightly condemn what seems to be the killing of a surrendering man; but we were not there at the time. We did not have to suffer the sometimes foulness of trench conditions, let alone the shelling and sniping and the death and mutilation of our comrades. (One man referred to the fact that the rats ran over the men when they were asleep;[16] another[17] told of rat hunts in the trenches.) By July 1916 some men had been at the front (though with periods of relief) for almost two years. Killing men who were surrendering or having been already captured was by no means uncommon and other witnesses refer to it, for example Robert

Graves.[18] One author[19] suggests that the troops had taken hold of the simple idea that they had been directed not to take prisoners and quotes the order of General Kiggell, Chief of the General Staff, issued on 28 June 1916 that reads in part:

> It is the duty of all ranks to continue to use their weapons against the enemy's fighting troops, unless and until it is beyond all doubt that those have not only ceased all resistance but that, whether through having voluntarily thrown down their weapons or otherwise, they have definitely and finally abandoned all hope or intention of resisting further. In the case of apparent surrender, it lies with the enemy to prove his intention beyond the possibility of misunderstanding, before the surrender can be accepted as genuine.

Even more extreme advice by a senior officer was recorded as given with 'homicidal eloquence' by Siegfried Sassoon.[20] One can sorrowfully add that this attitude was by no means confined to the Allies.

Kane had been born in Hastings early in 1885, so he was already 31 when he was at the Somme. The 1911 census records him as a single man living with his father and stepmother at 39 High Street. His father was a brewer's clerk, and Frank an ironmonger's assistant; his address was then given as 5 Harold Terrace. He went back to the line after each wounding; and he survived. He lived on to die at Battle late in 1965. Kane's father, a brewer's clerk, died before the war, in 1913; his mother lived to 1959. His brother Harold and sister Nina both married and had children.

Two Battle men were among the many dead on that terrible day.

Private Fred Skilton's death was reported in the *Hastings Observer* on 22 July, as was that of Private Boxall of the Royal Sussex on the same day. Given past practice, these reports were late. One must recognise that deaths and injuries on such a scale made it difficult for the army authorities to process information, especially when so many officers had gone too. It was rather easier to identify the officers, and news of their deaths came rather more quickly. Where a man was lost altogether – captured or having simply disappeared – things were even more difficult.

Skilton is recorded in the 1911 census as a poultryman aged 17, single and living with his parents at 8 Jubilee Cottages. After

1911 he was a groom and then a porter with a wholesale grocer in Watford. He became a regular soldier, joining the Bedford Regiment at Bedford in October 1913 and transferring to 2nd Battalion, The Border Regiment, early in 1914. He was at once sent to Ireland where he was based at Enniskillen, and went from there to France late that year.

Neither his health nor his army record was good. He was in hospital twice, at Mullingar in Ireland, and early in 1915 he was sent back to England with influenza, returning on 1 January 1916. There were numerous occasions on which he was guilty of some minor dereliction of duty – inattention, drunkenness, absences and the like – for which he repeatedly paid with loss of pay and being confined to barracks. The last occasion was as late as May 1916. He is buried in Dantzig Alley British Cemetery at Mametz, only just beyond the British front line of 30 June.

Skilton came from one of those large families so common at that time. The 1911 census records that his parents Caleb and Eliza had had 12 children, nine of whom had survived. Caleb, a roadman with the urban district, died in Rye in 1932; Eliza had already died shortly after the census in 1911. We know that brother Harry, born in 1897, served in the war with the RFA and survived, to die in Battle in 1972, and the death of his brother Eric, born in 1901, is recorded in Hastings in 1984. The siblings appear to have had no grandchildren in the Battle area.

The other man who died on 1 July, Frederick Boxall, lived at 11 Mount Street with his parents; father Albert was a tailor and Frederick was an apprentice tailor, presumably with his father. He was then 16, so he would probably have been 21 at the time of his death. It was a large family. Frederick had one elder brother and three younger ones as well as four sisters. One of them, Percy, is also known to have served. Frederick was active in sports locally, being both a footballer and a cricketer.[21] He enlisted in 13th Battalion, attached to 8th Battalion, The Royal Sussex Regiment and died in the Montauban area. According to the formal letter to his mother he was killed by a shell in the trench.[22] He has no known grave and is commemorated on the Thiepval memorial. The Montauban attack was one of the few successes of the day, the Pioneers working immediately behind the attacking forces to consolidate the ground won. The battalion suffered 'only' twelve deaths that day, out of the 19,200 of the British army as a whole.

Only one wounding is known for 1 July: Stanley Whiteman of Netherfield. His background is briefly described in connection with his first wound in 1915; he was to suffer another in 1917.

As July 1916 went on the reports of casualties grew. On 2 July it was the turn of Robert George Raper to die at Fricourt, a German strongpoint. Robert was one of two surviving sons of William Augustus Raper.

It is clear from all the records that the Raper family was held in the highest regard, and rightly so. Much of Battle's development in the early years of self-government was guided by William Augustus Raper. He had come to Battle as a young man from Portsmouth in 1870, where his father was Medical Officer of Health,[23] to practise as a solicitor and by 1879 had become a partner in the long-established firm of Ellman and Whitmarsh at 1 Upper Lake, in the building now occupied by Heringtons and almost opposite the house at 14/15 Upper Lake (later Pyke House) that he was to occupy for a long time.

The then young lawyer had made his name in the great Ashdown Forest case of 1876-82, which began when a commoner of the forest ordered his servant to cut bracken and other material from it. An agent of the landowner, Earl de la Warr, asked the man to desist, which he refused. De la Warr therefore brought a case to enforce what he believed were his rights. The commoner, however, was not only a barrister but also Deputy Lieutenant of Sussex, and not a man to be frightened. He engaged Raper, who meticulously assembled copious evidence, both local and legal, to support the rights of the commoners; and after a long time the commoners won the case.[24]

Raper was involved in the Sanitary Authority that preceded the Battle Urban District Council formed under the 1894 Local Government Act, when he was elected chairman of the new body. He remained in post until 1919 – as the Urban District was to be abolished in 1934, therefore, he was chairman for more than half its busy and useful life. He was also a county councillor. For long periods he was clerk of the Commissioners of Income and Assessed Taxes (this was before PAYE), and clerk and treasurer of the combined

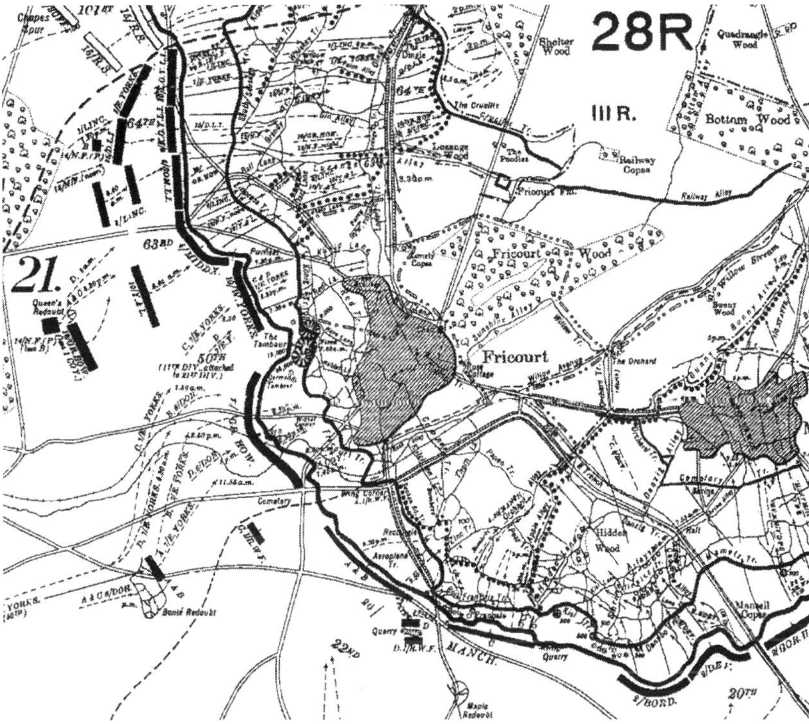

Map 9: Fricourt, 1 July 1916
The two unbroken lines are the British and German front lines before the battle began early on 1 July. During the following night 8th Battalion, South Staffordshire was brought up from the Morlancourt area at the south west for the attack on the next day. Lozenge Alley can just be picked out running east-west, about half a mile north of Fricourt town. The village on the right is Mametz; it is about ¾ mile from the middle of Mametz to the middle of Fricourt.

Battle charities. For years he contested with Charles Sheppard, no doubt politely, the leadership of the legal community in the town; they shared between them the various offices that were appropriate to the profession. His standing was so high that in January 1915, on his seventieth birthday, the bells of St Mary's rang specially for him.[25] He was also an active member of the Sussex Archaeological Society.[26]

But he had misfortunes with three of his four sons. The eldest, William, a solicitor like his father, had died in 1899. The next, Henry, had been a naval surgeon on HMS *Vulcan* who had died in Malta in 1904 (there is a plaque to his memory in St Mary's Church). Then came Robert, killed in the war. The last, Godfrey, also served, and with some distinction but survived. Their father died in Hastings on the last day of 1940, aged 95.

Robert had joined the territorial battalion of the Royal Sussex in 1896, and had been posted to garrison duty at Shorncliffe during the Boer War; he had been promoted Captain in 1908.[27] He was therefore subject to immediate call-up in 1914, and he applied for a commission in the Royal Sussex. There then followed a delay, and such was his enthusiasm that he decided to join a regiment with a quicker response, in this case 8th Battalion, The South Staffordshire Regiment.[28] By then he had married, in 1910, and had started his own family. He and his wife lived at Richards Hill, a large Victorian house on the south side of Powdermill Lane, shortly west of the entry to the Powder Mills hotel.

A detailed account follows:

> On the outbreak of war he transferred to a Service battalion, the 8th Bn. South Staffordshire Regiment, where he was also a company commander. Promoted Major and second in command at the end of May 1915, he remained with them until his death….
>
> Suffice it to say that the first attack on Fricourt having failed, 51st Brigade took over. Major Raper successfully led a patrol to clear the dugouts in the German front line and pressed on across no-man's land. Although the main German defence had retired it was still a tricky advance for the South Staffords as the Battalion took Fricourt village and pushed on through their second objective and on towards the third, getting ahead of their support as they did so. By this time Major Raper was leading the two forward companies and succeeded in taking the final objective of Lozenge Alley under heavy fire. But he was killed in doing so. Later his body was brought back by a friend and buried south west of Fricourt.
>
> Mrs Raper was determined to see her husband's grave remain where it was and by the end of 1918 was negotiating to buy the "small field or orchard, bounded on north and east by roads and on west by a light railway of no use for cultivation." (this is not quite right; the railway was to the south, roads to west and north) Instructions were given for the grave to remain where it was, the purchase was completed the following August and arrangements were made for the farmer's wife to look after the grave. In 1924 an almost horizontal stone cross supported clear of the ground on stone footings was erected over the grave inscribed:

> R.I.P. KILLED IN ACTION MAJOR R.G. RAPER 8th. SOUTH STAFFS. REGT. JULY 2nd. 1916
>
> As the years passed maintenance became more difficult, although CWGC gave much unofficial help, and in 1960 the grave was badly damaged by vandals. In 1965 the family decided the grave should be moved to its present site in the cemetery. When the grave was exhumed Major Raper's gold pins-nez [*sic*], cufflinks, gold studs and tie pin were found. No trace of the bridge or grave remain today.
>
> The Raper family contributed to the cost of rebuilding Fricourt church and the Twelve Stations of the Cross which adorn its walls are dedicated to him:
>
> CHEMIN DE CROIX OFFERT EN SOUVENIR DU MAJOR RAPER.
>
> Major Robert Raper was seen by the people of Fricourt as their liberator and they remembered him by naming the street leading from their new war memorial to the Church, 'RUE DU MAJOR RAPER'.[29]

After his death the Dean of Battle paid tribute to him on Sunday, 9 July, speaking of "a life without reproach crowned by a death of heroic self-sacrifice".[30]

Later still it was reported that the Commander-in-Chief, Sir Douglas Haig, had proposed special mention not only of Robert Raper but also of his brother, Temporary Captain Godfrey Curzon Raper ASC, and he did so again at the end of the war.[31] It was also reported that at the beginning of the war Godfrey had returned home 'to do his bit for the Empire', having handed over the management of his interests in Colorado to a friend.[32] Godfrey left Battle after the war, marrying in 1921 and having three children; the family lived in the west country where he died in 1951. His wife Stella (Hartcup) died there in 1957.

Robert and his wife Ida (Macadam-Smith) had children William, born in September 1911; Pamela, born late in 1912; Robert, born in August 1915; and the posthumous Josephine, born in September 1916. All were born in Battle except Pamela, who arrived in Elham, in Kent.

Ida remarried after Robert's death, to Reginald Fovargue, the solicitor who joined William Raper as a partner in 1922 when the firm's name was changed to Raper and Fovargue. They too lived at Richard's Hill. She died in 1979. There are still Fovargues in Battle. The firm itself was later joined by Robert's son William (1911–1987). In 1986 the growing alliance of various firms united under the name Heringtons.[33]

On the same day, 2 July, Charlie Blackman was badly wounded. As his battalion was split at the time, with many men having been withdrawn to recover after Richebourg, we do not know whether this was at Le Brébis or Béthune.[34] He was a Private in 12th Battalion, The Royal Sussex Regiment. He was aged 20 and was wounded 'in fifteen places',[35] and presumably this means that he sustained fifteen separate wounds at the same time. The army records the wounds as gunshot wounds to the right eye and to both feet. He was invalided out and after a period in hospital was discharged as physically unfit in February 1917. Charles was the son of a thatcher, Thomas Blackman. It was a large family – Thomas and his wife Adelaide had nine children, one of whom had not survived to be recorded in the 1911 census – and Charlie was the youngest; before the war he was a baker with King's of Mount Street. Adelaide died at Battle in 1927 and Thomas ten years later. Charlie himself went on to become a solicitor's clerk and died at Battle in 1959.

On 7 July the Battle teacher wounded on the previous Christmas Eve died in the attack on Ovillers: Private Cecil James Livesey Blackhurst, born in 1885 and unmarried. He had been an assistant master at Battle School and scoutmaster for the Battle Troop from September 1914 until he joined 7th Battalion, The Royal Sussex Regiment early in 1915, though his enlistment date is given as 31 August 1914. He died in action at Ovillers on a day of very heavy losses for his battalion. He has no known grave and his name is on the Thiepval Memorial.[36] Blackhurst's family lived in Blackpool, where his father was a wine and spirit merchant (later a grocer) and he and his brother had been born at Kirkham. There are no known Battle connections other than through his teaching post.

On the same day Lance Corporal James Whiteman died. He was with 7th Battalion, The Royal Sussex Regiment and was also in the attack on Ovillers. The Germans were perfectly prepared, and the battalion suffered its worst losses of the whole war. 25 officers and 650 men went into the attack; five officers and 220 men returned unhurt. 123 died.

In civilian life Whiteman was a poulterer living at Newlands Farm, Dallington in 1911. His parents George and Sally lived at Netherfield Place, which George farmed. They had had 19 children, of which 15 survived in 1911. They later retired to Eastbourne, where Sally died in 1925 and George in 1937. Except for his brother Charles, who also served but survived, it has not been possible to trace James's siblings from public records and it appears that the great majority moved away from the area. James himself, born at Warbleton in 1881, married Annie Bessie Mepham in 1900 and had two children, Albert and James. His widow moved away from Sussex and died at Plymouth in 1949. Neither son stayed at Battle, thus breaking the connection with the town.

Late in July, in the Bapaume sector, the town lost 23-year old Leonard Ernest McQuillan, a Corporal in the Royal Fusiliers and a son of a well-known Battle man. In civilian life Leonard was last living at Catford in the Lewisham area. His father James McQuillan, born in Kent in 1851 and formerly in the army (the 1881 census has him as a Colour Sergeant with troops on HMS *Ruby*), had been for some time the surveyor and inspector of nuisances for Battle Urban District. By 1916 the urban district councils had accrued more powers, but when they were set up in 1895 McQuillan's post would have been probably the most important of all. These councils were the direct successors to the urban sanitary authorities, and the inspector of nuisances was the key person in identifying nuisances such as overflowing cesspits and in providing remedies for them. The inspector was central to the drive to provide clean water, to ensure proper drainage and to remove sewage safely. The McQuillan family remained in Battle, and Leonard's father was buried there at the age of 80, in 1931. His mother had already died, in 1913. In 1901 the family was recorded as living at Starr's Green, but as it shrank James moved into smaller premises at 8 Lower Lake; at his death his home was at 28 Mount Street.

There was no early report of Leonard's death. The first mention in public was a statement that he had been wounded on 18 July and was missing; this reached the newspapers at least by 21 October.[37] In January the Red Cross reported that there was still no news of him, meaning that he was not in German hands and that he had simply disappeared. The family must then have assumed that he was somewhere dead on the battlefield, but at some point his remains must have been identified because he is recorded as being buried in Caterpillar Valley Cemetery, Longueval. This place is equidistant from Albert and Bapaume but south of the road joining them.

Leonard had six siblings, and five of them married. There were some children, but none remained in Battle. The youngest, Edgar, born in 1901, had a career in the RAF, retiring as Wing Commander. When he died in 1966 it was in Lincolnshire, but he is buried at Battle.

At the end of July three local men were reported wounded, without any specific information: A Mewett, Walter Cramp and Thomas Hoad.[38]

As to Mewett, we do not know whether the casualty was Arthur (born about 1892) or Albert (born about 1897), though we do know that 'Bert', presumably Albert, did serve.[39] The reports use a simple initial. Whoever the man was he was the son of Arthur Mewett who was a gardener to the Webster family at Powdermill, and the family lived on site at Park Dale. Arthur and Albert had one brother, George, who served as a Private in the RAMC and who lived to 1977. Their father died shortly after the Somme, late in 1916, and their mother at Battle in 1936. It appears that all their relatives are in Eastbourne.

Walter George Cramp was a Private in the Royal Sussex who lived at Fuller's Farm in Uckham Lane where his father was a waggoner; in 1911 Walter was a cowman there. Army records disclose nothing about him so we do not know his battalion but it was clearly on the Somme. He had been born at Ewhurst and was about twenty years old. Later in the war he won promotion to Corporal in the Trench Mortar Battalion when he was in Italy, and he received the Military Medal when war ceased. Cramp married Constance Eldridge in 1927 and had four children but he moved away and died at Newport, Monmouthshire, in 1978. His sister Gertrude, however, stayed in Battle and married Frederick French, having two children. She died in 1982. Constance appears to have lived to 1997.

The newspaper report gives Thomas Hoad's name as Head, which must have been a common misprint. There were no Heads at Battle in the 1901 or 1911 censuses, but there was a Thomas Henry Hoad, born about 1893, son of John Hoad, a carman's carter. He himself was a fruit gardener with Dannreuther's on Marley Lane. We do not at present know whether he was related to the Frank Hoad who was to die early in September.

Hoad was a Corporal in 5th Battalion, The Royal Sussex Regiment, which at the time was supporting the troops on the Ancre and towards Albert. He married Ellen Swabey late in 1917 and later a child was born. He died at Hastings in 1961 and Ellen at Battle in 1967.

On 31 July, probably at the Somme, Gunner Griffith John Morris of the Australian Artillery was wounded, though not seriously, while with the 106th Howitzer Battery. (He was to be wounded again in 1917, though we do not know where). Morris had been born at Battle in April 1891, son of Samuel, who was described in the 1901 census as a Congregational evangelist and who was to die at Guestling late in 1910. His widow Kathleen moved to Canada within months. Morris was a seaman and on arriving in Australia enlisted in the army at Sydney despite his defective vision. He embarked in January 1916 and arrived in France via Egypt. His military career ended early because he was sent back to Australia in January 1918, being discharged at Sydney in April. He then left for Canada.

Morris occupies a unique place in this record in that, despite his vision, he enlisted again for the Second World War, this time with the Canadian forces, and died on active service; he has a miliary grave in Vancouver.

On 5 August 1916 there was a report that Sergeant Bernard Anderson, already mentioned in this account, had been wounded in the thigh.[40] There were no major engagements on that day, and his wounds must be put down to the sporadic shelling and sniping that affected every trench at all times. The battalion was busy at Ovillers a little east of Albert, or at least at the remains of it, with work going on to strengthen trenches and barbed wire.

Anderson was in 5th Battalion, The Royal Sussex Regiment. In civilian life he was a plumber, and aged 24; he had joined the territorials at the age of 19 and so was liable for immediate call-up in August 1914. Nevertheless, as a territorial his contract expired in 1916, and he had spent two months at home before rejoining his battalion. He had been born at Battle and lived at 9 Mount Street with his father (a jam boiler with Newbery's), mother, two sisters and a younger brother. Three weeks after his wounding the report came that his condition, which at first had seemed manageable, had deteriorated and that he had died in Rouen military hospital. When his condition worsened the army told his parents, and his mother was able to be with him when he died.[41]

CQMS Roberts wrote of Anderson to his father. Such letters, however strongly felt, rarely strayed from a number of phrases; with the casualties mounting it must have been hard to find new ones. But Roberts's letter seems to go beyond the usual expressions of regret:

> I cannot tell you how grieved I was to hear the sad news of Bernard, and I hasten to offer you all my deepest sympathy in your great sorrow. You have lost a good son, and I a dear friend., for we had known each other for years, but more intimately since this horrible war. His death has come as a great blow to all of us, for he was well liked by everyone, and no-one thought he was so seriously wounded. In fact, he was quite cheerful on his way to the dressing station, and joked about going to England. Brave lad! He was none of the strongest, but stuck to his duty unflinchingly. Men like him, after all, are the real heroes, for to those of his kind of disposition this work is most repugnant, but it has got to be done, and, unfortunately, cannot be done without sacrificing precious lives. May God help you to bear your sorrow.[42]

Like those of so many others, Bernard's family appear to have died out. His mother died in Battle in 1925, and his father in 1941. His sister Ethel did not marry and died in 1949. Nor did his brother Frank marry; he died in Battle in 1936. His younger sister Elsie married and had two children; one died in infancy and the other, who lived to 1994, never married.

Also on 5 August it was reported that Private Victor Marchant of the Royal Sussex (battalion unknown), had been wounded in the leg. He was 18, born in Battle, and lived in Parks Yard off the High Street. His father was a coal carman and his mother one of those rare things, an employed married woman: she worked in Newbery's jam factory. Victor died at Battle at the end of 1965.

On 14–15 August, at the notorious Mouquet Farm, a Battle man won the Military Medal, along with his brother. That man was Walter Noakes, son of a farmer at Hooe, who had been born at Battle in 1874 and who had gone to Australia with his brother Levi Matthew. Levi was not from Battle, having been born elsewhere. The citation reads as follows, in an officer's handwriting:

> For gallantry + devotion. A duty as stretcher-bearers – on the night of 14/15 Aug 1916 these brothers repeatedly bandaged + carried in wounded men under heavy shell + machine gun fire. They brought a serious case down to the Bn Aid Post. Though much exhausted they volunteered to go out in response to an urgent call to Bn HQrs, passing through a heavy barrage + bandaging + helping wounded until completely breaking down from fatigue.[43]

The brothers were both living with their aunt at the Miners Arms, Bardoc, Western Australia, when they enlisted on the same day in July 1915. Walter gave his occupation as seaman and Levi as labourer. The Australian records show both as Privates, Walter in 52nd Battalion and Levi in 11th Battalion of the Australian Imperial Force,[44] so to be together there must have been some later change.

Walter married in Bermondsey in 1918, to Gladys Victoria Martin, and they went to Australia. A son was born there in 1929. Levi too married and returned, dying in Western Australia in 1954. Walter died there in 1969.

On 15 August Tom Hollands, a Private with 11th Battalion, The Royal Sussex Regiment, was wounded at Trônes Wood; he had to wait for his discharge for two years after that. Hollands was a general labourer in civilian life, and his family has been briefly described in connection with the wounding of his brother Walter earlier in the year. He was 22.

On 17 August[***] Richard Saunders of Netherfield (already wounded in 1914) was wounded again but quickly recovered. We do not know where this was, because at that point his battalion had been withdrawn from the front. Saunders was a professional soldier in 2nd

*** The Netherfield List states 22 August.

Battalion, The Royal Sussex Regiment, having joined up in 1905 and having reached the rank of Corporal in 1912. Called up in August 1914, he reached France on 21 August of that year. Three weeks later he was wounded; by the time of his third wounding in 1917 he would be a Sergeant. His brother Alfred had died in Egypt four days before. The public records are unclear as to Richard's future.

On 18 August Private Leonard Percival Stevenson, of the East Kent Regiment (The Buffs), died on the Somme. He was 19, and in 1911 had been an ironmonger's assistant, living with his family at 4 Leopold Road, Bexhill. All four children had been born in Battle to Walter and Emily Jane Stevenson; in 1911 Walter was a warehouseman. Stevenson is commemorated on the Thiepval Memorial.

Stevenson's father died at Battle in 1938 but his mother survived to 1970, when she would have been 96 or 97. A brother Raymond married in 1936 and died at Battle in 1959, having one daughter Janet, born at Battle in 1944. She had two sons, both born in the area.

On 23 August Frank Richard Ling also died in the attacks on the Mouquet Farm area on the Somme. He is remembered on the Villers Bretonneux Memorial and on the Australian War Memorial at Canberra. He was a Private in 23rd Battalion of the Australian Imperial Force. Ling had enlisted at Melbourne early in 1915 and had been sent to Gallipoli, where he suffered a serious shoulder wound in December; he was hospitalised first on HMS *Gloucester* and then in Egypt. By the time that he rejoined his unit in February the Allied forces had left Gallipoli. In May he embarked for France on HMS *Scotian*, arriving at Marseille on 18 May. (Consideration of his family is given above in connection with his brother Edward's death on 26 June.)

A week later William Dyer was killed. He had been born at Battle in 1882 and was a farm labourer, but in both 1891 and 1901 the censuses report him, his mother Jane (born at Battle) and his brother George (born at Westfield) as inmates of the Battle workhouse. His father George had died in 1885. The family is recorded as living at Westfield in 1881. William was a Private in 11th Battalion, The Royal Sussex Regiment and died on the Somme front. He is buried in the Engelbelmer Communal Cemetery Extension north of Albert.

The next summer death was Sergeant Frank Albert Hoad of 11th Battalion, The Royal Sussex Regiment. He had been born at Battle in 1889, though he did not live there afterwards. His family seem to have moved around considerably within the county, and he enlisted at Eastbourne in September 1914, arriving in France on 3 March 1916. At the time of his service his father was living at Little Lulhams farm at Ripe; we know this partly because in 1915 Hoad was released for five weeks to help with the harvest there. He had clearly caught the eye of his superiors because he was promoted from Private to Corporal in December 1914; the steps to Sergeant (via Lance-Sergeant and Acting Sergeant) all took place in eleven days of July 1916. He died on 3 September 1916 and has no known grave; he is commemorated at Thiepval (and at Ripe). His comrade Edmund Blunden (1896–1974), who was to be awarded the MC when a temporary Second Lieutenant in 1917 and who later still was to become famous as a poet, was with him when a shell splinter hit him:

Pillbox

Just see what's happening, Worley. Worley rose
And round the angled doorway thrust his nose,
And Sergeant Hoad went too, to snuff the air.
Then war brought down his fist, and missed the pair!
Yet Hoad was scratched by a splinter, the blood came,
And out burst terrors he'd striven to tame.
A good man, Hoad, for weeks. *I'm blown to bits*
He groans, he screams. *Come, bluffer, where's your wits ?*
Says Worley, *Bluffer, you've a blighty, man!*
All in the pillbox urged him, here began
His freedom: *Think of Eastbourne and your dad.*
The poor man lay at length and brief and mad
Flung out his cry of doom; soon ebbed and dumb
He yielded. Worley with a tot of rum
And shouting in his face could not restore him.
The ship of Charon over channel bore him.
All marvelled even on that most deathly day
To see his life so spirited away.

As far as one can see this is the only mention of the death of *any* named soldier in any 1914–18 war poem by a reputable poet. Blunden wrote much more, and included names, but appears not to have described further named deaths. He noted that he had written this poem on the 29th September 1917 on the battlefield at a place called Tower Hamlets near the Menin Road in Flanders.[45]

The scene of Hoad's death was typical of the war: a major attack against almost impossible odds, with the second and third waves facing an impassable barrage of shells. Hoad was clearly seen to die, and not in such a way that his body was destroyed; but he has no known grave. The authorities presumed him dead at once, which suggests that information was given that he had in fact died. The inference must be that his body was lost in the immediately subsequent fighting. Nevertheless some possessions were recovered: some letters, a pocket case, his wrist-watch and strap, a prayer book and a pipe. They were returned to his family.

Hoad's father Nelson had married a farmer's daughter in 1888, and from being a carter on his father in law's farm at Waldron in the 1891 census progressed to be a farmer himself in the 1911 census, at Payne's Farm, Warbleton. In 1911 Frank was recorded as a farm worker on an uncle's farm nearby. Nelson returned to Battle at some time between then and his death there in 1939; his wife Mary Ann (Luxford) died in Hampshire in 1942.

Frank's two brothers stayed in Sussex. Cyril, born in 1901, died unmarried in Battle in 1923. Herbert, born in about 1897, married in 1924 and had two children, neither of them living at Battle. There are, as noted earlier, other Hoads at Battle.

The last summer death was of Robert Kendall. His was a well-known name at Battle; he was the nephew of George Kendall whose medical practice was at 69 High Street. George had come to Battle in 1895. He was a popular and attentive doctor who was recorded as not collecting fees due when his patients could not afford his care, and no doubt his practice was busy. When he retired in 1928 a subscription was taken for him that resulted in his being able to retire in some comfort to Eastbourne.[46] In 1911 George was living with his wife and two daughters, and his mother had also come to live at Battle. But his wife died in September 1911, and his mother in

September 1914. Robert, born in London, was the son of his brother Alfred, who had himself died at Battle in 1902.[47]

Robert was a Sergeant in 10th Battalion, The Royal Fusiliers. He was severely wounded and died on 8 September 1916. He is buried in Loos British Cemetery. George died at Eastbourne in 1932; his daughters appear never to have married. Edith died in 1956 and Ellen in 1963, both at Eastbourne. Robert had two brothers and a sister, but they appear to have remained in London.

Also in September Jim Saunders was wounded on the Somme. He was a Private in 11th Battalion, The Royal Sussex Regiment, and had been born at Netherfield in 1898. His father Robert was a gypsum burner and his mother was Ellen Rose (Godden); Robert died at Hailsham in 1927 but Ellen lived on to die at Battle in 1963. After the war Jim married Kathleen Jenner, who predeceased him in 1969; he died at Hastings in 1990. There appear to have been no children.

On 27 September William Hiram Smith died at home of wounds received in action. He was a Private in 12th Battalion, the Royal Sussex Regiment, though one record has him as a sergeant; we do not know where he was when wounded. William appears in the censuses as having been born at Brede to William, an agricultural labourer, and his wife Elizabeth. There were three siblings surviving in 1911, by which time the younger William was a miller's carman at the King's Head Mill at Battle. In 1913 he married Minnie Pope, born at Battle in 1887. Due to the frequency of the surname it has been hard to trace what happened to any of the family, but it appears his father died in 1925. No children have been traced for William and Minnie. Smith is buried in the Hastings cemetery and his name is on the Hastings Memorial.

But the year was not over, and the Somme was to claim more local victims.

On 1 October it was the turn of Samuel Neeves (the man whose name appears on the plaque in the Memorial Hall but not on the churchyard memorial). Neeves had been born at Battle early in 1895 and was therefore 21 when he died. He was the son of Samuel Neeves, a wood dealer of Whatlington Road, and he worked at Newbery's. He was the only child of the family. He was a Private in 23rd Battalion, the Middlesex Regiment, enlisting at Hastings in December 1915 and being sent to France the following May. His army record states that he was a porter at stores, presumably a warehouse. We do not know how or where he died. No identifiable body was recovered and his name is on the Thiepval Memorial. After the war his parents left Battle for Cranbrook, where the elder Samuel died in 1930, aged over 90; Samuel's mother, much younger, lived to 1950 and died in Hove. Samuel had six half-siblings, and all but one stayed at Battle.

Private Arthur Neville Smith of 9th Battalion, The Royal Fusiliers, lived in Marley Lane, in the signalman's cottage close to the box from which the level crossing was controlled. His father Walter was a signalman for the South Eastern Railway and Arthur, only 14 in 1911, was then an apprentice grocer with International Stores at 61 High Street. He enlisted on 29 March 1916 and was wounded on 4 August. By the time of his death on the Somme on 7 October he was 19. On that day his battalion was engaged in the battle for the Transloy Ridges, a British attack that was broken by devastating machine gun fire. His father died in Hastings in 1927 and his mother there in 1942; and his brothers both lived and died in the area – Harry dying in Hastings in 1956 and Walter in Battle in 1973 or 1974.

On the same day and in the same action as Arthur Smith, Percy Eldridge was wounded. He was brother of Charles, wounded in July, and of Ernest, to be killed in 1917. He was shot through the wrist and invalided out; he was discharged as unfit late in 1917. He was a bricklayer who had enlisted at Hastings in February 1916 and had served in France only 31 days when he was wounded. He was a Private in 11th Battalion, The Royal West Kent Regiment.

The next day Sydney Clarence Meppem died. He was a Private in the London Regiment, born at Battle and aged 20. He is buried at Warlencourt, presumably close to where he fell. His brother Ormond was to follow him within a year. Although Ormond had been born at Ewhurst, both boys were educated at Battle. Their father (also Ormond) and mother Isabella lived in Imberhorne Lane at East Grinstead and also had two daughters. Before the war Sydney had been a clerk. The elder Ormond was an estate bailiff and died at The Hawthorns, Imberhorne Lane, East Grinstead on 1 January 1945. Isabella had died there in 1942.

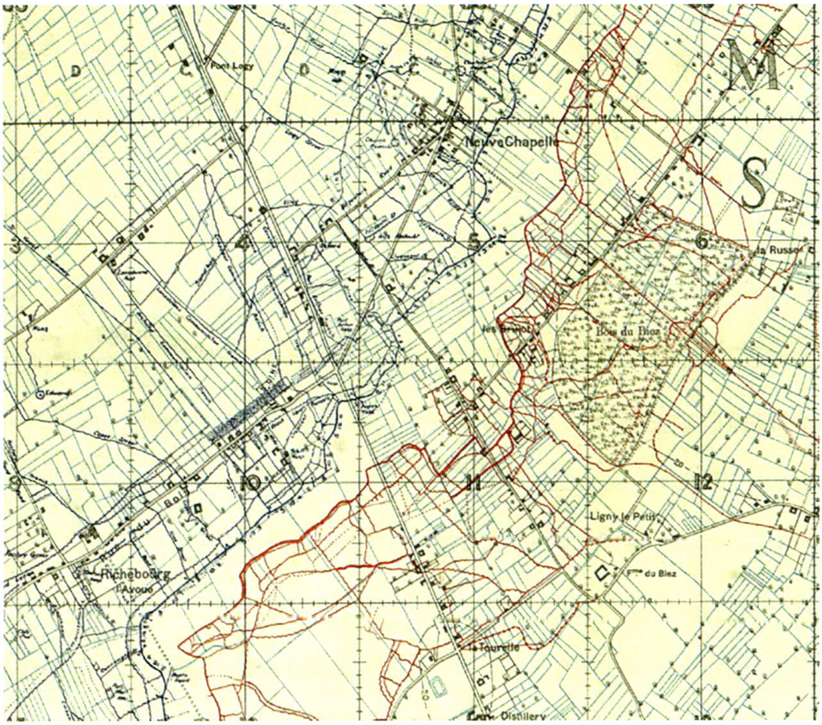

Map 1: Neuve Chapelle after its fall to the British in 1915. The German lines are in red. The British front line previously ran approximately northwards from the German line opposite Richebourg, turning north-east before reaching the top square. Each marked square is 1000 by 1000 yards. © Imperial War Museum

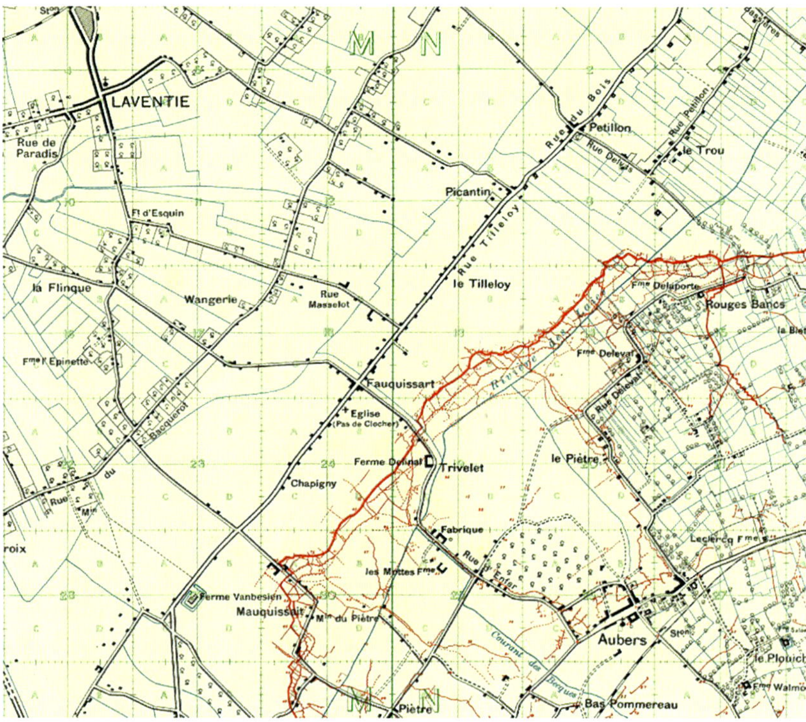

Map 4: Aubers Ridge on 27 July 1915, after the battle.
The German line here is in red; the British line is not given. Neuve Chapelle is immediately south of this map at the first square from the left. Each marked square is 1000 by 1000 yards.
© Imperial War Museum

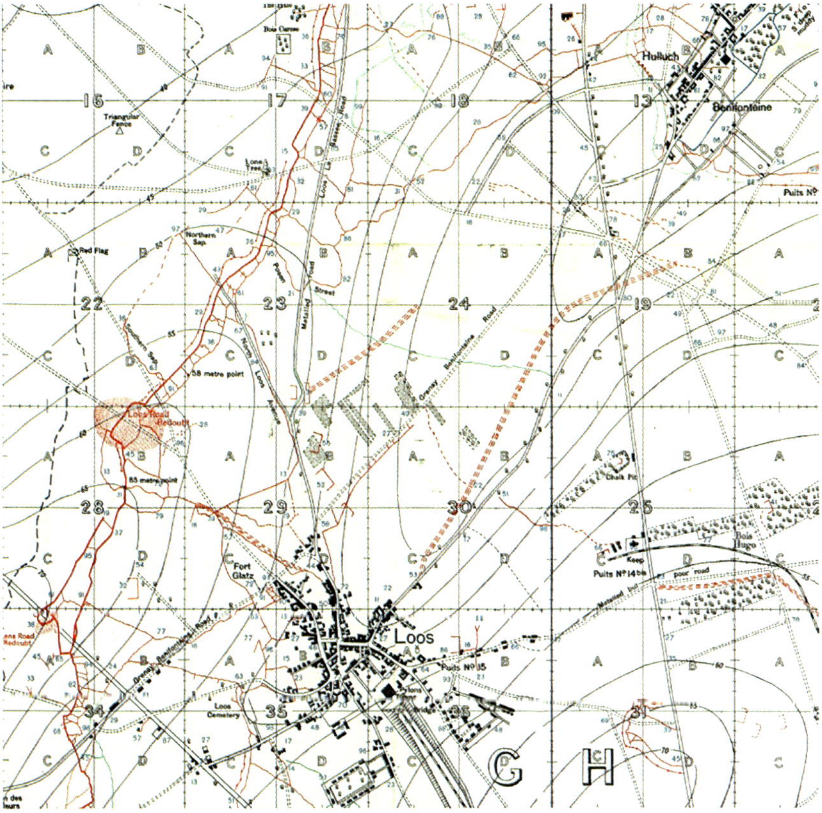

Map 5: Loos before the attack, 22 September 1915.
The German lines are in red, facing westwards (left).
Each marked square is 1000 by 1000 yards.
© Imperial War Museum

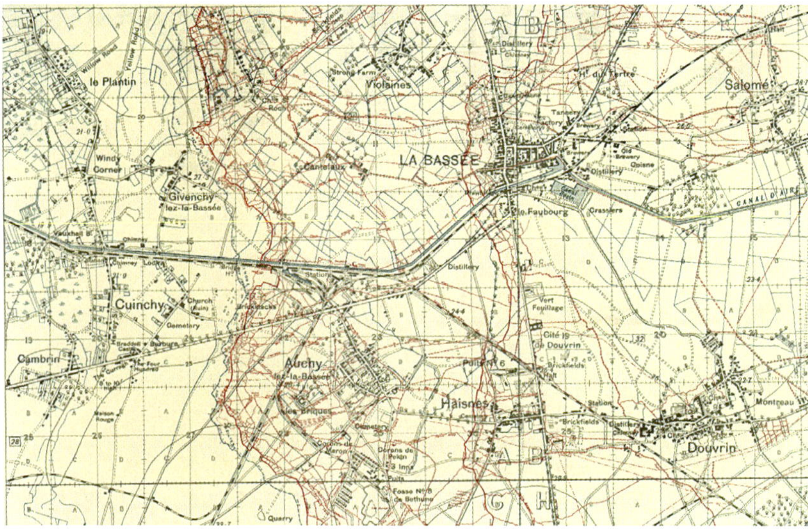

Map 6: La Bassée area, February 1916.
The map shows the area of La Bassée on 15 February 1916, with the German lines in red and the British front line in blue.
Each marked square is 1000 by 1000 yards.
© Imperial War Museum

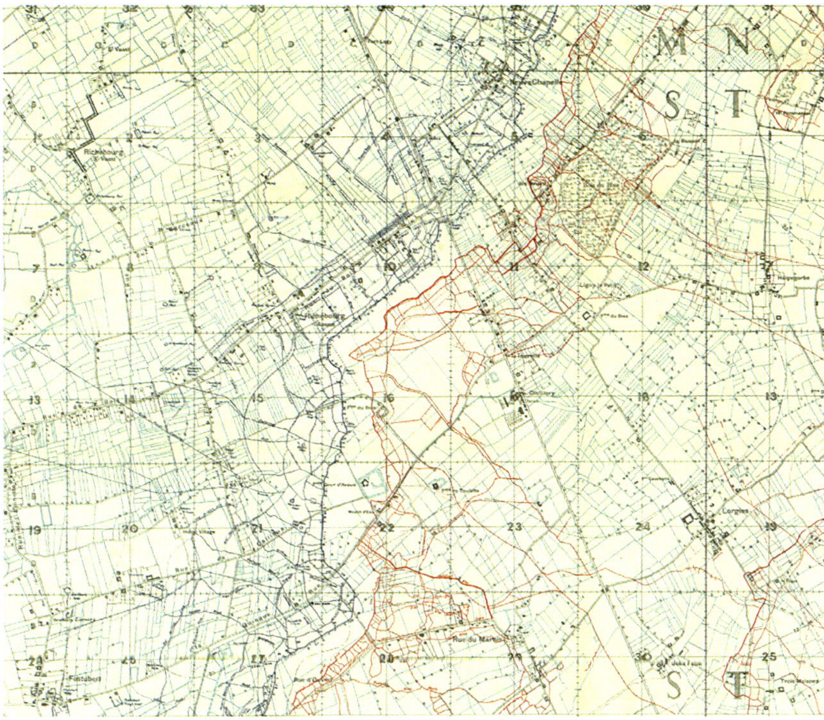

Map 7: Richebourg l'Avoue/The Boar's Head, June 1916.
This map, dated 12 June 1916, shows the German trenches in red and the British in blue. The Boar's Head salient is the point shown at six squares across and six down. The Ferme du Bois is marked as the first building southwards along the German line, next to the number 16. It is clear from a larger map that the ground rises from west to east. Each marked square is 1000 by 1000 yards.

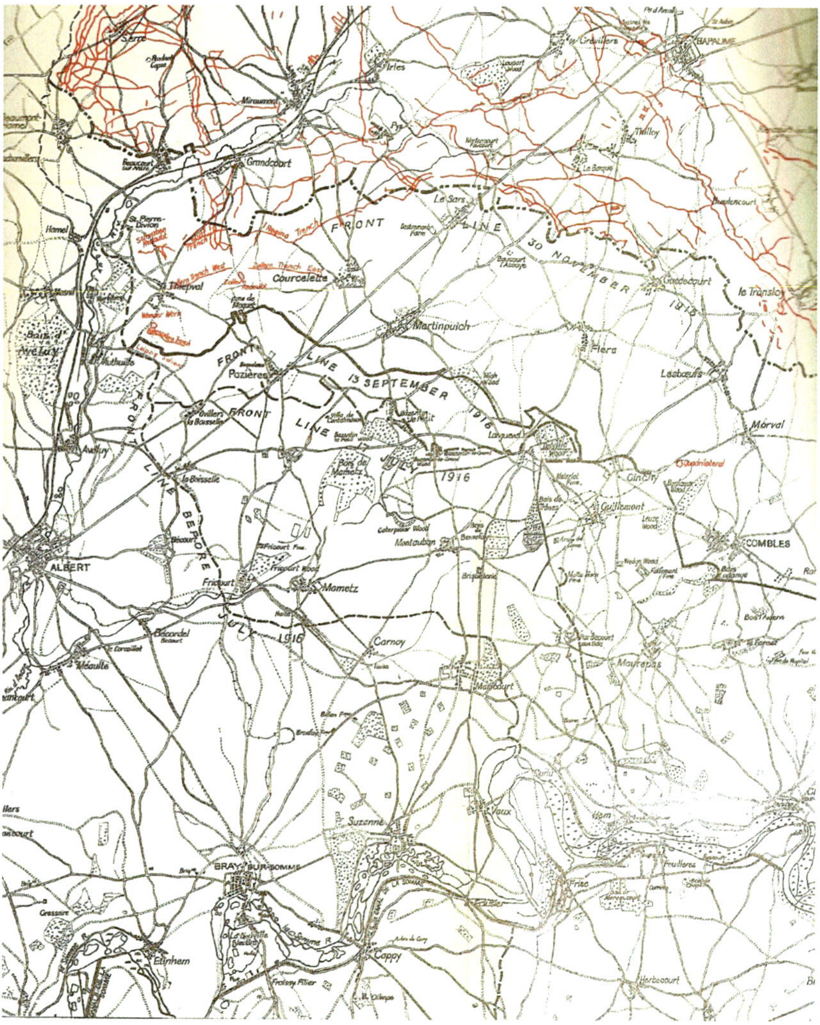

Map 8: The Somme Offensive, July to November 1916
The scale here is 0.5" = 1000 yards.
© Imperial War Museum

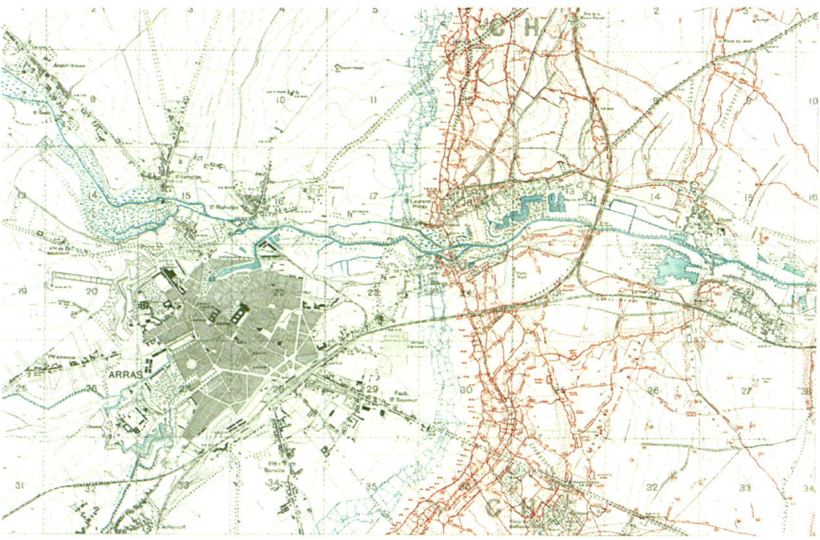

Map 12: Arras, 4 March 1917.
This map shows clearly the closeness of the lines and of the Germans to the city of Arras. The German lines are in red, the British in blue. Each marked square is 1000 by 1000 yards.

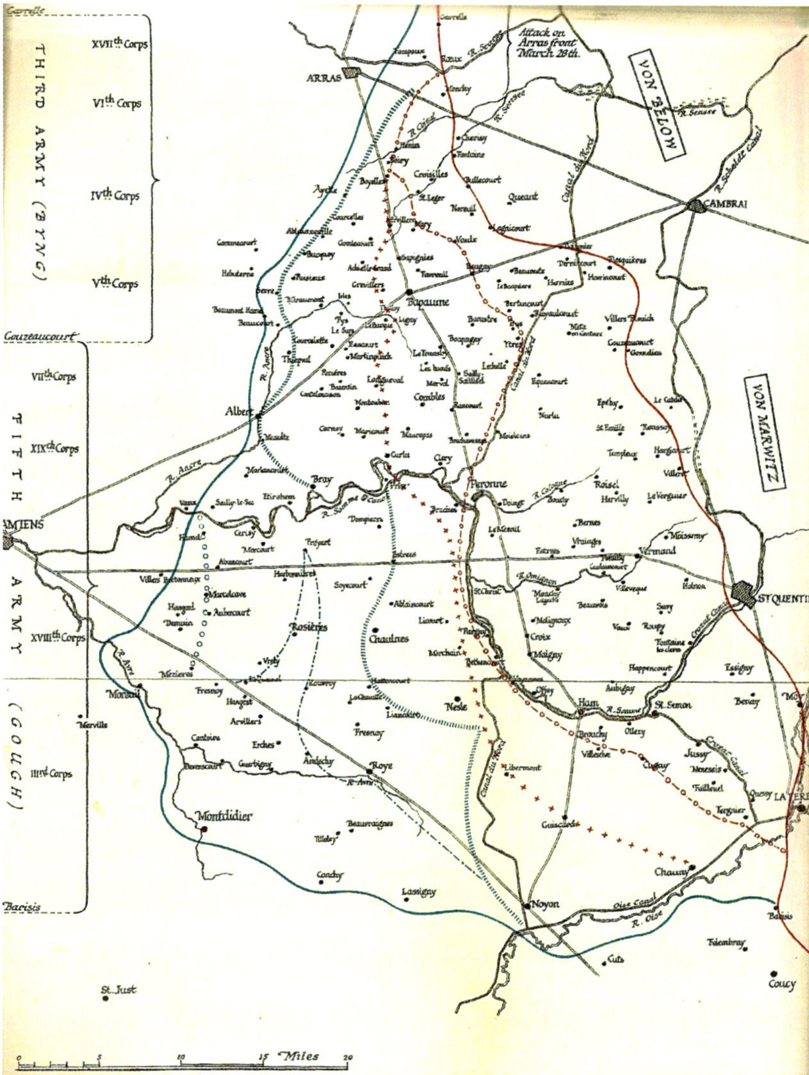

Map 15: The German offensive of March–April 1918.
The solid red line is the line of 21 March; the next to the left is the general line of 23 March and that with red crosses 24 March; the general line on the morning of 26 March is in hatched blue; the other two broken blue lines are successive defences; and the solid blue line is the front stabilised late in April.

Of the two surviving children, Adelaide died unmarried in 1927. Serena married and had two children, both in East Grinstead. She died in Lambeth in 1968.

Percy Brett was wounded on 14 October. He was a Private in 8th Battalion, The Royal Sussex Regiment and had been born at Battle in 1890 where his father, a Brightling man, was a police constable. His father's duties took him all over rural Sussex, however, and Percy went away very young. His mother, also from Brightling, died young in 1892. Brett married Lily Best at Hailsham in 1922 and they had a son. He died at Uckfield in 1969.

On 21 October Private George Henry Hobday died. He had been with 11th Battalion, The Royal Sussex Regiment and was aged 20 and unmarried. His death was again one of an enormous number suffered by his battalion that day in taking 'Stuff Trench' just north of Thiepval, an essential operation if the German Schwaben Redoubt was to fall.

In 1911 Hobday had been a farm worker living at Penhurst with his father William, an estate worker, and two of his three sisters. The third sister was in domestic service in Bexhill. Two of the three sisters married at Battle, though no descendants can reliably be traced. George's parents died at Battle, his mother, Mary Ann (Veness), in 1940 and his father in 1945. Their claim on Battle is that when George died the family lived at Battle Lodge, at the corner of the roads to Netherfield and Boreham Street and at the most easterly part of the Ashburnham estate but nevertheless inside the Battle boundary. George is buried at Grandcourt Road cemetery, close to the 'Stuff Trench'.

By a coincidence Harold Hobday was wounded on the same day; he may have been George's cousin. He too came from Ashburnham but in 1911 he was a farm labourer living at 1 Beechwood Cottages in Netherfield Lane. He was also a Private in 11th Battalion, The Royal Sussex Regiment, and must have been in the same action as George. He was invalided out to hospital at Lincoln and discharged in May 1917. The public records are silent as to his future. His brother and step-brother also served.

Also at some point in October Robert Whibley was wounded at the Schwaben Redoubt close to Thiepval. This German strongpoint had held out against bitter attacks but had fallen at the end of September. The vagueness of the date of Whibley's wound leaves open the question whether it was incurred during the actual capture of the redoubt or afterwards. Robert was a Corporal in 12th Battalion, The Royal Sussex Regiment. He was the son of Walter, a gamekeeper, and his wife Celia (Beal); Walter died at Hastings in 1928 and Celia at Battle in 1930. Robert lived to 1957. He was to be wounded again in 1917.

On 1 November Sidney Smith was wounded by gunshot to the wrist. He was 19 and had already served nearly two years. He had enlisted as a Private in 14th Battalion, The Royal Sussex Regiment but had transferred to 1st Battalion, The East Surrey Regiment, a few weeks before his wound. In civilian life he assisted his father William in a fish-hawking business run from their home at Gate Farm Cottage, off the London road. He too was to be wounded again in 1917.

Last of all the deaths on the western front in 1916 went William Leonard Curry, on 9 November when the battle of the Somme was dragging itself to a close. He was a Captain in the Royal Garrison Artillery, commissioned from Woolwich in July 1911. His father Thomas Elmitt Curry was engineer-in-chief to the Frontier Railways in India, and William and his brother Frank were born in Quetta (now in south-western Pakistan). In 1911 Frank was running Breadsell Farm off Hastings Road; he appears among the survivors of war service. As with many colonial births it can be difficult to trace their home connections, but we know from the 1901 census that the brothers were boarders at Colebrook School in Bognor, and from another source that William went on to Elmhurst School in Croydon, Tonbridge School and Woolwich Academy.[48] From there, presumably, he became a professional soldier.

Curry went to the front in January 1915 and served at Neuve Chapelle, at Loos and on the Somme. The report on his death states:

> On 28 October he went alone at night to obtain information as to the German front line trench opposite his Battery, and found it swarming with Huns, who attacked him with bombs. He succeeded in getting away, and crawled back to his trench in spite of a smashed leg and wounds in his head.[49]

Curry is buried in Puchervillers British Cemetery. As to the family, his father Thomas had been born at Ross on Wye in 1853 and had gone to India fairly early; he does not appear in censuses after 1861; nor does his marriage, which must have been contracted in India. He died at St Leonards in 1944 and is buried at the Church in the Wood at Hollington. His wife followed him in the next year. The only known solid connection with Battle is through his brother Frank. Properly Raymond Frank, he seems not to have married and he died at Tiverton in 1978. Frank's claim for war medals in 1921 asks for the reply to be sent to T E Curry at Breadsell Farm, so the parents were back home by then. The brother Frederick married in Hastings in 1917 and had two children, one in Hastings and one at Battle.

At some point during the Somme battle a Battle man won the Military Cross near Pozières. He was gazetted on 27 November. This was Thomas Whateley Rose, who when 5th Battalion, The Royal Sussex Regiment, was in Italy would also be mentioned in despatches and receive the Italian Silver Medal for Valour; and in 1919 he would be awarded the MBE (Military Division). At the time of his MC he was a Second Lieutenant, temporary Captain. He was to command B Coy of his battalion during the German retreat to the Hindenburg line early in 1917, in the Third Ypres later that year and then in Italy. The citation reads:

> For conspicuous gallantry. He marked out a communications trench for a distance of over 800 yards under very heavy fire. He displayed great courage and determination throughout the operation.[50]

Rose had been born at Westminster in 1876 (his father was a piano manufacturer) and was educated at Westminster School and then proceeded to St Thomas's Medical School. Soon he changed course to become a solicitor; he was for a time from 1906 clerk to William Augustus Raper in Upper Lake and from 1908 a lieutenant in the Territorials.[51] He emigrated to Australia in or before 1910, from which he returned to enlist in 1914. After the war he practised as a solicitor at Katoomba, New South Wales, but poor health resulted in his early death at Sydney in 1927.[52]

The Eastern Mediterranean and Mesopotamia

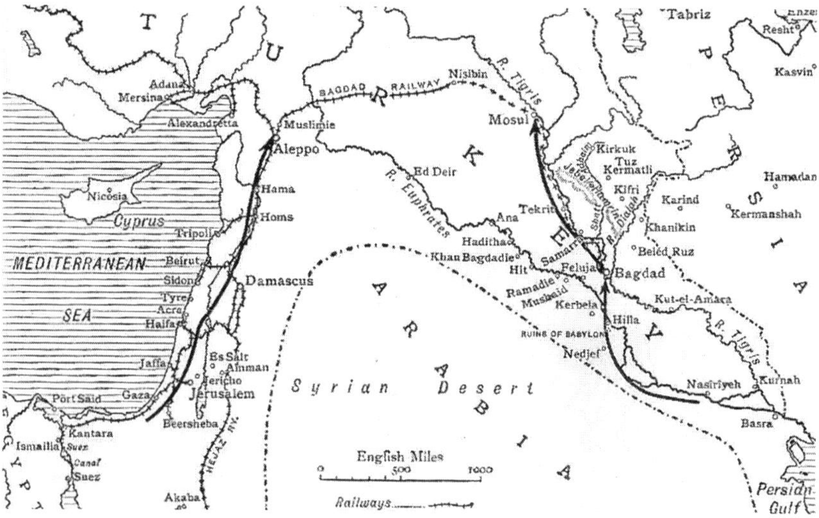

Map 10: the War in Mesopotamia 1916–18
This map shows in abbreviated form the war in the Near East from 1916.
The dark black lines show the British advances up to 31 October 1918.

The first local death was on 8 January. The Allies had already landed at Salonica in northern Greece, against the wishes of the King of Greece but with the support of his prime minister. The objectives were to keep the Turks and Bulgarians away from this useful port (which had been Greek only since 1912), and ultimately to be able to attack northwards. British troops reached the city by various means, mostly by troopship through the submarine-infested waters of the Mediterranean. However, the Adriatic was particularly dangerous, as enemy submarines had a major base at the Austrian port of Pola (now Pula in Croatia).

On this occasion a body of British troops had reached Brindisi, in southern Italy, by a long train journey from the north. They set out on the *Città di Palermo*, accompanied by two small coastal boats commandeered from the North Sea. The *Città di Palermo* was a modern vessel of 3415 tons built for the Italian state railways in 1910. It had served as a troopship in the Turkish–Italian war of 1911–12 and had been requisitioned for the same purpose in the middle of 1915. The British it carried were four officers and 139 other ranks, mostly from 605 Company ASC, including Victor Nelson Breeze of Battle. About six miles north-east of Brindisi it hit a mine, and the support vessels did the same. The mines had been laid shortly before by UC14 (Kapitänleutnant Cäsar Bauer). Detailed reports do not seem to be extant, but it is thought that 84 British survived. Breeze was not among them. He was reported missing and has no known grave.[53]

Breeze was a Private, 21 years of age, the son of Nelson Breeze who was a farmer at Little Park Farm. He had been born at Heathfield and was unmarried; as is usual in such cases he worked on his father's farm. His name is on the RN memorial at Hollybrook in Southampton. The farm still works, at the end of a lane running eastwards from Mount Street, very close to the centre of town. Breeze's family was relatively small in that his father had been a newcomer to the area, and his parents moved away before their deaths. Nelson's younger brother Stanley remained in Battle and married Lily Turner there in 1944 but had no children; he died in Battle in 1971. His sister Ivy married in 1930 and died in 1969; her three daughters all remained in the Battle/Hastings area. Two married in Battle and had children.

The next death was on the Mesopotamian front, of which little notice was being taken at the time – that is, until the disastrous British defeat at Kut-el-Amara.

As recorded above, the British were in Mesopotamia primarily to guard against a Turkish attempt to block oil supplies through the pipeline from Iran to the Gulf, and secondarily to forestall any attack on the Gulf itself that would imperil India. The British were at Basra, and there they sat until reinforcements came, largely from India. The Turks, meanwhile, were not idle and there were several engagements with them. They had made a major attack in April 1915, and although protection of the oil pipeline did not require a further British advance the local commanders decided to move forward. At a considerable cost in casualties they quickly reached a long way from the Gulf in the direction of Baghdad, whose capture would have been a real prize. At the end of September the Turks lost Kut-el-Amara on the Tigris, only some 80 miles short of Baghdad.

A further advance as far as Ctesiphon, very close to Baghdad itself, proved impossible to hold, given troop numbers and supply deficiency, and the British fell back on Kut. By 6 December 1915 the Turks had secured all land access to the town, and shortly thereafter it was under close siege. British forces were twice brought up from the south to break the siege but they failed. Supplies ran low, almost to starvation point, no attempt was made to break out, and Kut surrendered in April 1916.

It was on 23 February, during the second attempt to relieve Kut, that Gunner John French of 66 Brigade, the Royal Field Artillery, met his death. He took a bullet through the left side of his chest. He is commemorated on the Basra memorial.

French was a 22-year old regular soldier who at the time of the 1911 census was with the army in India. He had been an enthusiastic correspondent of the tobacconist Clark. His father Herbert was a carter on the farm run by Nelson Breeze's father and he lived at Little Park Cottages; he died at Hastings in 1942. His mother Annie (Weller) had died at Battle in 1934.

Attempts to trace the French family through official records have failed. His sisters had names that are too frequently duplicated, but his brothers (who are similarly afflicted) had at least their deaths recorded: Spencer in Tonbridge in 1950, Frederick in Battle in 1967, Percy there in 1968 and Ernest in Eastbourne in 1985.

Then Ralfe Whistler, newly promoted a temporary Captain and now in 1st Battalion, the Highland Light Infantry was wounded again. We have come across him before because this was the third occasion on which he was wounded; he was to die after the fourth, and his details are briefly explored in relation to that incident, in 1917. His 1916 wound was in one of the attempts to relieve Kut.

The second death in Mesopotamia was on 14 September: James Walter Sellens, a Private in 2nd Battalion, The Royal West Kent Regiment. This date was at just the point at which the British forces were actively preparing to relieve Kut and thereafter to march on Baghdad, but that campaign did not start until December. Sellens's battalion was part of 34 Brigade holding the Euphrates line based at Khamisiya, facing the Turks south of Kut and his body was later reburied at Baghdad. Sellens's family was one of those that spent little time at Battle (his mother Julia Spray was from Battle) and indeed moved around rather frequently. By 1891 they are in Hollington and by 1911 in Greenwich; the main focus then switches to the West Riding where his father James (a stoker, in the 1891 census) died in 1922 and his mother in 1929. Both his brother Percy and his sister Alice married and died in Yorkshire. The only member of the next generation was his brother George's son, born at Sevenoaks in 1930.

Elsewhere

There were two deaths outside the European and Near Eastern theatres.

First came Corporal Bertram Smith Donald. His connection with Battle is likely to have been slim. He was born at Benhall in Suffolk in 1881, where his father Joseph was a land agent. Joseph was originally from Cheshire and had lived in Cumberland and Buckinghamshire as well as in Suffolk, where he had married his wife Mary (Smith). They came to live at Pembury House on Battle Hill (now 115 Hastings Road) at some point after the 1911 census. Bertram had served in the 12th Lancers in the Boer War and had stayed in South Africa in the gold-mining business. In 1914 he had joined the Natal Light Horse and had taken part in suppressing the de Wet rebellion initiated by dissident Afrikaners in August of that year. He then joined the expedition to remove the Germans from their east African colonies of Tanganyika, Urundi and Ruanda (a process that lasted until two weeks after the 1918 armistice, the Germans remaining undefeated). On 9 May he was wounded while going for ammunition in an attack on a German fort; the location is unknown but is likely to have been rather north of Dodoma in central Tanganyika. He died of wounds on 12 May and is buried in the Dar es Salaam War Cemetery. The only known connection with Battle is late and through his family. Mary died in Battle in 1922 and Joseph in 1924. In 1926 a Miss C D Donald is reported as living at Pembury House; by 1927 she had gone.[54] This appears to have been a relative.

On 13 August there was a death in India: Ernest John Edgar Hayler died of pneumonia at Bombay. He was a Driver with the RFA, serving with the Indian Army. Previously a farm labourer, he had enlisted at St Leonards in November 1914, giving his address as Quarry Cottage, Blackhorse Road, Battle, and did not see active service before being posted to India in February 1916. Hayler had been born at Battle while his parents Alfred and Fanny (Edwards) had been living at Little Hemingfold; by 1911 the family had moved to Crowhurst but they returned later. His parents were at Yew Tree Cottage in Hastings Road in 1917; his father Alfred died at Battle in 1935 and his mother Fanny Edwards died there in 1942. Ernest had three brothers and two sisters, and none of their descendants appear now to have Battle connections.

Notes

1 *Hastings Observer*, 4 March 1916.
2 *Hastings Observer*, 13 May 1916.
3 *Hastings Observer*, 3 November 1917.
4 *Hastings Observer*, 1 February 1919.
5 The only evidence for this is the Netherfield List.
6 *Pike's Directory* for 1913.
7 Commonwealth War Graves Commission.
8 http://www.1914–1918.net/Diaries/wardiary-13sussex.html
9 Robert Graves: *Goodbye to all that* (Jonathan Cape, 1929)
10 http://www.royalsussex.org.uk/Richebourg.htm
11 Miller: *We wunt be druv*
12 *Hastings Observer*, 27 May 1916.
13 Netherfield parish record of baptism, which includes date of birth.
14 Capt Charlie May of 22 Bn, Manchester Regiment, in Malcolm Brown: *The Imperial War Museum book of the Somme* (Sidgwick and Jackson 1996)
15 *Hastings Observer*, 15 July 1916.
16 L/C Charles Longley in a letter to his sister: Sussex Express 12 March 1915.
17 Godfrey Webster in a letter to his mother, 6 April 1915.
18 Robert Graves: *Goodbye to all that* (Jonathan Cape, 1929)
19 Lyn Macdonald: *Somme* (Michael Joseph 1983)
20 Siegfried Sassoon: *Memoirs of an infantry officer* (Faber and Faber, 1930)
21 *Hastings Observer*, 22 July 1916.
22 *Hastings Observer*, 29 July 1916.
23 http://www.theweald.org/N10a.asp?NId=5380394
24 Brian Short: *The Ashdown Forest Dispute 1876-1882* (Sussex Record Society, 1997)
25 Brian Short: *The Ashdown Forest Dispute 1876-1882* (Sussex Record Society, 1997)
26 *Hastings Observer*, 16 January 1915.

27 http://www.nationalarchives.gov.uk/a2a/records.aspx?cat=179-raf_3&cid=-1 #-1
28 *The London Gazette*, 16 October 1908.
29 *Hastings Observer*, 8 July 1916.
30 http://www.westernfrontassociation.com/great-war-people/memorials/341-r-g-raper.html
31 *Hastings Observer*, 15 July 1916.
32 *Hastings Observer*, 9 August 1919.
33 *Hastings Observer*, 13 January 1917.
34 http://www.nationalarchives.gov.uk/a2a/records.aspx?cat=179-raf_3&cid=-1 #-1
35 Miller: *We wunt be druv*
36 *Hastings Observer*, 31 August 1918.
37 *Hastings Observer*, 12 August 1916.
38 *Hastings Observer*, 21 October 1916.
39 *Hastings Observer*, 29 July 1916.
40 *Hastings Observer*, 18 September 1915.
41 *Hastings Observer*, 5 August 1916.
42 *Hastings Observer*, 26 August 1916.
43 *Hastings Observer*, 9 September 1916.
44 http://static.awm.gov.au/images/collection/pdf/RCDIG1068748--20-.PDF
45 http://www.awm.gov.au/research/people/nominal_rolls/first_world_war_embarkation/person/R1736773/
46 http://www.oucs.ox.ac.uk/ww1lit/collections/item/9063?CISOBOX=1&REC=1
47 From *Battle in Pictures* (Battle Museum of Local History, 2012).
48 Death information from Battle Cemetery Records 1862-2007 (R A and K J Longley, 2007).
49 *Hastings Observer*, 11 November 1916.
50 *Hastings Observer*, 11 November 1916.
51 Richard Buckman: *The Royal Sussex Regiment: military honours & awards 1864-1920* (J&KH Publishing, Hailsham, 2001).
52 Cinque Ports Gazette, December 1933 (East Sussex Records Office).
53 http://trove.nla.gov.au/ndp/del/article/16428895
54 http://it.wikipedia.org/wiki/Citt%C3%A0_di_Palermo_(incrociatore_ausiliario_1915), accessed 27 February 2013
55 Pike's Directory for 1926.

5

1917: European Stalemate and Mud

For Battle as for the army as a whole, 1916 had so far been the worst year of the war. Again, the front lines in western Europe had not moved significantly. In eastern Europe the Russians had moved forward with Brusilov's offensive but had been as rapidly pushed back. Romania had entered the war on the Allied side but had been promptly subjected to German and Austrian invasion. There had been no sign of American involvement. Nevertheless there were some positive developments. The Allies were firmly established in Salonica and progress was being made in both Palestine and Mesopotamia. The tank had made a somewhat uncertain entry, and was to do more in 1917. The manpower shortage had been resolved, at least for a few months.

Two political events dominated the military year. In March the Russian revolution deposed the Tsar, after which there followed a long period of difficulty as more and more Russian troops began to desert and the Germans and Austrians continued to advance. The revolution was followed by one final, failed, Russian offensive and then in November by the Bolshevik coup at Petrograd and very soon by the armistice with Germany and Austria. In April the United States declared war on Germany. Neither event had an immediate effect on the western front because until peace with Russia was certain the Germans could not transfer large forces from the east to west front, and because it would take a considerable time before any large body of American troops could appear in Europe. But the American decision meant a much greater and more certain supply

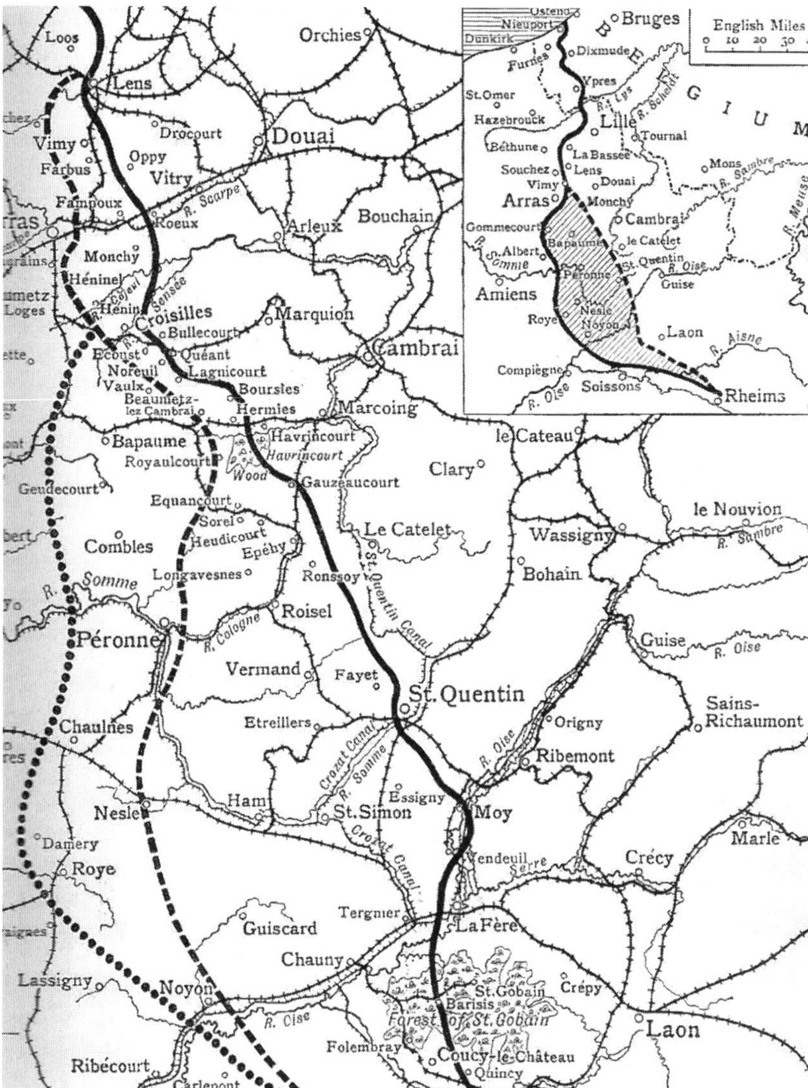

Map 11: the German withdrawal to the Hindenburg Line
Scale of main map 9.8 miles to the inch.In the main map the dotted line is the approximate winter line before the German withdrawal. The dashed line is the Allied position on 18 March 1917. The full line is the Allied position on 16 April 1917.The smaller map is in effect a summary of the larger.

of food and war material to the European allies, especially with the convoy system now operating in the Atlantic.

To a large extent the main battles of 1917 repeated those of the previous year but had to take account of a major German withdrawal. Aware that their forward lines left them exposed and were too long for effective defence, the Germans withdrew to the new, shorter and better-built defences known as the Hindenburg Line. The depth of the withdrawal varied considerably. At Croisilles near Arras it was only three miles; south of St Quentin it was almost twenty. The area given up was littered with obstacles and booby traps; the new line was even more solidly built. The withdrawal began on 13 March and was completed swiftly.

In April the British attacked at Arras and the Canadians took the important ridge at Vimy. Then matters stalled as fresh German reserves appeared. The Allied attack was primarily a diversion to let the French carry out their offensive further south, at the Chemin des Dames, which was a disaster and led to serious morale problems in the French army. In June the British blew up the Messines Ridge close to Ypres but were able to advance only a very short distance beyond it. On 1 August the third battle of Ypres began, just as a storm brought to an end the very dry weather that threw up clouds of dust in soldiers' faces; it stuttered to an end in the bottomless muds of Passchendaele in November in some of the wettest weather of the war. By then the Italian front had collapsed at Caporetto and had been pulled back 70 miles in some disorder; five British divisions, including 5th Battalion, The Royal Sussex Regiment were sent to shore up their ally. From late November the British offensive moved from Passchendaele to Cambrai, further south. Amid all these excitements the daily round of shelling and sniping continued everywhere on the western front.

The year cost a further 28 Battle lives.

Away from the Western Front

As 1915 had demonstrated, this was now truly a world war. Battle lost five men away from the western front.

The first was in Mesopotamia. Stalemate had ensued on the Tigris after the Turkish capture of Kut-el-Amara in April 1916, and it took time for the British to make arrangements to ensure a good chance of success. They attacked in December 1916, and the main point of contest was the Sanna-i-Yat position about sixteen miles east of Kut, the scene of heavy fighting until its capture on 5 February. By then the British dead included John Bertram Partington, who died on 3 February. His father Thomas, who had married Jessie Sheepshanks of Coventry (the daughter of a vicar), had been the second vicar of Netherfield, arriving late in 1868; his last signature was on the baptismal register before his death in November 1887, when John was not yet four. John Partington went to Radley College and then as an exhibitioner to Pembroke College, Oxford, from which he graduated in classics in 1907. He went to teach classics at St Edward's School, Oxford and while there he began military training, being a Second Lieutenant in the OTC. By the time that the war began he was teaching at Oakham School in Rutland.

Partington joined up in August 1914 and was gazetted Captain in 4th Battalion, The Devonshire Regiment, a territorial formation, in November of that year. He was sent to India; in January 1915 to Australia in connection with Germans interned there, until the autumn; then back to India; and on to Mesopotamia in October 1916. It was in February 1917 that his battalion moved to Amara[1] to support the capture of the Hai Salient and the Dehra Bend. Due to congestion the unit failed in its attempt to push two companies through in support of the 45th and 36th Sikh Battalions. In the fighting of 2 and 3 February Partington's battalion suffered 283 casualties. He is buried in the Amara War Cemetery.

There are none of these Partingtons left, at least in England. After his father's death the family moved to Frant and then to Paddington. His three sisters never married; one brother went to Kenya as a district commissioner and died there in July 1914; the other brother, a solicitor, died in 1937, and his one daughter died unmarried in 1997. The family was certainly not without means. The vicar left over £18,000 in 1888, the mother over £14,000 in 1922 and the brother over £16,000 in 1937. John himself left over £1100 in 1917, a comfortable sum for a young man in those days.

On the next day another Battle man died near Kut. He was Frederick George Booth, whose father Samuel was a labourer at Marley Farm when Frederick was born in 1889. He bettered himself in some way, however, later becoming a publican near Heathfield. Frederick was a Private in 2nd Battalion, the Royal West Kent Regiment and had enlisted at Maidstone well before the war: by 1911 he was in a barracks in India. At the time of his death his Division was holding the Euphrates front. Little is known about his family. His brother Samuel, born at Battle in about 1880, died in Hampshire in 1965. He also had a sister Fanny. His mother Ellen (Carver), from Petworth, died at Battle in 1945.

The third death was at sea. On 15 April the troopship *Cameronia* was making its way from Marseille to Alexandria. It was a large ship – just under 11000 tons – built in Glasgow for the Anchor Line in 1911 and requisitioned for military use only in January 1917. It was taking 2650 troops to Egypt, presumably on their way to fight either in Palestine or in Mesopotamia. One of these men was Gunner Thomas John Fuller, aged 34 and with 6th Reserve Battery of the RFA. About 150 miles east of Malta the *Cameronia* came into the sights of U33 under the command of Gustav Sieß, which torpedoed it. It sank within 40 minutes. Some men were picked up by the accompanying escort destroyer HMS *Rifleman*, but others remained in the water until the next day.[2] Among the 129 men who died was Fuller who, according to the Netherfield File, had been a keen cricketer. He is remembered on the Chatby Memorial in Egypt.

Fuller's father Stephen was a gypsum miner at Netherfield who had died in 1900 aged only 46. (His mother Mary Jane, originally Drury, lived on to 1946.) Thomas had married Rose Taylor early in 1914 and had had two children. The family stayed in the Battle area, and there are several descendants. Thomas's brothers Harry, Stephen and Ernest also fought, all of them being wounded later in the year.

On 28 May there was another death in Mesopotamia: Gunner Henry Frederic Flint of the RFA. Fighting had continued north of Kut towards Baghdad, and the Turks did not give ground easily. We do not know where Flint died. He is listed on the Basra Memorial along with John Jenner who had died in the previous year.

At the time of his death Flint's family were living at 18 Sidley Road, Eastbourne, but they were at Battle in the 1911 census and before that. Flint was one of three surviving children of Henry Frederic and Augusta Frances Phoebe (Rochford). He had been born at Battle in 1897, as was his sister Dorothy six years later; an intervening brother had been born at Hastings. His father was a coach painter born at Battle (his wife was from Athlone); they lived at Little Park, as did Nelson Breeze who had died in 1916. Flint's father died at Eastbourne in 1945, Augusta having predeceased him by nine years. There is no conclusive trace of his brother Arthur. His sister Dorothy married in Eastbourne in 1930 and had a daughter there in 1933.

The next eastern death was 25 August, according to the CWGC, though the memorial in St Mary's Church says 26 August. Frederic Noakes died in Palestine, in the campaign that in December was to bring about the capture of Jerusalem and ultimately to force Turkey out of the war. A Lieutenant in the Staffordshire Yeomanry, he is buried in Ramleh war cemetery but at the time of his death Ramleh was well inside Turkish lines; the British did not reach it for more than another three months. There was no major action in Palestine in August, though as always there were artillery exchanges and sniper fire.

Frederic Noakes was fairly old for service, having been born in 1877 and being therefore 40 when he died. He was the son of the tanner of Battle Hill, Frederick, who in the 1881 census is reported as living at 4 St Mary's Villas, and his wife Kate (probably Haffenden) from Hailsham. Later they lived in Lake House on the corner between Marley Lane and Lower Lake. The family clearly had money, because the son Frederick and the two younger daughters were sent away to school. In 1911 the younger Frederick was a farmer at Crippenden Manor, Edenbridge, with his wife Margaret (Carruthers). In 1917 they had twins. Ronald died young. His mother Kate had died in 1887 and his two sisters Kate and Edith in 1888 and 1894 respectively. Frederick's remaining sister Dorothy married an insurance broker and prompted the memorial plaque to Frederick in the church. She died in Sussex late in 1970.

Early Casualties in the West

The western front, of course, continued its bloody stalemate. On 4 January Arthur Reginald Abrey was wounded near Ypres. He had been footman to the owner of Beauport Park and lived in the grounds; his father was the butler; his brother William was serving; another brother Albert was to die in April. Arthur had joined up in 1915 as a Private in 12th Battalion, The Royal Sussex Regiment. He had gone to France in March 1916. On 30 June of that year, at Richebourg, he had disappeared and was presumed a prisoner of war or worse, and his surviving army record does not record how it was that he turned up again shortly afterwards. In 1917 his wounds were by gunshot to his right forearm, and he was discharged as physically unfit later in the year. Neither he nor his siblings appear to have married. Arthur died at Hastings in 1972.

On 9 February Charles Edward Frank Buss of Netherfield was taken out of the line after a gas attack. Born late in 1895, he had joined the Merchant Navy by 1911 but in 1912 enlisted with the Rifle Brigade, giving his occupation as plumber's mate, and went to France in October 1914, where he served throughout the war. He had frostbite in 1914 and shell shock some time later, being discharged as no longer physically fit in October 1918. His career was somewhat varied: Acting Corporal in August 1914, Corporal in February 1916, Lance Sergeant in October 1916; but in May 1917 he was found guilty of stealing the property of an officer and sentenced to six months imprisonment with hard labour, being reduced back to Corporal. Nevertheless he was awarded the Military Medal that December. Buss's parents were Charles and Nellie (Winchester). Nellie had died in 1912 but the elder Charles lived to 1950. The younger Charles married Lydia Pallister at Knaresborough in 1917 but died at Hull two years later.

The first death came on 11 February: Private John Henry Jenner of 1st Battalion, the Royal West Surrey Regiment. He had been born at Battle early in 1890 and was 26 years of age. The 1911 census gives William White as his stepfather and Eliza (Sheppard) as his mother. They had married in 1892, and it is clear from the records that John's father had been Joseph Jenner, who had died early in 1891. In 1911 he was listed as a farm carter, living at 2 Chapel Cottages close to the then Methodist Church. He joined up in May 1916 and was sent to France in August;[3] he lasted six months there. He died on the Somme front and is buried at Bray Military Cemetery. (*See Map 11*)

On the next day (or 13 February – authorities differ) 2nd Lieutenant Harry Ashley Willats died, having caught a chill on Salisbury Plain. He lived at Hemingfold Farm by the Black Horse, but had not been born at Battle or lived there long. In the 1891 census his father Henry was the manager of the Cliftonville Hotel at Margate, and Harry had been born in Margate in 1889. He was a stockbroker. He had enlisted in the ASC in September 1914, later transferring to the Royal Field Artillery. His death was registered at Battle. He was unmarried.

On 26 February James Buss was wounded at Zillebeke. He was a Private (from 1917 a Lance-Corporal) in 13th Battalion, The Royal Sussex Regiment, one of three Netherfield brothers who joined up and survived. Their father Charles was an agricultural labourer at Netherfield Place, who had died in 1908; their mother Jane (Pettit) was to live only to 1923. Another survivor was living with the family in 1901 and 1908 – Ernest Pettit, Jane's nephew. James worked on the land, too. There is no reliable record of a marriage for him; he was to die at Hastings in 1964.

Four weeks later, on 20 March Frederick Nelson Fletcher died. Fletcher was a Private in 6th Battalion, The Northamptonshire Regiment. He had been born at Battle at the end of 1887 or the beginning of 1888. His father Henry was a tailor living in Mount Street, and he had three brothers and four sisters. Frederick himself was that rarity of the time, a bus driver. He is buried at Croisilles British Cemetery near where he was killed. His battalion was engaged in filling the gap left by the German withdrawal to the Hindenburg Line, which was very close to Croisilles.[4]

Frederick's mother (Minnie Vidler) had already died, on 15 September 1916, but his father lived on to die at Battle in 1938. His elder brother William died in Hastings in 1945, having married and had children at Battle; one of them Thomas Charles, was to be killed in France in May 1940. His younger brother Clifford also married at Battle and had children there, but later moved to Eastbourne, dying in 1979. Neither of his sisters had children, and the older of them was to die as late as 1994.

Then, on 31 March, Private George Franklin Smissen died. Born at Mountfield, he was a Netherfield man with 7th Battalion, The Royal Sussex Regiment east of Arras. As always much digging had to be done to improve defences, a task that could only be done in a fairly exposed position and therefore had to be done at night. In the early hours of 31 March a German shell landed and killed eight men, Smissen among them. He is buried in Faubourg d'Amiens cemetery.

Smissen did not take part in the 1911 census but in his army records he declared that he was a labourer. He was quick to enlist, doing so at Hastings on 10 August 1914 and giving his age as 21 years and two months. He must have spent much of the following years in France. We know that he was in hospital in Surrey for most of March 1916, with trench foot. His father John Franklin Smissen was a labourer at the gypsum works, like so many in the Netherfield area. He died at Hastings in 1952, and his wife Sarah Ann (Whibley) at Battle in 1959.

Arras and the Somme again: Spring and early Summer

The continued fighting on the western front in April saw the deaths of more Battle men, one of them from a prominent local family.

Before them there was one wounded man: Private Arthur Osborn, born at Battle aged 21 and almost from the first in 14th Battalion, The Royal Sussex Regiment. By 1917 he had transferred to the Buffs, the East Kent Regiment. He had enlisted at Eastbourne in September 1914 and on 9 April 1917 he received a gunshot wound to his left leg that effectively put him out of the war. He was to be discharged later that year on grounds of shell shock. His father was a policeman, by now at Newhaven. Osborn died at Winchester in 1959.

The first death, on 9 April, was near Monchy le Preux in front of Arras. He was a Netherfield man: William Sydney Carter, a Private in 9th Battalion, The King's Own Yorkshire Light Infantry. He was 21, a son of Edward and Minnie (Selmes) of Ivyland Green. Edward was a gypsum sorter and William (known as Sydney) a farm labourer.

As he is buried at Wancourt, a little south-east of Arras, it is fair to assume that he was killed in that immediate vicinity. As so often with a common name it has been difficult to track down Carter's family with precision. His father died in 1920 and his mother in 1928; the public records attest that of his four siblings only his sister Mabel married and had children, in the area (*see Map 12*).

Two days later there followed Albert Thomas Abrey. He was 27 and had been born at Hollington, possibly in that tiny piece that forms part of Beauport Park. His father was butler to the owner of Beauport Park and his brother was a footman, so they worked within the parish of Battle and the 1891 census has them living there. Abrey had gone to Australia and enlisted there in 1st Battalion of the Australian Imperial Force; the account of his wounding in 1916 gives more information about the family. He was in action in the Lagnicourt section south of Arras and received a shell wound to the chest on 6 April. He died at the casualty clearing station five days later and is buried at Aveluy Communal Cemetery. He was unmarried. His brother Arthur also saw service and had been wounded only three months earlier. His father William and mother Robina (Watts) died within a few months of each other at Hastings in 1928/29.

On the same day, 11 April, Private John Patrick Kiley of 4th Battalian, the Middlesex Regiment was wounded in the hand and sent to hospital in France. Kiley had been born at Haggerston in Middlesex in 1884, son of John, a plasterer born in County Kerry. It was a large family, and by 1891 the father was a widower; his wife Ann died in 1887. He then appears to have married again to Katherine or Catherine Braban of Burwash, before dying himself, probably in 1895. Katherine then married Henry Hobday of Netherfield and brought with her John Patrick and his sister Minnie.

The newspaper report adds that his wife lived at 2 Beechwood Cottages, Netherfield Road.[5] The 1911 census has Patrick Kiley at 1 Beechwood Cottages, a labourer at the gypsum works: he remained in their employ as a gypsum miller. In 1913 he married a Brighton woman, Lilian Backshall (née Chant) at Hastings. She had previously married a David Backshall in Brighton and had one son.

Patrick Kiley died at Battle in 1971, and his wife Lilian in Hampshire three years later. Their first son Philip was born at Battle

Private Patrick Kiley

in 1914, followed by Arthur in 1919. Both married and had children, living at Battle. Philip died in 2002 and Arthur in 2004. Minnie Kiley married James Blackman, a survivor of the war, at Battle in 1919. Their descendants live in Battle today.

In the same house at Netherfield in 1911 was their step-brother Godfrey Hobday, who was to be awarded the DCM for his gallantry in 1918.

13 April saw Rifleman George Ponsford wounded again (and his final wound was to be on 1 December), probably near Croisilles. He has been more fully described in connection with his first wound, on 20 June 1916.

The next April death, on 22 April, was on the Somme: William Wait, a bricklayer's labourer who had lived at 17 Lower Lake. He was 38 or 39 and a Private in 2nd Battalion, The Middlesex Regiment, and he was another who suffered from the continual warfare on the Somme front. He too has no known grave and his name is on the Thiepval Memorial.

Wait was a son of William Wait, who in 1911 was living at 1 Parks Yard with his wife Ellen (Preston). William was to die before the war, in 1912, and Ellen in 1936. There were six children of his marriage – five sons and one daughter – and all the sons served in the war. Indeed, William asked for exemption when conscription came in but was finally refused. His argument was that with a widowed mother and all four brothers already at the front he needed to stay at home.[6] William was a bricklayer and carpenter in the building firm of John Thomas.[7]

The fourth Battle man to die in April was Ralfe Allen Fuller Whistler. He had been born in Glasgow in 1895; his father Fuller Whistler was an officer in the Highland Light Infantry though born at Battle from an old Battle family. His mother Gwenllian Annie (Robinson) was Welsh but born and raised in India, daughter of the headmaster of a large English boarding school there. Her uncle had been in the HLI in the Crimean War and was so badly wounded he was put out for dead but Florence Nightingale spotted his toes twitching and rescued him. The uncle fought again on the North West Frontier of India and the Whistler family have his medals from this campaign.

Ralfe joined 2nd Battalion of his father's old regiment on 24 March 1914. He went to France with his regiment in August and was wounded in the battle of the Aisne on 12 September and sent home for a few weeks to recover. He was wounded again, at Festubert, in May 1915. He was promoted Lieutenant and temporary Captain in February 1916 and Captain in August. In that year he transferred to 1st Battalion, took part in the attempts to regain Kut-el-Amara and was there wounded for a third time. Having recovered, he then contracted typhoid and was invalided out to Bombay. He rejoined his old battalion in France in March 1917. On 26 April 1917 he was wounded in the head at Oppy in attempting to rescue comrades under shell fire, about five miles north-east of Arras, and he died of his wounds on the next day. He was buried in a small wood with a few other men but very recently these bodies were exhumed and reburied in Aubigny Communal Cemetery.

Ralfe Whistler was unmarried. There is a memorial to him in St Mary's Church. His nephew Ralfe remembers:

> The vest pocket camera came back from Mesopotamia and my father kept it. When he died in 1943 it became mine. It is sitting on my desk while I write.

Ralfe Whistler on passing out at Sandhurst in 1913

> I have a photograph (rather faded) of Ralfe A. F. Whistler holding his vest pocket Kodak after leading an attack on a Turkish Redoubt in Mesopotamia. He had two bullet holes in his hat and four others in his uniform.
>
> After World War II, I was having some trousers shortened by a tailor in Hastings and he remembered a Ralfe Whistler in World War I coming to him to have the bullet holes patched up while he was on a weekend leave from the trenches in France. He could manage a weekend's hunting with the East Sussex hounds and get back to the trenches on Monday by the Newhaven Dieppe ferry.

The Whistler family, which has had distinguished members for centuries, is still active and well-known in Battle, from the same house in which Ralfe lived on Caldbec Hill. It was associated with the Websters in previous centuries but became better known in recent times from a believed relationship with the artist James Abbot McNeill Whistler (1834–1903) and much more certain and close ones with the artist Rex Whistler (1905–1944), who died in the Normandy invasion, and his brother Sir Laurence, the glass engraver and poet (1912–2000). Ralfe's elder brother Hugh was a well-known ornithologist. There were distinguished military men in the family, including Ralfe's father, Major Fuller Whistler, who was on Kitchener's staff in the first part of the war, and Sir Lashmer Whistler, who among other distinctions commanded the last British troops in India. There were also churchmen in the family.

Hugh Whistler also served, though in India as 2nd Lieutenant in the Indian Army reserve. He became a well-known ornithologist and a Fellow of the Zoological Society. After the war he married into the Ashton family of Mountfield and died at Battle in 1943. His son Ralfe is a well-known resident of the town. Hugh's wife (Margaret) Joan Ashton was herself distinguished. She served with the ASC for three years during the 1914–18 war, starting as a welder (at a time when the supply of effective welders' masks, made in Germany, were no longer available) and going on to drive empty lorry chassis to coachbuilders in England and then to transport shell supplies from the Rouen area to the front in France. She lived to 1981. Her service is peculiar in that she appears to have belonged to the ASC at a time when women could not join it.[8]

Lt Whistler's father died in London in March 1922, and his mother at Hammonds next to Caldbec House in 1950.

At about the same time as Whistler's fatal wounding Major Frank Vidler (he was a Gunner with the RGA – Major was his first name) was wounded in the chest and sent home; he had enlisted at Hastings in December 1915 and was sent to France in August of 1916. He was the younger brother of Tom, whose background is described in the chapter on 1918, and was 26 when he enlisted. Frank had already married, in 1914, to Annie Winchester, and they had two children: one in 1915 and the second in 1920. Frank was a grocer living at 6 Walden Terrace, Lower Lake. He died at Hastings in 1971.

Then on 3 May Private George Harris died. He had been born at Battle in 1884, son of a Kentish shoemaker and a washerwoman. Although there was an extensive list of siblings it is impossible to pick them out from later records, except for his sister Elizabeth who married in 1900. By 1891 the whole family had moved to the Dover area, and it was in Dover that George joined 8th Battalion, the East Surrey Regiment. At the time of his death his battalion was engaged in the third battle of the Scarpe, in an attack on Chérisy, south east of Arras. He had married Mary Jane (Bushell) in 1910 and had one son,

Reginald George, born in that year. George's name is on the Arras Memorial. Mary remarried in 1921.

A moment of relative calm followed for the men of Battle, at least in so far as deaths on the western front were concerned. On 5 May Sidney Smith, the fish-hawker, was wounded again, this time in the face; and within a month he had been discharged as no longer physically fit. There were three Sidney Smiths at Battle at about that time, so it has so far been impossible to determine what happened to this Sidney after the war. He is more fully discussed in connection with his wounding in 1916.

The war, however, went on, and a good example of continuing dangers to the men outside the named battles can be seen from the record of Sydney Roland Rose, a Sergeant in 12th Battalion, The Royal Sussex Regiment who on 3/4 June was at La Brique, a post just north and slightly east of Ypres. Rose had been born at Brightling to John Rose, a farmer, and his wife Jane (Wareham) and was to survive the war, dying at Battle in 1967. He won the Military Medal and the citation reads (in transcription):

> On the night of 3/4 June Sergt Rose was in charge of the Regiment Transport, coming up to La Brique Post in Ypres. La Brique was bombarded during the night with shells of all calibre, including a large number of gas shells. The limbers arrived at La Brique with the exception of the two that had taken petrol tins to Ypres Ramparts to fill with water. Sergt Rose then saw the limbers safely past Salvation Corner + sent them on; he had to leave his horse here, as it was badly gassed, + he returned to La Brique on foot to look after the water carts. Arriving there he found the mules had bolted with the water cart, having thrown the driver when a shell burst near them. Sergt Rose hunted for, + found the mules + cart, + himself mounted the mules + took the water cart to Ypres Ramparts to fill. Then he found the mules in the two limbers with petrol tins had also bolted, two of them being killed by a shell shortly after. Sergt Rose found the drivers of the limbers, filled the water cart, + took it back to La Brique, + then proceed [sic] to Ypres to hunt for the mules and limbers. The bombardment was still heavy + one of the men was badly wounded. Sergt Rose immediately went to the wounded man, + bandaged him up, + sent one of his men to get a stretcher. As the man did not return, Sergt Rose started for La

> Brique Post to get a stretcher; [on] the way he met his man bringing it down. Sergt Rose wore his respirator for six hours, + only took it off to give orders about the wounded man. During this time he was gassed, + was admitted to hospital next day. He returned to duty 2 days afterwards. Sergt Rose set a fine example to his men, + showed devotion to duty + a determination to carry all his work through.[9]

Rose married Bessie Tozer at Battle in 1924 and they had two children; Bessie died at Battle in 1969. Rose's parents had died there too: John in 1926 and Jane in 1954.

A few days later, on 15 June, the second Meppem brother died: Ormond Edwin, elder brother of Sydney who had died on the Somme in the previous October. He was a Private in the London Regiment (the Fusiliers) and died before Ypres; he is remembered on the Menin Gate. He had been born at Ewhurst and had lived at Battle, where he went to school; the family then moved to East Grinstead. (Family details are given in the entry for his brother.)

Acting Corporal Frederick Douch was wounded about 24 June (the record of the date is imprecise) and was invalided out on 4 July. Born in 1894/95, he was originally with 11th Battalion, The Royal Sussex Regiment but after March 1917 with 11th Battalion, The Bedfordshire Regiment. He lived in Mount Street with his father Naphtali (another of those Biblical references, but this time an uncommon one) who was a basket maker and Frederick followed him in the trade. He had six siblings, all younger than him. Frederick suffered a bullet wound to the chest and was discharged from the army in March 1919.

Frederick's father died at Battle in 1939 and his mother Elizabeth (White) in 1948. It seems that Frederick married Mabel Broadhurst at Battle in 1927 and had one son, Maurice, born in 1928. Frederick died at Battle in 1974. His two younger brothers also stayed at Battle, the last dying there in 1991.

On 26 June Private Stephen Noad died at Fulham. He was a Private in the Middlesex Regiment but without knowing his battalion it is impossible to pin down where he served. He had been born at Hamsterley in County Durham in 1877 and had followed his father, a Somerset-born coachman, around the country. By 1901 they had settled at Battle, living at Starrs Green. Stephen married Florence

Buck at Battle in 1910 and by 1911 they were living at the Lodge, Telham Court. Florence died in 1931, having left Battle. Two of their three daughters married in the Hailsham area and had children. Noad is buried at Kensal Green cemetery.

Just before the Third Ypres, on 28 July, Stanley Whiteman of Netherfield was wounded for the third and final time. His background is briefly given in connection with his first wound in 1915.

On 15 August Private Arthur Cecil Thomas died. He was about 31 – his birth record is elusive – and unmarried, a carpenter working for his father John, who was a builder. The family lived at The Briars, Caldbec Hill. Arthur had formerly been with the Royal Sussex but had transferred to 10th Battalion, the South Wales Borderers. It appears that he had trench fever[10] – not usually fatal – and was sent home; he is buried in Battle cemetery. It is unclear where he contracted the illness that killed him, and equally unclear why it was not a military funeral (though his grave has a military headstone). But the bearers were CSM Charles Thomas, ex-Staff Sergeant Santer, Corporal D Thomas and Private Mepham.[11] Two of them were his brothers. Tracing Arthur Thomas's relations is difficult because even in Sussex there are more than sufficient Thomases to create doubts, but we know that his father had died at Battle in May that year and that his mother Ellen would die at Hastings in 1927.

The Third Ypres (the Summer)

By August the next big push in the west was under way. The Third Ypres began on 31 July, and to a large extent it was a repeat of the Somme. There was bitter fighting and strong German resistance was evident from the start. By the end of the summer it was clear to many outside the High Command that continuing it would result in further loss of life for no appreciable gain. Lloyd George, the prime minister, tried to convince Haig that it should be called off. He failed, and the last part of the battle proceeded. It was the notorious Passchendaele. Lloyd George called it the battle of the mud.[12]

The idea of the third Ypres was not bad. The Allies wanted to push northwards to remove the Germans from the Belgian coast, from which in due course further assaults would be made. But it didn't work; after the very many deaths on both sides the front line remained where it had been, give or take a few miles. Serious rainfall began on 1 September; it cleared from time to time but became a real problem only in October.

The first Battle death was the heir to Battle Abbey and its estate: Second Lieutenant Godfrey Vassall George Augustus Webster.

The recent history of the Abbey is much that of the Websters and is well-known. Briefly, by the early eighteenth century the Abbey had fallen into some disrepair after more than a century and a half of ownership by the Browne family and their successors. Sir Thomas Webster, an Essex man, bought it in 1721 and thereafter steadily increased his lands in Sussex. Partly through gambling, the fifth and sixth baronets suffered enormous debts and in 1857 the seventh sold the Abbey estate to the Duke of Cleveland, who died without children in 1891; his widow died in 1901. In 1902 Godfrey's father Augustus Webster, by then the eighth baronet and married to an industrial heiress of much wealth, bought it back for about £200 000. In the same year he leased the Abbey itself and its immediate surroundings to Michael Paul Grace, who paid £1214 annually for the privilege. The Websters themselves lived at Powdermill House. Augustus had served in the Grenadier Guards for ten years and would serve again in 1914–18.

Godfrey was the eldest of the three children and the only male. Born in Hill Street in Mayfair in 1897, he was only 17 and still at Eton when the war began, and 20 when he died on 3/4 August 1917 as the result of a shell landing 'at his feet'.[13] He had entered Sandhurst in February 1916 and had joined his father's old regiment, the Grenadier Guards, in November of that year, being sent to France in the following March. He was a keen ornithologist,[14] and his letters home from Sandhurst and the front are full of accounts of his bird-watching; while at the front he was elected a Fellow of the British Ornithological Union.[15] After his death two of his essays on birds were published, written while he was still at Eton, and they show considerable knowledge and style for someone of that age.[16] The records say that he was buried on the battlefield but like so many others no identified body was recovered and he is remembered on the Menin Gate at Ypres.

Godfrey Webster

Only seven weeks earlier his mother Mabel (Crossley) had been drowned while bathing in Farthing Pond on the Abbey estate while reportedly trying to save her elder daughter Evelyn. There was a memorial service for her at St Mary's a few days later, and out of respect all the town's businesses closed at 2 pm on that day.[17] His father survived to August 1923 when he died at Hove. He had reached the rank of Captain in 2nd Battalion, The Grenadier Guards, before resigning his commission, and had served on the General Staff during the war.

With Godfrey vanished the sole heir to the baronetcy, and the estate would normally have descended to Evelyn, who had been declared insane. She survived to 1988, and her younger sister Lucy to the next year. Lucy had married but fell out with her husband and reverted to her maiden name. She too lived at Powdermill.

Inevitably the Ypres offensive slackened in mid-August, and Lloyd George, the prime minister, tried to have it called off. He failed and it was renewed in September, with the major attack being planned for October. The final attack ended on 7 November, when the original

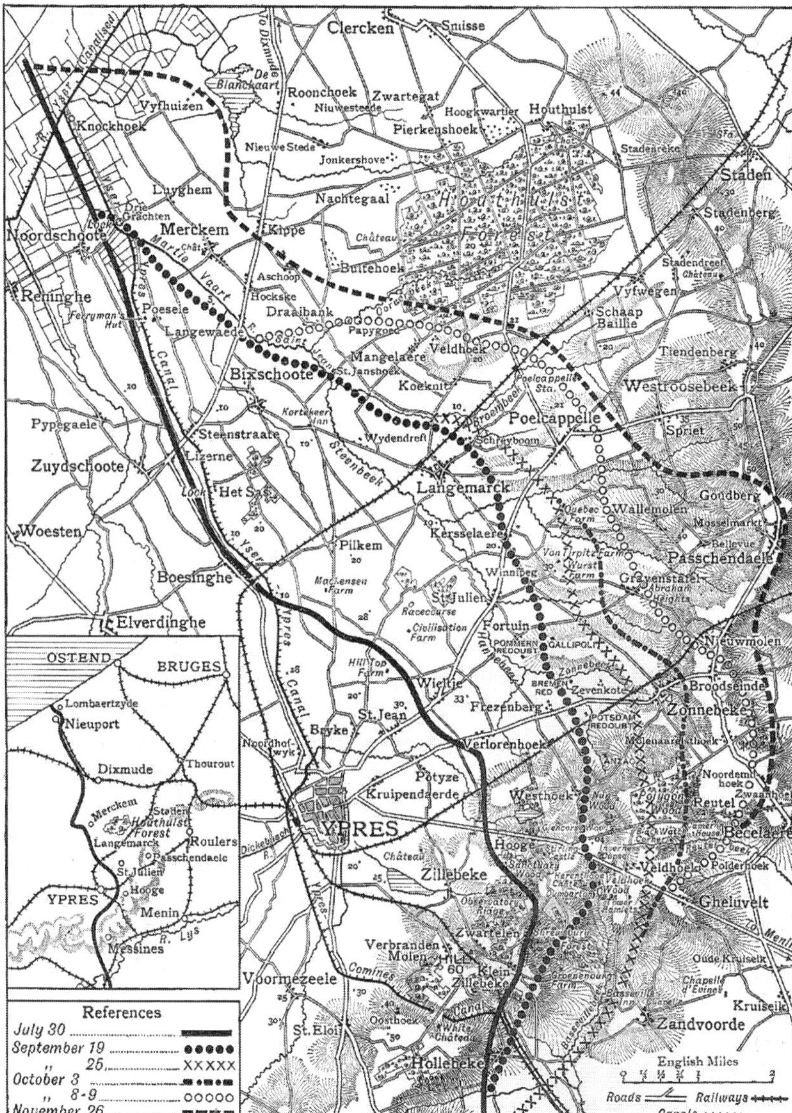

Map 13: the Third Ypres, including Passchendaele. The scale of this map is one half-mile to an inch. The distance from the original front line to Passchendaele is therefore about 4.5 miles, won over very nearly four months.

objective of Passchendaele was reached; the village no longer existed. All the gains were lost in the German offensive less than six months later. The casualties of third Ypres are unclear but it cost the Allies some 300,000 men and the Germans 200,000.

There are reports of further woundings. On 3 August Gunner William Lovell of Darwell Hill was shot in the left leg. He had enlisted at Hastings in February 1916 as a Gunner in the RHA/ RFA but had not been sent to France until 23 July 1917; his first tour therefore lasted about eleven days. He would have a similar experience in 1918. He was brother to George Lovell, who was to die in December 1918.

On 16 August Harry Fuller, also of Netherfield, was wounded in the left hand and sent back to England. The initial report was that his wound was 'mild' but he was not discharged from hospital until March 1918. He was serving as a Gunner with the RFA and had enlisted early in 1916, being sent to France in October that year. He was a brother of Thomas John Fuller, drowned when the *Cameronia* had been sunk four months earlier, and of the other Fullers wounded in this month. He was to marry Mary Hodgskin at Battle and have a son there in 1929. He died in 1972.

On 18 August another of the Saunders family was wounded outside Ypres, probably on Observatory Ridge: Private William Saunders of 8th Battalion, The Royal Sussex Regiment. He was the man who had appealed for magazines back in 1915, with what result is unknown. He was a bugler and later a Lance Corporal who was badly wounded in his right shoulder. Although wounded he did not suffer the fate of two of his five brothers, who were killed. The first of these had died only five days earlier, in Egypt: Alfred, from the No 6 Pack Wireless Section of the Royal Engineers. He died from appendicitis and is buried in the Cairo War Memorial Cemetery. Nelson, the other brother to die, lasted to the following April.

All these men were sons of Henry and Mary (maiden name not yet traced), of Ivyland Green, Netherfield, Henry had been an agricultural labourer but later worked as a labourer at the gypsum mine. There is at present no certain information as to the deaths of the parents or of that of William.

Also in August, but precise date unknown,[18] Ernest Edward Fuller was wounded near Ypres. He was a Netherfield man, another brother of Thomas who had died at sea in April, and his family is discussed in relation to that event. His two surviving brothers were also wounded in the same month. Ernest Fuller was a Private in 19th Battalion, The

Middlesex Regiment. After the war he married Matilda Stonestreet and they had children in the Battle area. He died at Hastings in 1978; Matilda lived on to 1987.

Ernest Fuller's brother Stephen was wounded near Ypres on 22 August; he was to be discharged before the end of the war. Stephen was an assistant engine driver at Newbery's and had joined 6th Battalion, the Duke of Cornwall's Light Infantry. He had been born in 1885; in 1911 he had married Annie Ballard and they were to have four children, all born at Battle: Nora, Edward, Arthur and Mabel. We do not have a date for Annie's death, but it is likely to have been at Battle in 1962.

In considering 1917 we cannot avoid the mud. The Third Ypres was infamous for it. It was not that mud was a new phenomenon. Its dangers must have been observed before, by officers as well as by the men. References to it were frequent. Private Picknell of 7th Battalion, The Royal Sussex Regiment, had written home towards the end of 1916 that he was

> Still all right in spite of the mud .... All the Battle boys are well.[19]

In January 1917 Private Tom Vidler had written:

> I don't know whether I shall take up mining or become a farmer's boy when I get the sack from this job, as no carter ever had more mud to go through than there is out here.[20]

Private Picknell of 7th Battalion, The Royal Sussex Regiment was James, born in Bexhill in 1896, like others a grandchild of Sarah Oliver and in 1911 living with her and many others in Battle Hill. He married at Battle in 1927 and had two children there; he died in Uxbridge in February 1949. Tom Vidler is mentioned later in this account, for August 1918.

If the mud meant that the British advance was slow, it also meant that the Germans had ample time to prepare for it. The Third Ypres was to be a bitter battle. Mercifully no Battle man died in it until September, but then there were six, four of them within seven days.

Fighting went on elsewhere, however, and two Battle men died in it.

The first was Herbert Smith Church, on 10 September. He was a photographer in Joshua Mathis's old premises at 12 High Street. Born in Battersea and at first enlisted in the Norfolk Regiment, he later transferred to 2/4th Battalion, The Royal Berkshire Regiment, and died of wounds. He is buried at Le Tréport on the Norman coast, so the wounds are unlikely to have been incurred in the Third Ypres. Church was 32 and had married Emily Gower, a Norfolk woman but almost certainly related to the Gowers of Battle. Emily died at Dartford in 1959; there were no children.

On the same day Stephen Claude Holland was wounded. Another Netherfield man, he was a brother of the Franklin Holland who was to be killed on 24 September. Stephen had been a policeman in London until disqualified by accident from further service; he is recorded in 1911 as a motor driver and in the war he was serving as a Private in the ASC Motor Transport section. He was invalided out to Birmingham. He died at Bristol in 1930. (His family is explored in connection with Franklin, below.)

The second death was Archibald Murdock of 3rd Battalion, the Buffs (the East Kent Regiment). He had served in the South African war of 1899–1902 and rejoined in 1914. He had been been wounded in 1916, and shortly thereafter achieved rapid promotion: Lance Corporal to Lance Sergeant in two days, Acting Sergeant six months later and Sergeant a month after that. He was awarded the Military Medal in July 1917 but was killed on 12 September; the records suggest a birth at Clapton by Hackney in 1886. His father, also Archibald, had been a milkman (dealer) according to the 1901 census; he and his wife Rosina (Jinks) were then living at 48 Priory Road, Hastings. They appear to have died before the war. Their son is buried in Philosophe British Cemetery at Mazingarbe, between Béthune and Lens.

The younger Archibald married Beatrice Maude in July 1905, and they had four children – Beatrice, Cissie, Emily and Archibald. His widow died in the Hailsham area in 1944.

On 22 September Percy Wait was wounded in his right arm and chin and later taken to the VAD hospital at Walmer. He was a Lance Corporal in 13th Battalion, The Royal Sussex Regiment and was 34 years old. A son of William Wait, his origins are explored in connection with the death of his brother William who had died earlier in the year. Percy had married Ellen Crouch in 1904 and was to die in an explosion while preparing fireworks at his house in Wellington Gardens in 1937.

Some time in September, too, Richard Hickmott was wounded. Born in Battle in 1884, he had enlisted in the RHA/RFA in 1904 and had served three years as a Gunner until he joined the Reserve in 1907. Recalled in August 1914 he went to France for three years, but suffered a gunshot wound to his left hip and came home. His ancestry is hard to find, but presumably during his first period of service he was stationed in East Anglia because he married there in 1909 and had four children before the war. He died at Ipswich in 1943; his wife had died in 1936. None of the family seems to have retained a connection with Sussex.

Then in September a further wounding: Corporal Kenneth Hannay, whose mother Harriet (Park) lived at St Mary's farm.[21] This is the old farmhouse immediately east of the railway line, north of Battle Hill. There is no Hannay in any Battle census; his mother and his brother George came to live in Battle after 1912, and their address was St Mary's Dairy Farm. According to directories, they had left by 1919. The man himself was Kenneth Hannay from Ulverston

Kenneth Hannay

in Lancashire, son of George Kerr Hannay, an ironfounder who had died when his son was only four; his exiguous army record – he was in the RGA – gives his address as Bedford Place in Bloomsbury, and adds that he was at first a corporal and then commissioned 2nd Lieutenant in August 1918 and sent to North Russia (presumably on the miserable Archangel expedition) in July 1919. It also suggests that Russia was his only theatre of war, which clearly cannot be true. Harriet died at Greenwich in 1933. Kenneth married Bessie Thompsett in 1919 and died in Middlesex in 1942; there were two sons and a granddaughter. Bessie died at Tunbridge Wells in 1968.

The Third Ypres: Passchendaele (the Autumn)

We then come to the aptly-named Passchendaele, an attack that like so many others should not have been ordered, and in which an uncounted number of men died in the mud rather than by enemy action. The Somme had been appalling; for rather different reasons so was Passchendaele. The Tate Gallery has a painting by Sir William Orpen, one of the official war artists, of what had been the village of Zonnebeke after the battle, and it remains harrowing after all these years, along with the many extant photographs.*

The village of Passchendaele was, or had been, less than five miles from the centre of Ypres, and the German front line not much more than half-way between the two.

The renewed push of 20 September gained some ground, with rather less than two miles in all being won by 4 October. By then the rains had returned, and with them the ever-deepening mud and the consistent advice from the Belgians that the offensive could not be sustained. Generals Plumer and Gough proposed delaying or even cancelling the next step but Haig insisted on it. It went ahead.

The first Netherfield man to die was Franklin Gilbert Holland.

* At this point it may be appropriate to mention Herbert Arnould Olivier the portrait painter (1861–1952), who had been born at Battle. It was in 1917 that he was appointed an official war artist. His father was rector of Crowhurst (1861–64) but in the censuses Herbert's Battle birth is carefully distinguished from that of siblings born at Crowhurst. His nephew Laurence was to take the family to even greater fame.

Holland was an Acting Company Sergeant Major in 11th Battalion, The Royal Sussex Regiment. He was 23 when he died on 24 September, having joined up at the beginning of the war. He was killed in heavy German shelling at Zonnebeke. His body was not recovered, and his name is on the Tyne Cot Memorial. Like so many others, Holland had been employed by Newbery's before his enlistment. He was clearly a good soldier, for on 3 September 1916, on the Somme, he had earned the Médaille Militaire with this citation:

> For conspicuous bravery and devotion to duty at Beaumont Hamel on September 3rd, 1916, when he ably led his team of Lewis gunners out in front of the enemy lines and opened fire with his guns. His splendid example and disregard for danger was the means of inspiring the men around him. In spite of the intense shelling and the casualties in consequence, he stuck [to his] gun for six hours and succeeded in [preventing] the enemy's counter-attack at [this] point. **

At one point he was buried by a 'Jack Johnson'*** but survived with "a few scratches". [22]

This Holland family of Netherfield was large: there seem to have been fifteen children, four of whom died young and all of whom had more than one forename (which was unusual for the time). The father, William, was a domestic gardener who had died at the beginning of 1915. We do know that Franklin had at least four brothers also serving in the war: Alfred, Ernest, Stephen and Herbert.

On 26 September George Johnston Martin was killed in action near Ypres; he is buried in the Tyne Cot Cemetery. Martin was born in 1894 at St Austell in Cornwall, son of Constantine Martin and Sarah (Durrant). George had pursued the same calling, being in 1911 the master's clerk at the Eastbourne Workhouse. Early in the war he joined 19th Battalion, The Royal Fusiliers and was sent to France in November 1915; he is reported as having then been commissioned as Second Lieutenant in the RFC and finally, with the same rank, in 13th Battalion, The Royal Sussex Regiment. He was unmarried.

** From the Netherfield File. Word in square brackets are missing from the extract and the text supplied here is likely to have been in the original.

*** A Jack Johnson was a black 15cm German shell.

Constantine Martin was Master of the Battle workhouse from 1896 to 1909. Late in 1908 his wife (who was the matron there) died and the Local Government Board regulations required him to leave, which he did in 1909. He had had something of a chequered history at Battle in any case. He died at West Ham in 1922. There were no other children.[23]

Jesse Kenward was wounded by gunshots to the thigh on 4 October. He was 29, born at Ore (though his military attestation states Norwich) and had lived in Whatlington Road where before the war he had been a bricklayer's labourer. He went to France in February 1915 as a Private in 5th Battalion, The Royal Sussex Regiment and suffered illnesses there in 1915. In October 1917 the battalion was engaged in making roads near Ypres. After his wounds he was transferred to the Labour Corps but remained in a poor condition. He survived the war, being discharged in 1919 with 60% disability through bronchitis and debility for which he was to receive a pension of 16/6d per week. He married in 1920 and had nine children, all born at Battle. He died in 1963.

The second Battle man to die was from Netherfield: Trooper Frank Carter of Church Lane. He was 24, a stockman on a farm and his father Edward was a higgler (a small trader without established premises); his mother was Annie Louisa (Wyatt) from Aston Clinton in Buckinghamshire. Carter was with 2nd Life Guards, part of the Household Battalion, and he died near Poelcappelle on 10 October. His body was not recovered or identified, and his name is also on the Tyne Cot memorial. He had married only in 1916, to Ethel Bowyer at Easthampstead in Berkshire, and their only child Frank had been born in May 1917.[24] In due course Frank married and had five children, none of them in Sussex. He died in 1975.

Carter's father died at Netherfield in 1932 and his mother in 1941. His brother Archibald married in 1931 and had three children at Lewes.

Also on 10 October Charles Crouch was wounded for a second time, on this occasion at the Yser Canal close to Ypres. His details are given in connection with his first wounding in 1916.

Among the soldiers who took Polygon Wood was very likely to have been Lance-Corporal Arthur Archibald Dengate. His battalion

Trooper Frank Carter, killed 10 October 1917 (see p. 127)

– 59th Battalion, the Australian Imperial Force – took a prominent part in the fighting, and he was awarded the Meritorious Service Medal early in 1918. Dengate had been born at Crowhurst and in 1911 was recorded as an under-housekeeper at Telham Farm. He married Caroline Playford at Battle late in 1913, which must have been only just before he emigrated to Melbourne: he left England on 14 October. Caroline stayed behind and gave birth to a son; she registered the birth only in the second quarter of 1915, which suggests that she had omitted to do so until then and remembered just before she too left. By 1916 the pair (and presumably the infant) were at Malvern in Victoria. Dengate returned to Australia after the war and died at Melbourne in 1959.

Probably just after the action at Polygon Wood a Netherfield man was wounded: Private Henry Tilden Smith. He had enlisted in 1915 but was not mobilised for some time. He first joined the Household Battalion, then the Coldstream Guards, and then the Guards

Machine Gun Regiment. It was while he was with the Household Battalion that he was wounded in the left arm on 9 October and sent home; he was back in action from the following October and was finally discharged in March 1919.

Smith was the son of Tilden Henry Smith, a general labourer, and his wife Frances (Harris) of Mountfield. Tilden died at Hastings in 1953 at the age of 97; Frances had died in 1909. Henry died at Hastings in 1959. He was married to Harriet Schnorr, and had three children. The two daughters appear to have married at Battle.

The third to die at Passchendaele was Private Arthur Gower, aged 26, son of H J Gower of Watch Oak. He was a gardener who in 1911 had been employed at the nurseries at Plumpton just under the South Downs.

Gower had already emigrated to New Zealand, and when he fought it was with 1st Company of the New Zealand Machine Gun Corps according to New Zealand records; the Roll of Honour has him as 2nd Company. He had left Wellington, in New Zealand, on the Manganui or the Tahiti bound for Plymouth, on 15 November 1916. We do not know the date of arrival, but it was probably at the time of the new year.[25] His parents, Henry and Jane (Blackman), lived at Watch Oak; Henry was a stationary engine driver in the tannery. Arthur was reported as having had a good position in New Zealand, which he left as soon as war was declared. He was part of a large tribe. His father told the press that Arthur had been one of five sons serving at the front, and in addition three sons-in-law and one grandson were there too.[26] Gower did indeed have five brothers – Harry, William, Charles, Frank and Percy – born between 1875 and 1892. His father and mother had both been born in Battle and had married there in 1874; they were both to die there too, in 1926 and 1930.

We have a record of the day on which Gower died, 12 October, albeit from 2nd Company. First from the official side:

> The officers of the barrage groups made the necessary reconnaissance of their positions, and throughout the 11th October the transport officers and drivers worked with indefatigable energy to get forward the ammunition required for the operation. The fiendish weather had performed its devilish task to perfection; the

> shell-torn areas that lay between the front, and the roads that had been pushed forward had become a seething mass of almost liquid mud. Wheeled transport was quite impossible, which necessitated the use of pack horses. In spite of all difficulties the transport did its job as it always did, and there was no shortage of ammunition during the following day....
>
> This group (all of the 1st Company) suffered 65 casualties on the 12th, including Lieut. Tansey. In spite of the heavy casualties, all the guns remained in the line until the 16th, when they were withdrawn. Although no casualties were suffered on the last two days, the gunners were completely exhausted. The terrible conditions under which they had to stick to their posts for four days and nights, and the nerve-wracking experience of the 12th, left the remnants of the 1st Company broken and worn out. Perhaps the most graphic illustration of the condition of the Company is contained in the entry in the War Diary for 17th October. Reference has been previously made to the fact that it was impossible to give details of the action of the 1st Company on the 4th October owing to the meagre report the O.C. made of it. The report of the 17th October is really much more meagre; it contains two words, but those words mean much; they are, "Company slept.[27]

And then from someone who went through it: Private W Smith of the NZMGC:

> ...the march up had been a nightmare, for the heavy shelling of the day had blown great gaps in the duckboards – too many to repair....
>
> It was a terrible night. We dug in as best we could at the bottom of the Bellevue Ridge – but the idea of 'digging in' was ridiculous. You can't dig water! My section managed to throw up a kind of ridge of slush, but the water from the shell-holes around just poured into it. You couldn't squat down, you just stood there in the rain and wind waiting for our guns to open up with the barrage.
>
> [On the next day] We made a bad 'blue' in sticking to that main P road [****].... As we started up the road we were being caught in enfilade fire... people were dropping all the way. Then, as we turned the corner at the top of the rise, we saw this great bank of wire ahead, maybe a hundred yards away. A rat couldn't have got through that. The bombardment should have cut the wire but it hadn't even

**** *blue* means *mistake*; P must mean Passchendaele.

> dented it. Not that we could get near it anyway, because it was positively spitting fire. The hail of lead we tried to go through was simply incredible. More than half of us fell.
>
> [Late morning] Now we were down to one NCO. When we'd finished laying out young Stewart to die, this NCO, a Sergeant Smith, suddenly issued the order, 'Prepare to advance'. Now this was just sheer suicide.... I thought to myself, 'Well, Sergeant Smith, if we're going, you'll go first!' Sure enough, up he stepped. As he showed his nose the sniper fired. He came crashing back on top of me with his face twisted in a look I'll never forget. That was the end of any advance in that direction.[28]

It must be in that kind of attack that Arthur Gower fell. He has no known grave and his name is on the Tyne Cot Memorial.

Also on 12 October Private Stuart Anthony Hale was wounded at Poelcappelle, which is now again a small village about four to five miles north-east of Ypres. He died the next day at 61 Casualty Clearing Station. He was a Private in 7th Battalion, the Royal West Kent Regiment. He had been born at Battle in July 1898, which means that he was 19 when he died. He had joined up in April 1917 and he was wounded on the first day of his service in the front line;[29] he died on the next. There are accounts of Poelcappelle from those who were there. The prevailing conditions can be summed up in what a man in the Rifle Brigade wrote later of the night of 9/10 October:

> Tea was all we had that night at Poelcappelle. There was no chance of getting the rations up..... we were just crouched in shell-holes waiting, and there was this one little chap. He made tea all night long, and kept nipping out and getting water out of flooded ground behind us and heating it up as best he could..... The next morning when it got light he looked over the side where he'd got the water and it was a bleeding shell-hole, and there was a dead Jerry in it and blood all floating around.... We heard screaming from another crater a bit away.... It was a big hole and there was a fellow of the 8th Suffolks in it up to his shoulders. So I said: 'Get your rifles, one man in the middle to stretch them out, make a chain and let him get hold of it.' But it was no use. It was too far to stretch, we couldn't get any force on it, and the more we pulled and the more he struggled the further he seemed to go down. He went down gradually. He kept

> begging us to shoot him. But we couldn't shoot him. We stayed with him, watching him go down in the mud. And he died. He wasn't the only one. There must have been thousands up there who died in the mud.[30]

Hale's father Charles was the coachman at the Railway Hotel (now the Senlac Inn) at the top of Station Road, and he had a younger brother and sister. They lived in the Railway Hotel Cottages, just behind the hotel on the Hastings Road. Hale is buried in Dozinghem Military Cemetery.

The father Charles died in 1937 and his mother Annie (Playford) in 1964. His brother Dennis married and had two children, one of whom died in infancy; he too was named Stuart Anthony.

There was a third man to die that day, another Eldridge: Ernest John, a Private in 11th Battalion, The Leicestershire Regiment. He was the son of Elijah Eldridge and his wife Ann. Elijah was a bricklayer who had died while the war was in progress (his widow would die in 1933). Ernest was one of six children born in the 1880s, and was 37 when he died. He too was a bricklayer and in 1911 was recorded as living at Sidley with his wife Ruth Amy (Wood), whom he had married at Battle in the spring of 1908. His widow, who had been born at Battle early in 1887, died at Uckfield in 1969.

We do not yet know the action in which Ernest died. He is buried at Dickebusch, behind the line and south-west of Ypres.

The last to die in October was Frederick Charles Blackman, a Lance Corporal in 13th Battalion, The Royal Sussex Regiment. Here there is a discrepancy between the Memorial Hall record, which has him as E C Blackman, and the churchyard, which has him as F C. The newspaper report of his death identifies the man as Private Frederick Blackman, son of T C Blackman of Mount Street.[31]

On 19 October he died near the Canadian Tunnels by Polygon Wood just east of Ypres, which was by then well in British hands, and because no precise record exists one must assume that his death resulted from shelling or from previously unexploded ordnance. On the day in question his battalion was heavily engaged in retrenching, burying the dead and laying new telephone lines.

Blackman had been a volunteer since 1910 and had enlisted at Battle as a territorial on 4 April 1914, for one year in 5th Battalion,

The Royal Sussex Regiment. The effect of the war on a small town is shown by the fact that his attestation forms were countersigned by Frederick Langham, who appears elsewhere in this account, and Ferris Grant of Crowhurst, who was to die in 1915; his medical examination was by Daniel Brough, who himself went to war later. In the manner of young men Blackman had a brush with the military authorities, being given seven days' CB for causing a disturbance in the barrack room late in 1914. He had gone to France on 18 February 1915; he was wounded by shrapnel in the ankle on 1 May 1915 and had spent two weeks in hospital. His promotion to Lance Corporal came on 10 May 1915. As territorials signed on for a limited period, in due course their time expired and Blackman declined voluntarily to re-engage; in April 1916 (apparently a year late) he came home. He rejoined in August and went back to France exactly one year before his death.[32] A letter describes him:

> He was a most efficient and reliable soldier, as might indeed have been expected by all who knew him at Battle.[33]

His body was never found or identified, and his name is on the Tyne Cot Memorial. His brother William had just been promoted Sergeant-Major.[34]

Blackman was 27, unmarried, and a carman in civilian life, son of Thomas Blackman, coal merchant at 66 High Street. The family home in 1911 was at 30 Mount Street, which he shared with his parents, two younger brothers and two younger sisters. There had been eleven children, two of whom had already died. Blackman's mother Harriett (Collins) died in 1919 and his father in 1947. There is a large number of descendants of those children around Battle.

Cambrai

5th Battalion, The Royal Sussex Regiment, was involved in the battle of Cambrai in November 1917, the last major engagement of the year on the western front. This was the imaginative attempt – rather too imaginative, as it turned out – to break the new German lines at a time when the Germans were heavily engaged around Ypres.

Cambrai was chosen as the objective because it was an important railway junction, and the land about it was reasonably well-drained. It began on 20 November without any preliminary bombardment and using a mass of tanks, and made quick work of the first five miles into German-held terrain. The command was of course unused to the use of tanks. The infantry failed to keep up with them and the

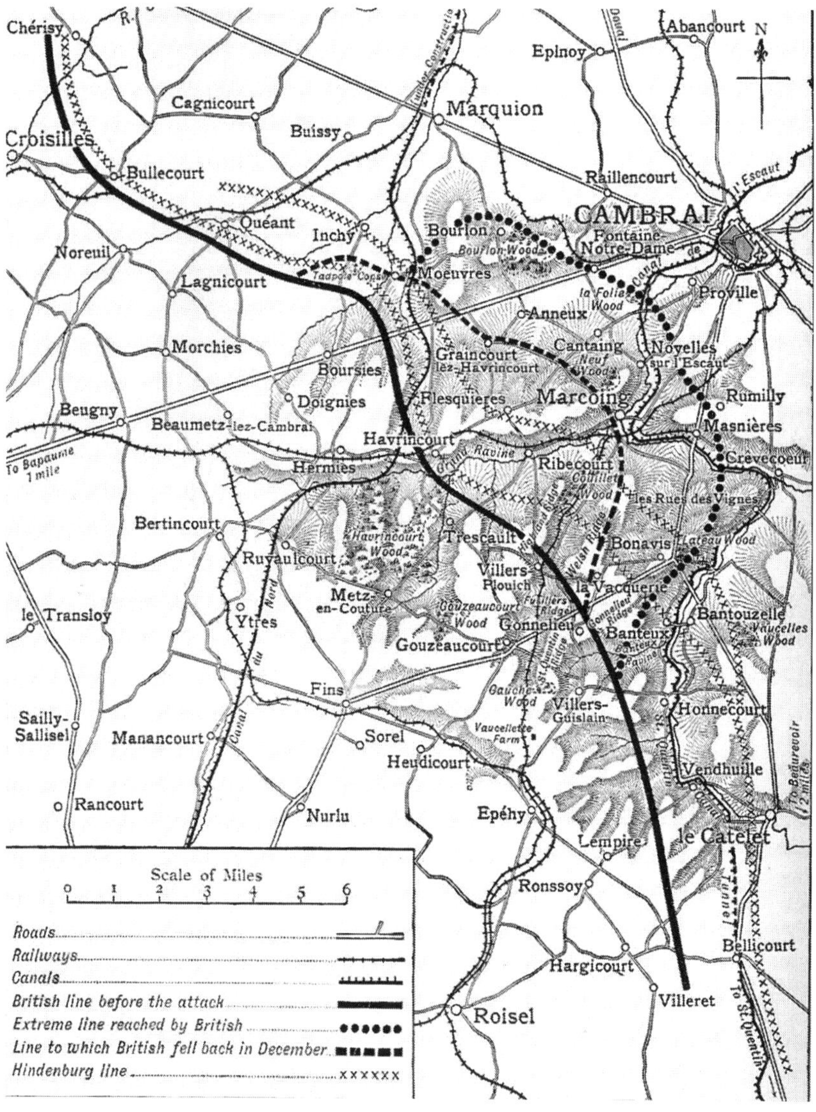

Map 14: Cambrai 1917

artillery failed to keep up with the infantry. Within a fortnight the Germans had regained all their land.

One of the men in 5th Battalion was Peckham-born Private George Radford, who in 1911 was listed as living at Kenward's Yard with the Smale family; another lodger was George Maplesden, who also served. A recent communication states that Radford was the adopted son of Emma Smale (along with Cpl Arnold Thompson), a widow whose six sons all served and survived the war.[35] A letter from Radford (by then Radford-Twyman) to the Battle and District Historical Society has survived, dated 6 May 1968.[36] In it he said:

> ...as a lad I belonged to the Boy Scouts & after that the Church Lads Brigade, headquarters the Deanery, Territorials the Drill Hall ... I volunteered to serve my country overseas in France & Belgium 4½ years until I was demobilised from the Rhine Army of Occupation in 1919. Actions were Neuve Chapelle 1915, Ypres, Arras, Battle of the Somme 1916–17, & Italy. Parve [*perhaps Piave?*], near Gorizia, La Bassée Bapaume & Bourlon Wood.... I was wounded & gassed at the Battle of Cambrai and also shell-shocked.

Bourlon Wood was right at the front on the furthest British advance, and was a German strongpoint. It was taken after four and half-hours of fighting on 23 November but the new line was untenable. The British withdrew from the wood and brought their advance lines back to a defensible position on 4–5 December. Bourlon Wood was particularly difficult to hold because of concentrated gas attacks.

He joined up early: there is a report of him among the former Church Lads who were serving in July 1915.[37] Unfortunately his official military records have not survived.

Radford's father was a furniture salesman living at Camberwell in 1911; he died at Eastbourne in 1943. His mother Emily (Holman) had died at Camberwell in 1914. Radford married late in life, in 1957, and died at Eastbourne in 1973. He does not appear ever to have had children, and neither did his sister Diana.

Robert Whibley was wounded again at Cambrai (see 1916 for his family and for his first wound).

Notes

1 http://www.wartimememoriesproject.com/greatwar/allied/devonshirergt-gw.php
2 http://www.rmslusitania.info/related-ships/cameronia/
3 *Hastings Observer*, 3 March 1916.
4 http://www.wartimememoriesproject.com/greatwar/allied/northamptonshire regiment6-gw.php
5 *Hastings Observer*, 19 May 1917.
6 *Hastings Observer*, 11 March 1916.
7 *Hastings Observer*, 26 May 1917.
8 Information from Ralfe Whistler
9 From a press cutting in the Netherfield file.
10 *Hastings Observer*, 25 August 1917.
11 *Hastings Observer*, 25 August 1917.
12 The historian A J P Taylor provided a characteristically vitriolic account in his *The First World War* (Hamish Hamilton, 1963).
13 *Hastings Observer*, 18 August 1917.
14 Keith Grieves: *Sussex in the First World War* (Sussex Record Society, 2004)
15 Correspondence preserved in East Sussex Records Office.
16 Pamphlet produced by Hugh Whistler and in the possession of Hugh's son Ralfe.
17 *Hastings Observer*, 23 June 1917.
18 Netherfield File
19 *Hastings Observer*, 2 December 1916.
20 *Hastings Observer*, 13 January 1917.
21 *Hastings Observer*, 8 September 1917.
22 Document (unsigned) held by East Sussex Records Office.
23 Information on Constantine Martin from Adrian Hall of Battle.
24 *Hastings Observer*, 17 November 1917.
25 http://muse.aucklandmuseum.com/databases/Cenotaph/5746.detail?keywords=Gower%20Arthur%20World%20War%20I,%201914-1918
26 *Hastings Observer*, 10 November 1917.
27 Major J H Luxford NZMGC: *With the machine gunners in France and Palestine*, 1923
28 Lyn Macdonald: *They called it Passchendaele* (Michael Joseph 1978)
29 *Hastings Observer*, 3 November 1917.
30 Lyn Macdonald: *They called it Passchendaele*
31 *Hastings Observer*, 3 November 1917.
32 http://1914-1918.invisionzone.com/forums/index.php?showtopic=169303
33 *Hastings Observer*, 3 November 1917.
34 *Hastings Observer*, 3 November 1917.
35 Information from Mrs J Macvicker of Battle.
36 BDHS records at Battle Museum.
37 *Hastings Observer*, 10 July 1915.

6

1918: The Final Months of the War and its End

One might think that the men of Battle might have endured a less difficult year in 1918, particularly in that the war ended six weeks before the year did. But in fact 35 Battle men died, more than in any other year of the war.

The year on the western front was dominated by two major offensives, the first of which unlocked the trenches and created a real war of movement for the first time since 1914, but as in previous years fighting continued on a lesser scale elsewhere. Forward movement continued in the Near East, leading to the final defeat of Turkey in its Arab possessions; nearer home the Allies began to move forward from Salonica towards Austria. The demand for manpower had of course increased with the losses of 1916 and 1917, and the conscription net had been widened to cover older men. It was now even to cover Ireland, though to no identifiable effect.

The first offensive was the Germans' final attempt to win the war, in that short period between their no longer having to fight on the eastern front and the arrival of American troops in large numbers. They began with an overwhelming assault on Allied forces on 21 March. The German army attacked first the British and then the French lines. The second offensive was the Allies' reply, from August, which ended with German acceptance that they could not continue the war any longer. By then the narrow window open in March had closed and the strategic position had changed. In the east the Russian front may have been peaceful but the Austrians and Bulgarians were now under pressure from the south, and in the west there was a steadily growing American presence.

The 1918 losses on the western front were huge, even by past standards. The two great campaigns – the defence against the Germans in the spring and then the attack against them in the late summer and autumn – were particularly costly.

Before then a Battle man won a commendation. He was Albert Collins of Netherfield, a Driver with the Royal Engineers. On 29 January he won a certificate, presumably for actions late in the previous year, that read:

> Whilst taking RE stores forward into the Line his transport came under very heavy shell fire and gas. Driver Collins with most commendable courage stuck to his horses, although they had been wounded in several places and were difficult to manage he succeeded in bringing the transport safely back to the wagon lines.[1]

Collins was 38, the son of John Collins, a gypsum miner, and his wife Eliza Anne (Brabyn). They had lived at Mountfield, where Albert had been born, but had then moved to Netherfield; later they moved back again. Albert was a gypsum miner too. He had married Elizabeth Jane Harris in 1907 and they had two children. Albert died in 1938 and Elizabeth died late in 1962. Albert's father John was one of the many Cornish miners who left their home county to mine elsewhere; both he and Eliza, also from Cornwall, died in 1924.

The War nearly lost: the German Offensive

Of course there were casualties before the great German attack, and one of them was James Harris of Netherfield, one of three brothers who joined up and survived. He was a Corporal in 13th Battalion, The Royal Sussex Regiment and was wounded near Heudicourt. This is a small place between Péronne and Cambrai, just behind the front line. No postwar trace of James can be definitely found. He was stepson of Thomas Harris, a gypsum worker living at Watch Oak in 1911 and son of his wife Caroline, who appears to have previously been married to a brother of Thomas. By occupation he was a bavin maker: this now obsolete term seems to have referred to the twigs used in constructing the head of a broom or to an assemblage of twigs to be used as kindling or fuel.

Probably just before the attack – the record is unclear – Gunner Thomas Mercer received a gunshot wound to the thigh; he was discharged as no longer physically fit in the following year. Mercer had enlisted in the RGA at Bristol in 1911 and had been made Lance Bombardier only a few weeks before his wound. He was a gamekeeper like his father William, who was at Netherfield Place Farm but moved to Catsfield before the 1901 census. We can find no reliable trace of his parents. His brother George, having moved to Canada, was one of the Battle survivors.

The German offensive of 1918 had been expected, but the British were in a poor position to resist it. They had remedied their old and now obvious weakness: previously their front lines were strong but the second and third lines thin, but now they used the concept of 'defence in depth', allowing attacks to succeed but to be broken by strong points. Unfortunately they had not yet strengthened some sections recently taken over from the French. The German objective was to drive large holes through the front line, after which they might go for the Channel ports or bottle up the British forces in the Pas de Calais or both. The German method was new: to attack artillery and machine gun posts and British communications and to make powerful infantry assaults not on known strong points but on those sections where a breakthrough was likely. It worked. By the time that the line began to stabilise at the end of April the Germans were in some places very much further forward than six weeks earlier; they had swept the British (and in this case the Portuguese) from the hard-won fields of Passchendaele and were close not only to Arras but also to Amiens. But there the forward movement ceased and the Germans were unable to make further progress. Within a short time they were being pressed back. A war of movement had been restored, for the first time since 1914. The Allied response was no rapid onslaught, akin to the German offensive of March, but it was sustained: it took three months for them to reach the symbolic town of Mons from which the first British retreat had taken place in 1914.

The precise moment of the attack on 21 March was a surprise, because it was a day of thick fog and because the opening barrage was relatively brief. Using very heavy shellfire of high explosive and mustard gas, the Germans made immediate progress and broke the Allies' front line despite desperate resistance. For some time it appeared that this was the campaign that would end the war, for the Germans made very successful progress. Within two days they had advanced up to 15 miles and had retaken Péronne and crossed the Somme; when they ground to a halt their furthest advance had been 40 miles, not only retrieving the whole of the 1916 Somme battlefield but pushing far south, including the capture of Montdidier. Though they had failed again to take Ypres they were within a mile of what had been the city's centre; the killing fields of the previous November were theirs again. As always before, however, the advance faltered and stopped. (*See Map 15*).

One result of the rapid retreat for the families at home (and for later historians) was that in the early days of the push the officers, or rather those who survived, failed to keep up with the casualty lists, and when they were finally completed it was unclear who had died on which day. Dates for deaths recorded for the period between 21 and 31 March, therefore, must be taken as approximate.[2]

Among these undated deaths were William Eldridge, Frederick Holden, William Santer, Henry Vitler, Percy Relf, Alfred Stephens, Sidney Sellman, Frederic Newman and Albert Holland.

The Bexhill Roll of Honour records William Eldridge as being born there but no such birth was recorded in the formal records; instead, it seems clear that he was in fact born at Battle in 1883. The Roll of Honour gives his parent as Mrs A Eldridge. This must be the Ann Eldridge, recently widowed and previously married to Elijah who had died in 1917. His brother was Ernest, who had been killed in October 1917. William was a Private in 2nd/6th Battalion, The North Staffordshire Regiment and lived with his mother and brothers Percy and Charles Elijah at Sidley. The 1911 census describes him as a housepainter. His unit was in the line at Longatte, near Croisilles, where the heaviest German blows fell on 21 March. His name is on the Arras Memorial.

Frederick Holden was a Private in the Canadian infantry who had been born at Battle in 1896. The Canadian records have the briefest mention of him, unlike those others for whom there is a considerable amount, but we do know that his father was Thomas Holden, a domestic gardener, and his mother Mary Ann (Alderton). In 1911 the family was living at Phillips Buildings in Mount Street where (another) William Eldridge, who was to die in August, had also lived. Although Holden had several siblings the records are largely silent about the family after 1911, and it would appear that all, or at least most, of them went to Canada. Holden is buried at Wanquetin Communal Cemetery a short distance west of Arras.

Private William Aubrey Santer of 9th Battalion, The Royal Sussex Regiment died near St Quentin, a town that had remained in German hands but which the front line almost touched. His company was at Hesbecourt east of Péronne and that area was not subject to heavy attack; but there was heavy shelling and it killed Santer and a good few more. Santer was 28. He had married in 1909 and had a son, Frederick William, and a daughter, Maude. In 1911 he lived with his wife Annie (née Bean) and Frederick at 2 Carriers Yard; his job was as a confectioner's assistant. Frederick William, born late in 1909, married and lived at Bournemouth. He had three children and died there in 1986.

Santer's father William, a carpenter, lived at 9 Upper Lake with his wife, also Annie (Bodle); he died in 1947 and she in 1926. They had had two children, William and his sister Annie. (The recurrence of names makes their holders hard to distinguish from each other in the public records.) Santer's body was never identified, and his name is on the Pozières memorial.

In the same period Private Henry James Vitler of the Royal West Kent Regiment died; his name, too, is on the Pozières memorial. That his name is there suggests a death near St Quentin, and indeed his battalion were active in resisting the German advance there.[3] His family are unusually hard to trace. His father Henry, who was a farm labourer and carter, died in 1899 and his mother Ann Elizabeth (Waite) in 1934. In 1911 they are recorded as living at 9 Harold Terrace. Henry James had eleven siblings, some of whom stayed at Battle but most of whom – including those with children – went elsewhere. His brother Thomas was to be killed in Mesopotamia in October; another brother, Francis, also served.

Then perhaps a little later Private Percy Edward Relf of 23rd

Battalion, The Middlesex Regiment, was killed near Arras; his grave too is unknown, and he is remembered on the Arras memorial. The recent movements of his battalion have been set out as:

> In November [1917] the Division was ordered to Italy, moving by train to Mantua. The Division took the front line near the River Piave, north west of Treviso. In February they were summoned back to France and departed from Campo San Piero, travelling by train to concentrate near Doullens and Mondicourt.[4]

We do not know when Relf enlisted, but from the above it is more than likely that he had served in Italy, in one of those battalions sent there to shore up the Italians after the disastrous collapse of the their armies at Caporetto.

Relf was 20. In 1911 he had been living at Squirrel Hill at the western end of North Trade Road with his father Charles, his mother Kate (Fuller), two elder brothers Charles and Ernest and three older sisters; two other sisters had left. His father described himself as a woodman/dealer; the two brothers were woodsmen.

The elder Charles died at Battle in 1938 and his widow Kate in 1946. The younger Charles married and had one daughter, and there are descendants in Kent.

It has so far proved impossible to find out very much about Alfred William Holman Stephens. He was born at Battle late in 1882 but he does not appear definitively in a census until 1911, when he is a tailor living at Norbury, just north of Croydon, with his wife Ethel (Briggs), and recording himself as born at Battle. There is no available record of any child. This man may have been the Alfred whose father Alfred and mother Ellen (probably Brown) were living at St Leonards in 1901, but the younger Alfred is recorded as having been born there and not at Battle. He enlisted at Kingston in 2nd Battalion, The Middlesex Regiment, and was killed in the onslaught of the German forces. The CWGC give the date as 27 March. His body was never found or identified and his name is on the Pozières Memorial.

Sidney Sellman was 19 and a Sapper in a tunnelling company in the Royal Engineers. He is buried at Hangard, which is some 14 miles south-east of Amiens. He was the only child of James and Mary

Ann (Jenner) of Croucher's Cottages, Crowhurst and in 1911 was living on Spital Hill. He was then a butcher's assistant. His father had already died, and his mother lived only to 1924. Sellman was unmarried. James had married twice, and by his first marriage in 1864 he had had a number of children.

Frederic Charles Newman was a Gunner in 'Q' AA Battery of the Royal Garrison Artillery when the German attack killed him. The official date is 27 March, though this may not be true. He was not identified and his name is on the Pozières Memorial. Newman had been born in Battle towards the end of 1882; his father William was a groom and gardener at 1 Upper Lake. His mother was Fanny Louisa (Boxall) and they had both been born at Battle. After 1901 Frederic went to London and married Kate Hodgson in 1904; they had had three children by 1911. His mother died at Battle in 1930, and his father in 1938. Newman's younger sister Edith married Horace Stentiford at Battle in1926 and had two children.

Albert Holland from Netherfield also died reportedly on 27 March, and he too has no known grave. Albert was a Private in 9th Battalion, The Royal Sussex Regiment, attached to 73rd Light Trench Mortar Battery. By 27 March the British had been forced back well to the west of Péronne, and it was close to Méharicault that Holland was killed. His company had no grenades until the evening, and the Germans had entered its trenches, being kept at bay by bayonets alone. Holland was 36 and the second of two brothers from Netherfield to die in the war, sons of Walter and Harriet, whose details are given in connection with Albert's brother George, killed in 1915. Albert had married Annie Maria Kemp in 1908 and lived at Bracknell in Berkshire. Their son Albert Thomas had been born in 1909.

A local man was also wounded in this chaotic period. He was Albert Carter of Netherfield, son of Edward Carter, a gypsum miner and brother of William Sydney Carter who had been killed in April 1917. Albert was 23 when he was wounded. He was a Gunner in the RFA who had gone to Australia but had returned to join up in November 1914. He returned to Australia in 1922. Family details have been given in respect of his brother's death.

There were seven deaths in April as the British continued to fall sharply back: Horace Cockett, Frederick Holt, Tom Marsh, Albert Stemp, William Highwood, Nelson Saunders and Sydney Markwick.

Private Horace Edward Cockett of 12th Battalion, The Royal Sussex Regiment, had the distinction of having been awarded the Military Medal and bar, the only bar awarded to a Battle man in the whole war. The medals arose from his conduct at the end of July and the beginning of August 1917. The report describes him as a brigade runner. In the first instance he "during a very heavy engagement displayed conspicuous gallantry and devotion to duty in carrying on during very heavy shell fire";[5] and in the second, again under heavy fire, he rescued colleagues from a shell-hole that had opened up next to them.

In 1911 he was living with his widowed grandmother Sophia next to Mill Cottages in Hastings Road, with Sophia's daughter, also Sophia, and his younger brother Charles Walter. Cockett was born in Battle in 1892, and he was 25 when he won his medals and indeed when he died. A gardener at Battle Abbey, he had enlisted at Hastings and he died near Amiens in the German push to the west, on 3 April. His body was not recovered and he is commemorated on the Pozières memorial. His grandfather Joseph, born about 1833, had married in 1859; but we do not know for certain who the father of Horace and Charles was. Both in 1901 and 1911 they were living with their grandmother and her daughter Sophie, and in 1901 also with their grandfather. His mother was the younger Sophie, but to have two illegitimate children seems slightly odd for the time and place. The 1911 census yields no very convincing father, however. Charles stayed in Battle and had a son John, born in 1927.

Three men died on the same day, 5 April: Frederick Holt, Tom Marsh and Albert Stemp.

We know that Frederick Holt died in Aveluy Wood.[6] Aveluy was a large rectangular wood on the west side of the river Ancre, just north of Albert, and stood in the way of the Germans as they moved both north and south of the town to force a further British retreat. The wood was held by 7th Battalion, The Royal Sussex Regiment, and they had already suffered so many casualties that the officers were burning paperwork to prevent useful records falling into German hands once they were surrounded. In due course, after very heavy fighting, the wood was lost.[7] In fact Holt was a Second Lieutenant with the Queens West Surrey Regiment, which was almost as heavily involved with the wood by trying to hold the line immediately behind it. He has no known grave and is commemorated on the Arras memorial.

Holt was the son of John George Holt, a grocer and retailer of wines and spirits at 82–83 High Street, and of his wife Mary Ann (Bradley). He had been educated at Highbury School, St Leonards, and was in business with his father. He had only appeared in the newspapers once before his death: in November 1914 he was fined 2s 6d, with 6s costs, for letting off a firework in the High Street on 5 November. He enlisted as a Private on 1 January 1916 and was wounded on the Somme. By November 1917 he was at home awaiting his commission, which arrived shortly when he was gazetted to join the Queen's West Surrey Regiment. He left for France on 27 November. His commanding officer wrote to his father:

> We were heavily attacked, and your son was killed instantly by a machine gun bullet.[8]

This was one of the stock sentences and it must all too often have been true. One hopes that in this case the officer was not glossing over a worse death. There is a memorial plaque to Holt in St Mary's Church. His parents, both of whom had been born in London, died at Battle in the 1920s; he had only one sibling, a sister Elsie.

Private Tom Marsh was killed in action near Senlis Mill. Senlis is about 6 km north west of Albert, where the British were still desperately resisting the German advance towards Amiens and the coast. He was a Private in 7th Battalion, The Royal Sussex Regiment, some of whom had been deployed behind Aveluy Wood and had managed to avoid capture. Aged 23 at death, he is buried in Bouzincourt Ridge Cemetery.

Marsh was the son of the publican at the Squirrel Inn, also Tom Marsh. His mother had died in June 1915. His father lived to 1926 and is buried in Battle cemetery. He had three sisters, all of whom married. One of them had children at Battle who appear still to be living, and another had children elsewhere.

Albert William Stemp was a Private in the 51st (Western

Australian) Battalion of the Australian Imperial Force 13th Brigade. He was killed somewhere between Albert and Amiens and his name is on the Villers Bretonneux memorial.

In 1911 Stemp was recorded as the younger son of William, a wood-hoop maker of Mill Cottages, Hastings Road, though in 1916 his address was 3 Virgin's Croft; his brother Wilfred was a jam boiler's assistant and he was a market gardener. There were no other children in the family, and both sons were single. Albert emigrated to Australia at some point between the census and 1916. He enlisted at Fremantle, and embarked from there in October 1916 on HMAT *Suffolk*.

The Australians were in fierce fighting around Villers-Bretonneux on 5 April 1918; the village stood squarely on the main road between Albert and Amiens. An account from the 12 Brigade describes first-hand the attack that they faced. Private Stanley Sutcliffe recalled:

> At seven o'clock in the morning [5 April] such a barrage started as I have never seen before or since. Jerry had his guns registered on all our batteries, and was even knocking guns out miles behind the line at Warloy. It was a very foggy morning and we couldn't see much. He started this barrage on our front line and gradually lengthened his range until he got back on our artillery, and then he would shorten it gradually until he got on the front line again.
>
> He did this three times until eleven o'clock, with the idea of killing every living thing in its way. He put three shells within thirty yards of our post, but did no more damage than covering us with mud and giving us a good shaking up. Then he came over in full marching order, evidently with the idea of reaching Amiens without a stop. They say they had four divisions against only two of our brigades.
>
> The first wave of Germans came in massed formation, and they were cut down by machine-gun fire just like a scythe cuts grass. But his second wave appeared, so the 52nd Battalion and our 12th Brigade hopped up and met it. That was the first time I experienced hand-to-hand fighting with the bayonet, and it was heavy! But the Germans kept being reinforced, with the result that we were pushed back about 1,000 yards.[9]

Albert's father died in 1921 and his mother Ellen Sarah (Smith) in 1935, both at Battle. His brother Wilfred married in 1924 but appears to have had no children. He died at Battle in 1953 and his widow in 1966.

At some point in this catastrophic attack by the German army James Percy Woodhams was wounded. Aged 35, he was a Hastings man but worked at Battle where his father, also James, had been an auctioneer in the cattle market. The father had died in 1903 and his mother Agnes (Hunter) in 1916. He began the war as a Second Lieutenant in 2nd Battalion, The Royal Sussex Regiment, later becoming a Captain in 8th Battalion. His wounds appear to have been suffered in the Noyon/Compiègne area, though without a date one cannot be sure: 8th Battalion was keeping pace with the rapid retreat. Woodhams had married Muriel Abbott at Battle in 1910 and they had one child, also James, who died in 1984. Woodhams occupied several public posts at Battle and chaired the Battle branch of the British Legion. He died at Hastings in 1953. Muriel died at Canterbury in 1978.

The next to go was William Highwood. He was a Private who had enlisted at Hastings in September 1914. He had been with 11th Battalion, The Royal Sussex Regiment and had been wounded on the Somme in 1916. Having transferred to the Lincolnshire Regiment late in March 1918, Highwood was reported missing on 16 April and is regarded as having died on 10 April. But it may well have been 16 April, when the Lincolnshires suffered serious losses at Wytschaete. His death was formally presumed in March 1919.[10] As with so many others his body was never found and he is remembered on the Tyne Cot memorial.

Highwood had been born early in 1894 and so was 24 when he died. In 1911 he was living 6 St Mary's Villas with his father James and mother Henrietta (Fullagar), his brothers Frank and Harold and his sister Edith. His father was an insurance agent with the Prudential, but in March 1916 he had suddenly disappeared, only to be found a few days later in the New Pond in the Abbey grounds. No explanation was given, and the verdict was suicide during temporary insanity. He is buried in Battle cemetery.[11] William's brother Frank was in the RNAS, and Henrietta's nephew Frank Green was also on active service, reminding us that many of the Battle families were closely connected. Henrietta lived on to 1956.

Unlike many Battle casualties, Highwood had posthumous remembrance through his family. All three siblings married and had children.

Frank, the eldest, married Annie Santer in 1921, who seems to have been the widow of William, killed earlier in the year, and they had a child in 1924. He was Peter, who later married and had two children, both of whom left the town. Edith, his sister, married John Smale in 1924 and also had children, though it appears that there are no descendants at Battle. Harold, the youngest, married Florence Dean and had two children; he died in Croydon in 1968, and his family appear not have lived in Battle.

On 18 April Percy Champion was wounded, for the second time, and taken prisoner. This was at Beaumont Hamel, one of the most notorious fields of the war. Champion was in the Notts and Derby Regiment and returned to Battle as early as 3 October; one may therefore assume that he had been held just behind the line and that his location was overrun by Allied forces.[12]

Champion is described in the 1911 census as a paper boy aged about 13, son of William, a farm labourer at what was then called Pepper in Eye Farm and his wife Matilda. He had been born at Crowhurst. He married in 1924 and had three children. Two – John and Charles – married and had children of their own at Battle. Champion died there in 1960. His mother had died in 1925 and his father in 1936.

Nelson Saunders died on the day after Champion was wounded. He had enlisted at Hastings into the Royal Sussex but had later transferred to 9th (Glasgow Highland) Battalion of the Highland Light Infantry. He was a Private. Apparently he had been wounded on 14 April, but we know that his unit was heavily engaged on the previous day, on the Belgian/French border south of Nieuwkerke. He was taken to Etaples, the major British base on the French coast. He is buried in Etaples Military Cemetery. His family is discussed above in connection with his brother Alfred, who died in the previous year.

Nelson's brother Albert was wounded on the old Somme front on 9 May. He was a Private in 12th Battalion, The Royal Sussex Regiment and a gypsum labourer living at Netherfield. It is not clear from the records whether he married after the war, but he returned to the mine, where he was killed in October 1951, crushed between two trucks on the railway there.

Then there was Sydney Markwick. He was a Rifleman with 2nd Battalion, The Rifle Brigade, and aged 18. He was wounded in the German attack and died at Rouen base hospital on 28 April. In 1911 he was living with his father George and mother Mary (Dawes) at the entrance lodge to Normanhurst, where George was a gardener. By the time of his death his parents had moved to 1 Lower Lake. He had one sister, Edith, who later married Charles Gander at Battle in 1925; she died, apparently childless, in Hastings in 1988. Their parents died there in 1947 (Mary) and 1953 (George). He is buried at St Sever Cemetery Extension at Rouen.

On 15 May Private Robert Franks also died at Rouen of wounds received in action. Born at Battle in 1884, he lived initially at 6 Upper Lake. His father was a gardener who died in 1895, and Robert, his mother and his two sisters moved to Streatham in Surrey where Robert was a potman in a pub. His military record states that he was in the Royal Fusiliers and then the Labour Corps. Franks's mother Emma (Clarke) appears to have remarried after the war and returned to her birthplace Ipswich, dying there in 1934. Like Sydney Markwick, Robert is buried at St Sever Cemetery Extension at Rouen.

On 18 May there was the report of another wounding. Sydney Carter was one of the prolific Carters of Battle. His father Charles, of 7a Mount Street, was reported in 1915 as having three sons and four brothers serving in the army.[13] All of them returned. Sydney was 20 and a Private in 13th Battalion, The Royal Sussex Regiment when he was seriously wounded in the right leg and sent to hospital in London. He recovered and appears to have married Annie Crouch at Rye in 1933, but no children can be identified. The rest of the Carter family have continued to people Battle. In 1911 the family reported themselves as heavily dependent on the jam factory: father Charles was a warehouseman, and mother Lilly and two of Sydney's sisters were also employed there. Sydney was then a newsboy. Lily died at Battle in 1928 and Charles in 1929, but no certain report of Sydney's death can be established.

Pte. C. Smale,
d Scots Guards. In France.

Trooper H. G. Smale, 1st Sussex Yeomanry. At the Dardanelles.

Pte. A. Smale, 21st Lancers. In India.

Pte. T. A. Smale, Motor Transport. In France.

Petty-Officer T. W. Smale, Husband of Mrs. E. Smale, Battle.

Driver J. Smale, R.E. For Foreign Service.

Pte. G. Radford, 5th Royal Sussex. In France.

Cpl. A. Thompso 5th Royal Sussex. France.

Six sons and two adopted sons of Mrs. E. Smale, Market Green, Battle.

The Carters were not the only family to send a large number to the war. The Potters did so too, and also the Smales.[14]

If the Carters were unlucky, the Potters and the Smales were not: none of the seven younger men above died in the war, or their brother Frank. (The father Thomas, had already died in 1898. The mother Emma died at Battle in February 1918.)

The next local man to die was only just local: 39-year old Private Percy Ripley of 9a Lower Lake. He is reported as living there in 1911 and at his enlistment in April 1915 but his family was based in Kent. Ripley had first joined the ASC but then transferred to 1st/7th The Middlesex Regiment. He had been born at Smarden; his father was a blacksmith. Both his parents had died before the old century ended, and his various siblings, though impossible to track reliably from public records, appear all to have avoided Battle. Percy was unmarried. From the location of his grave he must have died in the battles around Arras as the Germans were still pressing forward. This was on 26 May.

If Ripley's connection was slight but real, the next death in the great German assault was in most senses not a local man at all, though he is listed on both the Battle memorials. Henry George Congdon was born at Dunbar in East Lothian in about 1867 and had evidently followed an army career because censuses list him as an army pensioner. Absence on military service would explain his absence from the 1891 and 1901 censuses. His father Samuel had been a militia officer at Dunbar, where he is listed as living in the militia barracks in 1871, and he stayed there when he became a school attendance officer. He had nine children, including Henry.

By 1911 Henry had been married for some 20 years to Mary Ransom Hollingsworth, daughter of a labourer at Fuller's Farm in Uckham Lane. Congdon was then a publican running the White Hart beerhouse at Fifield in Berkshire, between Maidenhead and Windsor. Three of his four daughters had been born at Chatham and one, in about 1901, in St Lucia in the West Indies.

Congdon was RSM in the Royal Engineers when he died on 28 May, and he was clearly highly regarded. He held the Long Service Medal and the Belgian Croix de Guerre. He is buried in Varennes Military Cemetery.

After Congdon's death his widow returned to Battle, dying there in 1922. His first daughter Gwen married in 1920 and had two daughters, but they appear to have left Sussex. His second daughter Daisy followed her mother back to Battle and was to die in the German bombing of Hastings in May 1943; she was then reported as living at Hertford.[15] Edith married but not at Battle; Mabel did not and appears to have died in Derby in 1991. The formal records therefore suggest no further involvement with the town by way of marriage or death after Gwen's daughters were born in 1921 and 1925.

The last of the spring deaths was on 31 May: Sapper Charles Stuart Bothwell of the Royal Engineers. He is buried at Lijssenthoek Military Cemetery near Ypres, meaning that he died in front of that city. He had been born in Kingston, Surrey, as had his brother and two sisters, to Charles, an upholsterer, and his wife Mary. They lived at 6 St Mary's Terrace. Stuart was 20 and single.

Bothwell was in 255 Tunnelling Company, which lost 17 men that day. This suggests either a cave-in or a gas attack.

Charles Stuart's father died in 1929, his mother Mary Ellen (Nurse) in 1945 and his brother (apparently unmarried) in 1968, all of them in Sussex. His two sisters married away from Battle.

For reasons that remain generally unclear the *Hastings Observer* did not mention any of the April and May deaths from Battle except that of Holt. There could be family reasons for this, and it is true that the paper was short of space in which to report every casualty but it remains odd, given the attention that the paper usually gave to casualties.

Congdon was not the only man to merit remembrance at Battle despite his poor connection with the town. On 19 June a Canadian was wounded who up to that year had no such connection (as far as we know) but his wound brought him to Sussex. Allan Hall Forbes was from Ontario and had enlisted there in November 1914, being sent to Britain in May 1915 (where he was promptly hospitalised with gonorrhoea) and to France that September. He had steady progress up the ranks, reaching the rank of Sergeant in 21st Battalion of the Canadian infantry, despite having survived a severe reprimand for overstaying his leave in 1916. On 19 June 1918 he was shot in the chest and was declared dangerously ill. He was then removed to hospital in England. His new base was Seaford. One can only surmise that it was there or at Battle he met Emily Kate Ponsford (sister of George, who served in the war), and they were married in St Mary's Church, Battle, that December. In 1919 they both went to Canada.

On 23 June 1918 a Battle man was wounded, but it was a self-inflicted wound. He was Private John Luck of 7th Battalion, The Royal Sussex Regiment, who reported that he was cleaning his rifle when it accidentally shot him in the foot; he had left it empty the night before. Similar tales had in the past led to court martial and possibly to death, but his story convinced his officers and he went to hospital to have a toe removed. He had enlisted at Uxbridge in January 1916, and had previously had bad attacks of trench fever, sufficient for him to have long stays in UK hospitals, and he was now discharged as physically unfit, with a 30% disability, early in 1919. In 1911 Luck reported himself as a domestic coachman living at 4

Lower Lake; he had been born in Baldslow in 1887. His father James was a gardener who died in 1943, and his mother Jane (Sargent) died in 1932. By the time of his enlistment he was living at Hayes in Middlesex, working for the Gramophone Company. He married in 1916, had four children and died at Lambeth in 1963.

At some point before July a Battle man won the Distinguished Conduct Medal. He was Company Sergeant Major Charles Edward Thomas, a bricklayer of Virgins Croft, a son of the builder John Thomas and a brother (and pall-bearer) of Arthur Thomas who had died in 1917. The newspaper report reads:

Charles Thomas, photographed probably early in the war

> When the officer in charge was down he took command of the small party which hardly numbered a hundred, but by skilful handling held their own against at least 2000 of the enemy.

It adds that Thomas had been a volunteer and had been mobilised at the outbreak of the war.[16]

The full citation gives much more information:

> For conspicuous gallantry and devotion to duty. This W.O. displayed conspicuous courage throughout two days' hard fighting in defence of a post which he held to the last. By his own example of gallantry and coolness he kept his command well in hand when all the officers had become casualties. Under the stress of circumstances the men broke temporarily on one occasion, but he rallied and reorganised them and putting fresh heart into them by his example, led them back to the trenches. He was thus able to hand over the position intact to the troops who were sent to relieve him, the very large number of enemy casualties lying in front testifying to the stubborn manner in which it had been defended.[17]

Thomas had been a volunteer before the war, serving from the age of 14 in 1890 in the 5th Cinque Ports Battalion. As a territorial and a Colour Sergeant in 1913 he won Queen Mary's Gold Prize at Bisley, £50 and a rifle from the manufacturers. In the war he became a Company Sergeant Major and then Acting Regimental Sergeant Major in the Royal Sussex. Thomas had three daughters. He died at Battle late in 1953.

At some point in July Charles Edwin Whiteman was wounded in the hand, an injury that presumably led to his prompt discharge. He was a Private in 3rd Battalion, the Royal West Kent Regiment, who had been in the Royal Sussex before he re-enlisted at Hastings in 1915. He was one of several brothers of James Whiteman, who had died in the first week of the Somme in 1916, and his family is described in connection with that event. When Charles came home he married at Hastings in 1921 and had two children; he died in Surrey in 1966.

So far in this account we have not come across anyone suffering from the poison gases released by both sides. But on 5 August Charles Spray had this misfortune. He was an Acting Lance-Corporal in the Machine Gun Company, 15th Battalion, The Royal Fusiliers, but he cannot have been badly affected because he returned to duty very soon. Born in 1892, he was son of William, an agricultural labourer of Watch Oak and brother of Harry who had been wounded in 1915. In March 1916, as a stockman with a hip defect, he had asked for exemption but had been refused. In 1919 he was posted to the Rhine Army where he overstayed his leave and was reduced

Charles Spray MM, of Watch Oak (1892–1923). Charles was recorded as an agricultural labourer. He died at Battle without leaving trace of marriage; the report of his death describes him as a gardener.

to the ranks. He was discharged in the ordinary way in November.

Charles had won the Military Medal on 25 April 1918: the citation reads:

> For bravery and coolness under heavy fire and devotion to duty.

Then on 6 August Tom Crowhurst, a Gunner in the Royal Garrison Artillery, received bullet wounds to his head near Amiens and lost an eye; he was invalided to Wimereux near Boulogne and then to London and discharged as unfit to continue in service. Crowhurst was 35, and in 1911 had been recorded as an ironmonger's labourer living at Netherfield. Crowhurst had enlisted at Hastings in December 1915. He had married Beatrice Blackman at Netherfield in 1909 and had one son, Thomas Eric, born in 1912 (who died at Battle in 1971). Crowhurst himself died at Battle in 1939, and Beatrice in 1976. His father Samuel was a firewood merchant and his mother was Sarah (Croft); both died a few years before 1914.

The Tide Turns

The Germans made their last thrust on 15 July, on the French lines further east, which was met by French tanks. Fearing encirclement, they pulled back. Thereafter they barely stopped pulling back. On 8 August the British began a major offensive using hundreds of tanks (an instrument that for some reason was never effectively copied by the Germans in this war); the German commander Ludendorff was to call this the 'black day of the German Army'. In fact the Germans, in withdrawing, simply established a more solid line and Allied losses were enormous. However, after further fighting the German command accepted that it could not realistically win the war and that Germany must seek peace by negotiation. From 29 September, when Bulgaria obtained an armistice, its own allies started drifting away. Turkey followed suit on 31 October and Austria–Hungary on 3 November. The German armistice came into force on 11 November.

There were nine more Battle deaths before the end of September and three, the last, in the few later weeks before the armistice took effect.

On 9 August it was the turn of Percy Edward Stapley, a Private in 6th Battalion, the Royal West Kent Regiment. He died in the attack eastwards from Amiens, designed to take back the ground lost so expensively earlier in the year. He was 31 or 32. The records place him at St Leonards and having been born there. In 1901 the family was living at 157 Perth Road, just off Battle Road north of Silverhill. By 1911 he had married and he and his wife Louisa and son Frank Richard were at Old Roar Cottage, Silverhill. Stapley enlisted at Hastings. The Battle connection is that he was gardener to Charles Sheppard, the Battle solicitor, who lived at Loxbeech in Mount Street. Sheppard was the father of Frederic, who appears elsewhere in this account. Stapley is buried at Dernancourt Communal Cemetery, just outside Albert.

Also on 9 August there fell Clarence Chrismas, a Private in 28th Battalion, Canadian infantry, aged 20, who had won the MM in the previous year. He was a stretcher bearer at the time of his death. Chrismas had been born in Battle, third son of Thomas Chrismas.[18] None of the family appears in English records after 1911 and all

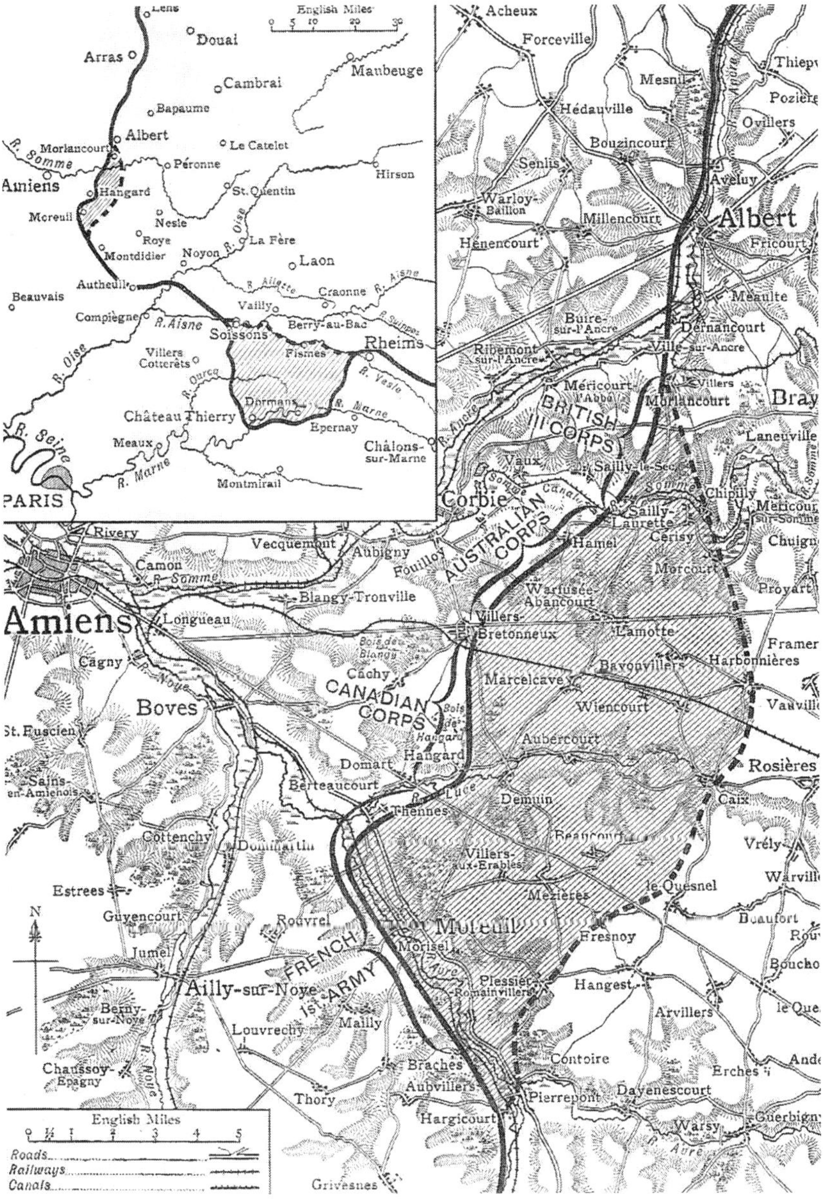

Map 16 The Battle of Amiens - land won by the Allies

must have gone to Canada at some point after that census. Clarence enlisted on 15 January 1916 at Moose Jaw in Saskatchewan, giving his home address at that town. He gave his next of kin as his mother Mrs Elizabeth Chrismas at Mossbank, Saskatchewan; her address was recorded later by the Army as 1346 Connaught Avenue, Moose Jaw. He described himself as a mechanic.[19] His father Thomas had been a butcher at 9 Market Green in 1901 but a boarding-house keeper at 18 Station Road, Hastings, in 1911. The family had long been concerned with the meat trade in Battle. Chrismas is buried at Rosières Communal Cemetery close to the German Hindenburg Line.

Another man died on 13 August.

Private Arthur John Miller was 28. Born in Pevensey and the son of a postman, he had been a rural postman in Battle from September 1910 until he joined 7th Battalion, The Royal Sussex Regiment on 5 February 1915. He had gone to France for the first time on 4 March 1916, had been wounded twice at Richebourg on 30 June that year and had then transferred to the Pioneers. In France again in May 1917, he contracted trench fever and was sent home in October. He returned to the front in May 1918. His death was part of a tragic incident. A local operation near Morlancourt, a few miles south of Albert, was scheduled for 0455 on 13 August, but as soon as the company rose to advance they were shelled by the British from behind. The artillery had not had time to register their guns before the attack begun. Miller is remembered on the Vis-en-Artois Memorial.

Miller was only too typical of a small number of families in that one brother was also killed in the war and another died of pneumonia contracted while on service. Miller's great-nephew Hugh is the author of *We wunt be druv*, a remarkable and complete work.

These four were followed on 22 August by William Herbert Eldridge, a Driver in 491 Field Company, the Royal Engineers. He had enlisted at St Leonards in April 1915 at the age of 20 (the attestation is signed by 2nd Lieutenant J W Ticehurst, a Battle man who was to serve with distinction, part of a family performing considerable offices in the town) and had been posted to France on 4 August 1915. He then served until, apparently, being slightly wounded in April 1916. He had eleven days home leave in March/April 1917 and fourteen in August 1918, during which he married Ida Pocock Mitchell at Battle. He was killed one month and one day later. His address is given as 3 Chapel Cottages, at the foot of Battle Hill. He is buried at Gommecourt military cemetery, which suggests that he died in the attempt to dislodge the Germans from the line that they had established there in April/May; Gommecourt is roughly halfway between Albert and, to the north, Arras.

In 1911 William was recorded as living with his grandparents, William and Mary, at Phillips Buildings, Mount Street, the elder man being a carman and the younger a farm labourer born in Battle, and that he was 16; he was born in the third quarter of 1894 and would therefore have been about 23 when he died. As the only other relevant census, 1901, lists him as a boarder at a house in Sedlescombe one is left none the wiser as to his parentage. The elder William and his wife Mary had four children, three of them daughters. Their son William, born about 1879, would have been only fifteen when the man was born who was later to be killed in action. It is of course just possible that he was the father, but the finger points at one of his older sisters: Emma Mary (born about 1874), or Sarah Ann (1877). There is no point in investigating further. Emma seems to have married later but there is no clear entry for Sarah. William's widow remarried in 1925, in London.

Then on 24 August Donald Victor Scotton died. He was the son of William and Hannah Scotton of Netherfield and was a Private in 4th Wellington Reserve Regiment of the New Zealand Expeditionary Force. He was killed between Albert and Bapaume as the German advance was being finally brought to a halt, and is buried at Adanac Military Cemetery at Miraumont. He was 25.

Scotton was not a Sussex man, having been born at Claybrooke Magna in Leicestershire, like most of his siblings. His father William was a farmer, in 1901 at Earlswood by Tanworth in Warwickshire, but by the time he died in 1908 he had moved to Ticehurst. His widow Hannah, from Caernarvonshire, is listed as a visitor to Netherfield in the 1911 census, along with three of her eight children; Donald was living with his brother Horace, a publican at the Grapes in Milton Road, Gravesend. It would appear that Hannah then took up employment and residence in Netherfield. But the family did not last long there. Donald's siblings left the area and are later recorded in Thanet. Hannah returned to Leicestershire where she died in 1925.

Four days later, in Rouen, nineteen-year old Lance Corporal Stanley Victor Sadler, of 7th Battalion, The Royal Sussex Regiment died of wounds received near Hardecourt. This was the third time that he had been wounded.[20] Hardecourt is down on the old Somme battlefield, only two miles or so from Mametz and Fricourt where Fred Skilton and Robert Raper had been killed two years before. Sadler's battalion reached the area on 26 August and it is probable that he was wounded then, by heavy and sustained machine gun fire. Sadler is buried in the St Sever Military Cemetery Extension at Rouen.

Like Scotton, Sadler was not himself a Battle man, having been born in Mortlake, but his grandfather was. He was Thomas Blackman, a thatcher of Virgins Croft, father of Charlie Blackman who had been so badly wounded in 1916. Sadler was with his grandfather at the time of the 1901 and the 1911 censuses, which raises a question. His mother was Ansley Blackman, born at Battle in 1876 and whose name appears in the records as Ansley, Ainslie and Annesley. She married James Sadler, a coachman, at St Marylebone in 1896 and Stanley was their first child. A daughter arrived in 1900 but died almost at once. James himself died shortly afterwards, probably in late 1903. Ansley did the inevitable thing short of the workhouse: she went into service, as a cook. She died at Croydon late in 1942.

Stanley Sadler had enlisted at Hastings. In civilian life he was a baker, like his uncle Charlie.

Lance-Corporal Tom Vidler of the Royal Engineers distinguished himself on 28 August when he and his men were in a bathing parade in the Aisne Canal. (A bathing parade was an organised event designed to get men to wash and simultaneously to have a little bit of fun away from the actual fighting.)

> a Sapper Coleman sank and became stuck in the mud. Discovering this, Lance-Corporal Vidler dived and searched for him, and after great difficulty succeeded in rescuing him. Artificial respiration proved successful, and it was the gallant action of Lance-Corporal Vidler, that undoubtedly saved his life.[21]

Vidler was 29 at the start of the war and was described in his discharge certificate as a plumber. When he died of influenza and pneumonia in 1927 his occupation was stated to be a house decorator and sign writer. He had begun as a Sapper in the RE under Major Cecil Ticehurst of Battle and had served throughout the war except for a brief period when his voluntary service expired. At some point, he wrote in a note that his life had been saved by his New Testament that he carried – the shell fragment had hit the book and had not reached his body. The testament and his war medals are among the material preserved at the Battle Museum.

Vidler lived with his widowed mother at 4 High Street; his father, like him, had been a house painter but had died in 1904. His mother Harriett (Foster) was to die at Battle in 1922. Vidler married Florence Foord at St Peter's, Bohemia, in 1923 but they appear to have had no children. His brother Major (the name, not the rank) also served and had been wounded in 1917.

30 August saw another Netherfield man wounded. This was Private James Henry Blackman, who had enlisted at Hastings in December 1914 and had gone to France with 11th Battalion, The Royal Sussex in April 1916. In June 1916 he transferred to 1st Battalion, The Worcestershire Regiment. The nature of his wound is not clear from the records, where the handwritten term *gs* (for gunshot) can easily be confused with *gas*. In civilian life Blackman was a labourer on Crowhurst Farm, Netherfield, to which he returned after the war. He did, however, re enlist in the Reserve for a year after his discharge in February 1919. He married that year and had five children, all in Battle, where he died in July 1965.

On 5 September another Eldridge died: Private Basil Richard Eldridge, in 7th Battalion, The Norfolk Regiment, in which he had enlisted in Hounslow. The 1911 census has him as a boarder at 10 Hill Street, Penygraig, Rhondda and lists him as a single man and a confectioner. In 1901, aged 13, he was living with his mother Caroline Bodle in Parks Yard, Battle, with his brothers Alfred, Percy and Charlie; the 1891 census gives him three more brothers – John, William and David, and a sister Cecilia. His father David had died in Battle in 1893, aged only 39, and his mother had remarried in 1899. Basil had also married, to Annie Irish, in Portsmouth the autumn before his death and was living at 104 Londesborough Road in that city. They did not have children.

Basil is buried in Péronne military cemetery. Péronne was taken by Australian forces on 2 September, and on 5 September Eldridge's battalion was attacking Nurlu, about five miles NNE of Péronne. One record[22] states of his battalion that "In September they were in action in a successful attack on Nurlu and pursued the enemy back to Sorel Wood. They were in action during the battles of the Hindenburg Line, including The Battle of Epehy and The Battle of the St Quentin canal."

On 18 September, Private William Marchant died. He was in 2nd Battalion, The Royal Sussex Regiment; previously he had been in 3rd Battalion and before that a reservist. That date was when the British broke through the outer defences of the Hindenburg Line before Cambrai, and it was near there that Marchant died. This was a single day's attack to keep pressure on the Germans, then beginning what turned out to be their final retreat. The place was close to Vadencourt about thirteen miles north east of St Quentin, and the attack was mounted by 2nd Battalion in association with Australian forces. It was successful, not only keeping the Germans busy but securing several mortars, nine field guns, about 300 prisoners and much further war material.

Having been a reservist, Marchant had enlisted at Hastings on 28 August 1914 and had served continually since then. He is buried at Jeancourt Communal Cemetery, which is due east of Péronne and well south of Cambrai.

He lived at 3 Beechwood Cottages, Netherfield Lane; he was 30 when he died. In 1911 the census describes him as a farm labourer, though the newspaper report of his death describes him as having worked for Newbery, a local builder. His father, who had been a carter and general labourer, appears to have died late in 1917, as did his mother.[23]

There was one last wounding before the last phase: on 21 September. This was to Lance-Corporal Robert Suggitt, born at Hastings in 1878. He had served in the South African war of 1899–1902 and had re-enlisted in 1908. He was promoted to Lance-Corporal in May 1914. Suggitt was a bricklayer and his father Robert a carpenter. In 1899 he married Elizabeth Soan and they had four children, three of them born at Battle. He sustained gunshot wounds to the left thigh and buttock that removed him from action until the war was over. When he was discharged in March 1919 he gave his address as Phillips Building, Mount Street. He died at Hastings in 1962.

Probably in late September, but we do not have a precise date, Thomas Harris was wounded at Thiepval. He was originally a Netherfield man, and his family is described in connection with the wounding of his brother James earlier in the year. He was a Private in 8th Battalion, The Royal Sussex Regiment, but other than that we know nothing of him other than that he died at Battle in 1959.

Late in September the end was in sight. We now know that on 29 September the German commander Ludendorff recognised that the fight could not continue and instituted changes within and without Germany. The new German government would negotiate for an honourable peace, but while their representatives did so the fighting continued, as indeed it did right up to eleven o'clock in the morning of 11 November. So there were three local deaths in this final period, a stage of the war even less necessary than the war itself.

Before that, two more woundings. First it was the third Abrey brother of Beauport Park: William Charles, a Private in the Northamptonshire Regiment. He suffered gunshot wounds to the chest on 10 October. He had been living at Eastbourne before enlisting at Redhill in February 1916; he was sent to France in April of the next year, exactly a week after his brother Albert had been killed there. He was sent home two weeks after being wounded and discharged the next year as 40% disabled. William died at Eastbourne in 1978.

Then it was Gunner William Lovell again, who had spent eleven days in France in 1917 before being wounded and sent home. He returned to France on 14 August 1918 and lasted rather longer this time: on 13 October he was shot in the left arm. He left France and did not return. Lovell later married Edith Rose Parfitt at Reigate and had two children in the 1920s. He died at Netherfield in 1965.

On the next day, another Battle death: William Henry Noel Strevens. He was a manservant at Battle Abbey, aged 30. He would never have known his one child, Joan, born in London on the day before his death, which took place in the General Hospital at Calais. He was suffering from broncho-pneumonia "due to field operations, fatigue, privation, exposure etc while on Military Duty". Strevens was a Gunner in an anti-aircraft section of the RGA and had been in France since November 1916. He is buried at Les Baraques Military Cemetery, Sangatte. It appears that Joan married at Maidenhead in 1941. Strevens does not appear in any census, so it is impossible to trace any ancestry or siblings, but on 30 March 1912 a William Strevens arrived in London on SS *Orsova*, having embarked at Toulon; he is described as a valet. He married at Kensington late in 1916. His widow Evelyn Mary (Flack) died in Berkshire in 1966.

On 17 October Robert Marchant received gunshot wounds to his shoulder and was sent to Sefton Park hospital in Liverpool; by the time he emerged the war was over; he was discharged in January 1919. Marchant was only 17 when he joined up in 1917, at Brighton, giving his occupation as a pit prop sawyer. Born at Catsfield, he was the son of Robert Marchant, a brickmaker, and his wife Caroline, and at the point of enlistment lived at Starrs Green. He was a Private in 51st Battalion, the Royal West Surrey and died at Hastings in June 1975.

The second death of this final period was Private John Brown of the ASC. He was 37 and had almost certainly been born at Catsfield. In 1911 he was a gypsum miner living at Netherfield, married to Annie Fuller (whose brother Robert lived at Darwell Hill). The Roll of Honour reports him as having been in Mechanical Transport and that he died of wounds on 3 November. He is buried in Busigny Communal Cemetery. Busigny is near Le Cateau-Cambrésis, well east of Cambrai. The Allies had reached the area and taken Le Cateau itself by 18 October.

Brown's own birth seems hidden. The Roll of Honour reports him as being from Cuckfield (though the census of 1911, in his own hand, states Catsfield) but also says that he was 48 when he died (in 1911 he states 33). There are no relevant births close to either year in either village. His daughter Bessie married Frederick Plummer in Battle in 1929, but there appear to be no local descendants.

Another man was then wounded, on 22 October. This was

Thomas John Edwards, a Gunner in the Royal Field Artillery. Born at Etchingham in 1896, in the 1901 and 1911 censuses he is shown as living with his grandparents Thomas and Mary (Coppard) Edwards; his grandfather was a farm labourer, formerly a gamekeeper, who worked at Hemingfold. The family lived at Cherry Tree Cottage by the Black Horse. It has not been possible to identify his parents. He had joined up in August 1914 and had arrived at Le Havre in June 1915. He had lasted nearly to the end of the war without serious mishap. His injuries – bullet wounds and shrapnel – were sufficient for him to be returned to Britain, where he stayed in hospital until January 1919, when the main fighting had already ceased. He was demobilised in March. Edwards married Ethel Mizon at Battle in 1923 but no children are recorded. He died in 1966.

There was one final Battle death in France immediately before the armistice. On 9 November Lance Corporal Charles Andrew Fuller died. He was in the Machine Gun Corps and formerly with the Royal West Kent Regiment. He was 24 and had been born in the Warbleton area; in 1911 he was listed as an apprentice saddler. He lived then at Newbery's Cottages off the High Street with his father Frank, his stepmother Charlotte (Noakes) and his brothers Percy and Laurence. Charles had enlisted in 1914. His brother Frank also served.

On 9 November 1918 the Allies were pushing the Germans sharply back, though there was considerable resistance up to the last minute and in no case did the German line break. Discipline held, at least in the army; the German navy had already mutinied at Kiel and on that very day a republic was declared in Berlin.

Fuller is buried at Wimille, which is near Boulogne and far behind the lines. He died in hospital of pneumonia.[24] His father Frank Fuller was, like so many others, employed at Newbery's jam factory, in this case as an engine driver. He died in 1938. Charles's mother Jane (Fairall) had died in 1901 and his father had married Charlotte in the next year. Of his two sons, again the frequency of the surname defeats an ordinary search, but it is clear that Laurence, born about 1905, died at Tunbridge Wells in 1982.

We do not know when or where another of the Battle solicitors had to be invalided out, except that it was in France. Nor do we know his regiment, though he is recorded as being in Signals. He was Major Charles Buckwell, a Brighton man born in 1885 and himself the son of a solicitor. He had come to Battle shortly before the war. Afterwards he returned to his practice and to his wife Dora (Peirce) whom he had married in 1911. Buckwell served on the east coast defences between 1914 and 1917, going out to France later that year. His only child John was to be killed in action in Italy in 1944, and Charles was to die at Battle early in the following year.

Africa

The Germans did not surrender in east Africa until late November 1918; reliable communication with them must have been difficult. They had fought tenaciously and with great cunning throughout the war. In one late action Godfrey Hobday of Battle was wounded and later awarded the DCM. The citation reads:

> For gallantry at Medo, on 12th April, 1918, in remaining at his post when wounded and thereby setting a fine example of courage to all ranks. In addition, he had commanded a platoon with exceptional ability and courage, and has been of the greatest assistance to his company commander.[25]

Medo was one of those hard skirmishes between forces that were European-commanded but largely African in composition. In this case the German commander, von Lettow-Vorbeck, had moved into northern Mozambique and could have constituted a threat to the coastal ports of German East Africa captured by the British – not without difficulty – early in the war. The British attack at Medo forced the Germans back inland.

Hobday had been born at Ashburnham and before the war was employed as a farm labourer, living in Netherfield Lane. His mother Harriett (French) had died in 1897 and his father Henry, an agricultural labourer living at Ashburnham Furnace, had remarried.

He joined 2nd Battalion, The Royal Sussex Regiment in September 1914 and was sent on attachment as Acting Sergeant to 1st/2nd King's African Rifles. He already held the MM, but records are unclear as to how or where he won it. There are no public records of Hobday's marriage, if any, or of his death. His brothers Robert and Harold also served, the latter having been wounded in 1916. His step-brother Patrick Kiley was also wounded.

Mesopotamia

Far away from France was the last death in the East: Thomas Vitler, a Private in the 7th Hussars was killed in Mesopotamia on 28 October. He was a brother of the Henry who had died in the great German onslaught in March, and the family is described above in relation to him. The battalion had gone to India in 1912 and to Mesopotamia in 1917; we do not know when Vitler joined them. Defeat in Mesopotamia in 1916 had been turned slowly into victory. Baghdad had been captured in March 1917. Thereafter there had been an advance northwards towards Mosul, against sometimes very stiff opposition, and indeed there was a serious Turkish counter-attack in October that pushed the British back between Tikrit and Samara. Vitler's battalion was part of this engagement.

The Armistice and the final casualties

News of the armistice reached Battle at about mid-day on 11 November and it spread quickly.

> From nearly every house flags were displayed, and in many instances streamers, interspersed with Union Jacks, red and white ensigns, etc, were strung across the road with such suddenness as to suggest the gift of prophecy. Proudly floating from the Abbey towers were the emblems of the Allied nations....
>
> Shops were closed at an early hour, and the relaxation of the Lighting Order was apparent as soon as darkness fell. In spite of the drizzling rain, the streets were full of people, most of whom made their way to the Market Green,* where a big bonfire was in course of construction. Taken altogether, the day was reasonably spent, and without any extravagant expression Battle showed its delight that the beginning of the end was so near.

* Now Abbey Green.

On 13 November there was a special service at St Mary's.[26]

This was how small towns celebrated the day; there was a closeness and a lack of anonymity in a small place. Hastings had parades; central London, by many accounts, went wild.

But there were still three local deaths to come. Britain was still in a state of war and the armed forces were still at work; the wounded and the ill did not suddenly recover on 11 November. The first man concerned was Gunner George Lovell of the Royal Garrison Artillery, who had been with 49th Anti-Aircraft Company. His name is on the Roll of Honour for Netherfield, but not on that inside the church there, nor on the memorial itself. This is a little odd, given that he is buried under a military headstone very close to the memorial, clearly showing his date of death. He was 34, and the son of William and Mercy Lovell. He was a farm labourer when he enlisted on 3 April 1916, and in fact never left England during the war. He served in Shoeburyness and Darlington and finally in Chelmsford, where he died as the result of a bicycle accident on 18 December. It is arguable that he was a war casualty; but in December Britain was still at war and he is on the Roll of Honour.

The 1901 census listed him as a general labourer and his father as a gypsum miner, clearly a cut above the usual because they also had a resident servant. They lived at Darwell Hill. George had been born at Brightling, as had his elder brother William; their two sisters Rhoda and Mabel had been born at Netherfield. In 1911 all three men were gypsum miners but there was no servant; Mercy had died in 1909. There is no public record of Mercy's marriage, but a *Mary Smith* married a William Lovell at Battle in 1882. George's sisters both married, and both in Battle. However, Rhoda's two daughters both married men called Morris, which makes determining relationships difficult. One of them appears to have continued to live in Battle or Hastings and to have had children there. The other, Mabel, married John Cloke in 1925, and died in 1976, probably. She had two children and has grandchildren, all born in Hastings.

The same argument about lateness of death can be made for William Spray, a seaman who died of disease on 3 January 1919 aboard HMS *Mersey* in Romania, but here it is clear that the ship was on active service. Spray had been born at Battle in 1888 but had moved early to St Leonards and then to Hollington. His father Aaron was a woodcutter and dealer from Mountfield, but his mother Jane Elizabeth (Blackman) was from Battle. Although he had six siblings the frequency of the family name in the area means that it is impossible to say more of them with certainty other than that his younger brother Frederick Albert died at Hastings in 1987 and that his father and mother died at Hastings in 1945 and 1946 respectively. William was buried in Conotan Lane Protestant Cemetery at Braila, an inland port on the lower Danube; the CWGC now record him as being in Bucharest War Cemetery. It may be questioned why the Navy was on the Danube at all (as indeed was the army), but Braila was an important port that had fallen to the Germans in 1917 and the British were responsible for securing their evacuation and no doubt for guarding against any Bolshevik infection from the north-east.

The last death recorded was of Captain Rashell Montague Rashell Davison, known as Monty. He had been born at Battle in 1886, along with three sisters and two brothers. His father, also Rashell, was a Northumberland man whose father had been a substantial landowner at Tritlington, and his mother Frances (Smith). From at least 1879 elder Rashell was a physician in the town working from Langton House, 81 High Street, now appropriately the Memorial Halls; it is a pity that his son's death in particular is not commemorated there. The younger Davison was educated at Epsom College and had been in India at the time that the war had begun, as an agent for a company.[27] He returned from Colombo on the *Gloucestershire*, arriving at Tilbury in May 1915. He joined up as a Private in 3rd Battalion, The North Staffordshire Regiment in the next month, and was promoted Second Lieutenant in October, being sent to France on 5 July 1916. In March 1918 he was attached to 8th Battalion, The Leicestershire Regiment. He was seriously wounded in the head at Epehy and captured by the Germans. Epehy is a small village near Le Catelet, and on the front line attacked by Germans on 21 March. We do not know the date of his wound, but it is very likely to have been inflicted in that attack. He wrote to his parents to explain that he had been shot through the head, with the result that his right arm was paralysed; he had other wounds too.

On his repatriation after the armistice the decision was made in London to operate, but he did not survive the operation and died on 27 January 1919 of pneumonia and post-operative cerebral meningitis.[28] He is buried in Kingston on Thames Cemetery, and there is a memorial to him at Christ Church, New Malden.[29]

The Davison family had left Battle for New Malden before the 1901 census, at about the time that George Kendall arrived, though in fact Kendall succeeded Hugh Hudson rather than Davison. Their contact with the town ended then. The elder Rashell was in general practice at New Malden and later became medical officer of heath for the Urban District of Malden and Coombe. He died in London in 1936. His wife Frances had died in 1927. There are no easily-discernible descendants of any of the younger Rashell's siblings.

In December 1917, sitting dutifully awaiting the final order to go over the top and fearing the result, Davison wrote a poem; and in the belief that he would be killed in the morning he entrusted it to a friend. It was the friend that died and the poem that survived. Davison's father sent it to the *Hastings Observer* after Rashell's own death in 1919.[30] It may be noted that in the seventh verse he refers to 'Eppy': he was to receive his fatal wounds at Epehy.

The poem may be a fitting conclusion to this account.

Vale! A soldier's farewell

So I lay dying – while the hours of Life
  Slowly welled forth, straining the shattered ground,
The poor shell-shocked ground, victim of strife,
  Which rocked and crashed and screeched and echoed round.
Dim velvet shadows veiled my aching head,
And in a few short hours I would be dead.

Dead! Yet to me Life gave with both her hands.
  Joyous I strayed down paths with pleasure strown:
Laughed lightly, lightly loved in many lands,
  And reaped in fields which fairy hands had sown:
Drinking deep draughts of joy that had no end,
And once at any rate I found a Friend.

A Friend! Ah! Yes, I have plumbed the deep
  Of Friendship's passioned moments, calmer hours.
I have snatched happiness from gentle sleep,
  Culled the sweet blooms of Night's exotic flow'rs;
Won too great joy – a joy which stifled breath –
And lost it in a moment to chill death.

E'en as I lie I see the Bridge of Fate
  Linking me in the Future to the Past,
And, as I strain my dimming eyes, the Gate
  Of life-through-Death flings open wide at last.
There limned in colours that may never fade
Are all the treasures of my mind portrayed.

The poor grey battered bastions which remain
  Of all the glory Ypres gave to mankind,
The sacrifice of him without a stain
  Which faithful souls at countless cross-roads find,
A narrow road-strip leading to the sea –
All these are living memories to me.

Orion leaning down to greet the morn,
  As daily round the outpost line I go,
His golden belt fast fading while, forlorn,
  He vainly strives to meet the new Sun's glow –
The pale French grey of dawn and mist and sky
As Flanders' battle days go grimly by.

Street scenes in Arras – "Eppy's" coat of snow –
  A Red Cross ambulance at eventide,
Speaking to weary wounded of the slow
  And comfortable homeward motor-ride –
Glories of old gold on the puddled way –
Sun flashes of a washed-out winter day.

Dear memories that live, though I must die!
  Mind paintings that are still a part of me!
Let no one grieve – for it is willed that I
  Must pass through Life through Death to Victory.
Grieve not – for Life had been too sweet for Grief.
I go quite happy in this sure belief.

Notes

1 Roughwood.net/GenealogyData/f36.htm
2 Hugh Miller: *We wunt be druv*
3 http://www.wartimememoriesproject.com/greatwar/allied/westkentregiment7-gw.php
4 http://www.wartimememoriesproject.com/greatwar/allied/middlesexregiment2-gw.php
5 *Hastings Observer*, 13 October 1917.
6 His plaque in St Mary's Church states this.
7 Lyn Macdonald: *To the last man* (Viking, 1998)
8 *Hastings Observer*, 20 April 1917.
9 Macdonald: *To the last man*
10 *Hastings Observer*, 8 March 1919.
11 *Hastings Observer*, 1 April 1916.
12 *Hastings Observer* 16 November 1918.
13 *Hastings Observer*, 24 July 1915.
14 Picture by courtesy of Mrs J Macvicker of Battle.
15 Battle draft roll of honour for 1939–45
16 *Hastings Observer*, 20 July 1918.
17 London Gazette, 3 September 1918.
18 *Hastings Observer*, 31 August 1918.
19 http://www.collectionscanada.gc.ca/databases/cef/001042-100.01-e.php
20 *Hastings Observer*, 31 August 1918.
21 *Hastings Observer*, n.d.
22 http://www.wartimememoriesproject.com/greatwar/allied/norfolkregiment7-gw.php
23 *Hastings Observer*, 2 November 1918
24 *Hastings Observer*, 16 November 1918.
25 Richard Buckman: *The Royal Sussex Regiment: military honours & awards 1864–1920* (J&KH Publishing, Hailsham, 2001).
26 *Hastings Observer*, 16 November 1918.
27 *Hastings Observer*, 1 February 1919.
28 http://archive.epsomcollege.org.uk/First_World_War/Known%20to%20have%20served.pdf
29 http://www.nationalarchives.gov.uk/a2a/records.aspx?cat=074-ds_2&cid=1-16-8#1-16-8
30 *Hastings Observer*, 19 April 1919.

7

The Survivors

Damage to the military records makes it hard to establish how many men went to war in 1914–18 and came back, let alone who they were. In August 1919 it was thought that nearly 200 men might be eligible to attend a proposed welcoming-back party, with another 70–80 still awaiting demobilisation.[1] We do not know the source of this estimate or the method of calculation: in particular whether it was based on the very wide boundaries adopted by the Dean (and similarly in this account) or on some more restricted basis. But the number currently known of those who survived is 393, and there must have been many more. From the extent that the military archives were destroyed one might well assume the number to be well over 500. Catsfield church records about 110 men who survived, against 21 who died; and on this formula there should be some 600 survivors from Battle. The Netherfield List contains 72 names (73 are listed but two appear to be the same man), which is an underestimate, and the same proportion would yield more than 457 survivors for Battle town rather than the 393 now known. Among the unknowns must be those who are known to be fairly local but whose connection to Battle, though suggested, has not been demonstrated.

There are various sources available to us in this search. Clearly when a man is reported wounded then we can check to determine whether he came from Battle or from somewhere else, for example Catsfield or Westfield. There were not many of these reports, and some were of wounds to men who were later killed and therefore cannot appear among a list of survivors. The military records held by www.ancestry.co.uk, despite their partial destruction in the second world war, are very helpful.

(James Henry) Guy Duke, 1892-1975. Private and ultimately Sergeant in 7 Battalion, The Royal Sussex. Military Medal 1917. Hospitalised in January 1918 and discharged as medically unfit in September 1918; Orderly at Normanhurst VAD hospital during that last period.

Then there are published lists and occasional mentions in the *Hastings Observer.* The longest list is that given by the Battle schools and published at the end of 1915.[2] It contains 137 names; but of course this was before conscription and so must have missed many yet to come. In any case there may well be problems of transcription and of duplication of names. After the war the schools followed this up with a list of those who died, which contains 34 names, at least some of which should without doubt have been on the memorials.[3] There is also the Netherfield List, referred to earlier in this account.

There are other published lists, probably of less reliability. There was the Railway Hotel Slate Club, of 70 members, eight of whom were in the forces by the end of December 1914 but not all of whom can be identified.[4] Three months later Sergeant Bernard Anderson (who was to die on the Somme) sent eleven names, all of whom are clearly known.[5] In July of that year there was a report of 26 men serving who were present or past members of the Church Lads Brigade.[6] And for the first few years a fair proportion was supplied by Thomas Clark, tobacconist, who received letters of thanks from the grateful addicts at the front. But the lists and Clark's names generally disappeared after the end of 1916, possibly because by then it would have been easier to compile a register of those who were *not* serving. Clark's longest list is of 65 names.[7]

These lists and references must be of variable reliability. In particular with Clark's correspondents, it is not clear whether the men were actually from Battle, and in any case the process of recording them was fraught with the possibility of error. There were many points at which error could have crept in, but it is remarkable that so many men are fully identifiable from this trail. But in many cases any mention of a man must be pursued through official records before an identification can be made. Here something of the same problem can occur.

1 The original record may itself be faulty.

2 The record is often hard to read and needs careful deciphering.

3 The heads of the families or the enumerators were sometimes very casual about spelling. Years of birth are also variable.

4 Location data are not necessarily precise. This is mainly because the Battle registration district was wider than the town itself, but also because some of those completing the returns – enumerators up to 1901 and the householder in 1911 – were themselves erratic in their memories or their transcriptions. And sometimes www.ancestry.co.uk will think that Battle is in Hampshire or that Battle has been set down as Bath.

5 Sometimes the records agency omits a name altogether.

Even when it is clear that a name is correct there can be ambiguities because of the very common incidence of a surname. Some merely have an initial, leaving it impossible to distinguish between (say) an Albert and an Arthur of the same generation in the same family.

C.Q.M.S. BLACKMAN,
Champion Shot of Sussex, 1930.

William Blackman (1891–1969), who finally retired from 5th Battalion, The Royal Sussex, in 1936.

There are also mentions that cannot be tracked down using conventional methods because the connection with Battle was established by simple residence between census points or after 1911, and none of the family is recorded as having been born or having lived there. Then there is the possibility of emigration. The latter is more easily identifiable among the dead, where some were living outside the UK, and it may be that in due course a higher proportion was likely to have obtained.

This means that there is an element of assumption about some of the records in appendix 2. Where there is truly no evidence, or a choice to be made for which neither side has any stronger call than the other, the person concerned is not listed as a definite. But some of those so listed may be misplaced.

Those mentioned as connected with Battle but who cannot be placed at present are as follows. The possibility of some having been mistranscribed and already known under different initials cannot be ruled out.

Name	Date of report
Baily, Gunner P C	01.06.18
Bonds, Pte J	25.05.17
Butler, C R	02.10.14
Dawson, Pte N G, 8 RSR	1919
Eldridge, Pte A	14.05.15
Farmer, A H	02.10.14
French, Pte P J, RHA	05.11.15
Fuller, Vic, 16 Lancers	12.03.15
Jones, A L	02.10.14
Marchant, A	02.10.14
Marchant, P	25.12.15
Marchant, R	13.09.19
Pearce, Pte Thomas, RFC	28.07.16
Rooke, Jack	12.03.15
Smith, G	13.09.19
Stuart, L/Sgt J F, E Kent	30.08.19

Taylor, Pte R	22.04.16
White, W	13.09.19
Willard, F	13.09.19
Williams, Tim	12.03.15
Wise, Sgt W W, 8 RSR	21.07.16

There are several other instances where it is likely that a Battle individual served but the records cannot demonstrate it.

Some of the survivors may also have fought in 1939–45; certainly many would have been in civilian defence. We cannot identify from the public records those who served again unless they were killed – and, as far as we know, thankfully only one of them was – because for highly questionable reasons the military records of that conflict are unpublished, and successive governments have refused to open them to general public view.

Notes

1 *Hastings Observer*, 16 August 1919.
2 *Hastings Observer*, 25 December 1915.
3 *Hastings Observer*, 24 May 1915.
4 *Hastings Observer*, 26 December 1914.
5 *Hastings Observer*, 27 March 1915.
6 *Hastings Observer*, 10 July 1915.
7 *Hastings Observer*, 4 September 1915.

8

Afterwards

The war with Germany was not over until the peace treaty of 28 June 1919, the fifth anniversary of the murder of the Archduke Franz Ferdinand. Treaties with other enemy states followed, and until then a state of war remained with them: Turkey was the last, late in 1920.

Nevertheless the main fighting had ceased on 11 November 1918 though it was some days before the news allowed German troops to cease fire in east Africa. British forces remained in combat in various theatres after the armistice, and in occupation in others. There were troops in Russia and Ireland, for example. For a few years they were involved in the occupation of the Rhineland area of Germany, and initially in various other places whose future was being determined by the Paris peace conference, quite apart from any continuing imperial commitments. But there is no evidence that more than a very few men of Battle were asked to do their duty away from the battlefields, although the Royal Sussex did see service in both Russia and Ireland. (One man died in France in 1919, after the real end of the war, but as the result of an air accident, and I have not included him in the war service dead: Thomas Charles Blackman, son of the coal merchant who had lost another son late in 1917.[1] Thomas was an Aircraftman Second Class in the RAF and the accident was near Paris. He is buried in the City of Paris Cemetery, Pantin, and appears as a survivor in Appendix B.)

The war and the end of the main fighting could not but dominate the news. There were returning prisoners of war and further decorations. The two policemen who had joined up in 1917 came back. That life was returning to normal was itself news.

The peace treaty with Germany gave another opportunity to celebrate the end of war. Battle and the country generally did it much more soberly than they had greeted the armistice of November 1918. There were flags and bunting, of course, and fireworks in the street (to some alarm),[2] and an interdenominational thanksgiving service at St Mary's.[3] The Abbey gateway was lit up for the first time.[4] In due course, on 10 September, there was a welcoming party for returning servicemen. The number that attended was not given but it had been estimated earlier that some 200 men would be available, in addition to the 70-80 who were still serving.[5]

By the end of 1919 Britain was returning to normal, or what could pass for normal where so many men were missing, so many of those who returned were disabled and the economy had suffered such enormous blows. In the public mind the war was over, even if the custom of the two-minute silence had been instituted that November. (It may have been an idea that originated in South Africa,[6] though several other sources have been claimed.) Some returners would have been near-strangers to their families: one man born in 1915 and much later a resident of Battle recalled late in 2013 that he hid behind a dresser when a strange man came in and embraced his mother – of course the newcomer was the child's father.[7] Many families will still remember men who never quite recovered from their experiences.

Now, almost a hundred years later and even after the second major war, let alone after all kinds of conflict at other times, the first world war is far from having lost its capacity to shock and to inspire a mix of feelings: horror at what happened, deep revulsion at what appears to be the callous and brutal attitudes of the high commands, enormous sympathy with those who died as cattle (as the poem put it), and at least some understanding of what it must have been like on the home front as the telegraph boys on their daily rounds approached the houses of families whose men were at the various fronts and as the big guns could be heard in Battle itself, some two hundred miles from the front line in Belgium and France. Generals on both sides in the second world war tried hard not to repeat the mistakes of their predecessors, under whom almost all of them had served.

In 1914 the revolutionary and Napoleonic wars were very distant from the public mind. A century later it is hard to see when the first world war will attain the same distance.

Notes

1 *Hastings Observer*, 27 September 1919.
2 *Hastings Observer*, 5 July 1919.
3 *Hastings Observer*, 12 July 1919.
4 *Hastings Observer*, 19 July 1919.
5 *Hastings Observer*, 16 August and 13 September 1919.
6 See Ronald Blythe: *The Age of Illusion* (Hamish Hamilton, 1963)
7 Letter from Eric Holliman, December 2012.

Appendix A
Those Who Died

The following abbreviations are used in addition to those used generally in this account:

A, B, C and D (each upper case) refer to the quarters of the years, starting with A meaning 1 January to 31 March. In all cases these are civil registrations not actual events. Birth/marriage data drawn from public sources generally refers to registration districts and not to places. This means that unless determined by other means an event in Netherfield is recorded as Battle and (later) one in Battle is recorded as in Hastings. It also means that an event taking place late in one quarter might be registered, and therefore recorded here, in the next following quarter, or sometimes even later.

b born
BC on the churchyard memorial in Battle
BM on the plaque in the Memorial Halls in Battle
c (lower case) about
d died
e enlisted
m married
N on the churchyard memorial in Netherfield
s son

Abrey, Albert Thomas b Hollington 1889, s of William, butler to Beauport Park. Little Bethanga, Victoria. e Rosehill, Sydney 23.09.14. Pte 1101 then 1170, I Aus Infantry. Embarked Melbourne 22.12.14, HMAT *Themistocles.* Gallipoli 1915–16. France 28.03.16. Wounded in thigh 25.04.16. Wounded 06.04.17. d near Albert 11.04.17. Aveluy Communal Cemetery Extension. Hastings Memorial.

Anderson, Bernard George b Battle 25.12.92, s of Bernard, jam boiler. Plumber. 9 Mount Street. e Battle. Sgt TF3488, 5 Bn RSR. To France 18.02.15. Wounded near Albert; d at Rouen Military Hospital 21.08.16. St Sever Cemetery, Rouen. BC BM.

Beaney, Albert Edward b St Leonards 17.05.79 A1877, s of William, white-smith. Postman. 154 Old Lane, Hollington. Wife at 6 Chapel Cottages. m Mary Jane Poole 1912. AB 182377 Royal Fleet Reserve/Ch/B/5833 HMS *Hogue*. Torpedoed off Dutch coast and d 22.09.14. Chatham naval memorial. Hastings PO memorial. Hastings Memorial. BC BM.

Blackhurst, Cecil James Livesey b Kirkham, Lancashire 05.06.85, s of John, grocer. Teacher at Battle School. 5 Lower Lake. e Hastings 31.08.14. Pte G/567, 7 Bn RSR. L/C 21.09.14. Cpl 01.05.15. To France 30.05.15. L/Sgt 04.11.15. Wounded 24.12.15. Sgt 10.3.16. d at Ovillers 07.07.16. Thiepval Memorial. Baines Endowed School Memorial, Blackpool.

Blackman, Frederick Charles b Battle 03.05.90, s of Thomas, coal merchant. Coal porter. 30 Mount Street. e Chichester. Pte G16405, L/C 10.05.15, A/Cpl 01.04.16. 13 Bn RSR. France 18.02.15–31.03.16 then home on expiry of service. Wounded 01.05.15. Rejoined. d near Canadian Tunnels, Polygon Wood, Ypres, 19.10.17. Tyne Cot Memorial. BC BM.

Booth, Frederick George b Battle D1888, s of Samuel, agricultural labourer then publican. Soldier. Marley Farm. e Maidstone. Pte L9131, 2 Royal West Kent Regt. d Mesopotamia 06.02.17. Baghdad (North Gate) Cemetery.

Bothwell, Charles Stuart b Kingston C1896, s of Charles, upholsterer. 6 St Mary's Terrace. Gunner then Sapper 28670 RE. To France 07.03.15. d near Ypres 31.05.18 (wounds). Lijssenthoek Military Cemetery.

Boxall, Frederick Edward b Battle C1894, s of Albert, tailor (maker). Apprentice tailor. 11 Mount Street. e Hastings. Pte G2801, 13 Bn (Pioneer) RSR. 8 Bn (Pioneers) in 1916. d Montauban 01.07.16. Thiepval memorial. BC BM

Breeze, Victor Nelson b Mountfield D1894, s of Nelson, farmer. Little Park Farm. Pte M2/082721, 605 Heavy Transport Coy, ASC. On *Città di Palermo* troopship bound for Durazzo. Lost at sea, Adriatic, 08.01.16. Hollybrook Memorial, Southampton. BC BM

Brown, John b Catsfield A1881, s. of George, builder's labourer. Gypsum miner. Netherfield. m Annie Rachel Fuller, Battle, A1905. Child. e Hastings. Pte M2/178333 ASC MT. d of wounds east of Cambrai 03.11.18. Busigny Communal Cemetery Extension. N

Buckle, William b Garboldisham, Norfolk B1885, s of Robert , gamekeeper. Gamekeeper. Netherfield Place. e Bury St Edmunds. Pte 24942, 13 Suffolk Regt. d Norfolk 30.04.16. Greenwich cemetery.

Carter, Frank b Netherfield 06.09.93, s of Edward, higgler. Stockman on farm. Church Cottage, Netherfield. m Ethel Florence Bowyer, 1 Warfield St, Bracknell. Son Frank b 1917. e Croydon. Trooper 726, 2 Lifeguards, Household Bn. Was 3287, 2 Lifeguards. d Passchendaele 10.10.17. Tyne Cot Memorial. N

Carter, William Sydney b Netherfield D1895, s of Edward, gypsum sorter. Farm Labourer. Ivyland Green. e Hastings. Pte 44002, 9 Bn KOYLI. Was Pte 164581 RH/FA. d near Monchy le Preux 09.04.17. Wancourt British Cemetery, Pas-de-Calais. N

Catton, Frederick b Battle C1893, s of James, gamekeeper. Gamekeeper. Great Wood. e Hastings. Pte SD2879, 12 Bn RSR. d Richebourg 30.06.16. Loos Memorial. BC BM

Chrismas, Clarence Henry b Battle 23.06.1897, s of Thomas, butcher then boarding house keeper. Mechanic. Family emigrated to Canada after 1911. 18 Station Road, Hastings formerly Abbey Green. e Moose Jaw, Saskatchewan 15.01.16. Pte 781900, 28 Bn Canadian Infantry. MM 1917. d Hindenburg Line 09.08.18. Stretcher bearer at time of death. Rosières Communal Cemetery Extension.

Church, Herbert Smith b Battersea 1884, s of John, butler. Photographer. 12 High Street. m Emily Gower 1912. e Bristol. Pte 7009 Norfolk Regt; Pte 202771 Royal Berkshire Regt. d of wounds 10.09.17. Mont Huon Military Cemetery, Le Tréport. Overstrand church memorial, Norfolk.

Cockett, Horace Edward b Battle B1892. Gardener. Next to Mill Cottages, Blackhorse Road. Pte SD1017, 11 Bn, RSR. MM and bar 1917. d near Amiens 03.1918. Pozières memorial. BC BM

Congdon, Henry George b Dunbar c1867, s of Samuel, soldier, school att officer. Soldier then publican. White Hart beerhouse, Fifield, Berkshire. Married Mary Hollingsworth, Battle D1891. Children. RSM 44469 RE. Long Service Medal. Croix de Guerre (Belgium). d near Albert 28.05.18. Varennes Military Cemetery. BC BM

Curry, William Leonard b Quetta c1891, s of Thomas, railway engineer, India. Breadsell Farm. Capt, Royal Garrison Artillery. d Somme 09.11.16. Puchervillers British Cemetery. BC BM

Davison, Rashell Montague Rashell b Battle 31.05.86, s of Rashell, physician/surgeon/registrar. 81 High Street. Lt then Capt 3 Bn N Staffs att 8 Bn Leicester Regt. To France 05.07.16. Wounded in head at Epehy, captured, repatriated, operated on. d London 29.01.19. Kingston Cemetery, Surrey.

Donald, Bertram Smith b Benhall, Suffolk A1881, s of Joseph, land agent. Soldier, goldminer. Pembury House, 115 Hastings Road. Cpl 9838 SA Infantry. Previous service in 12 Lancers, SA war. Natal Light Horse 1914, de Wet rebellion. d Tanganyika 12.05.16 (wounded 09.05.16). Dar es Salaam War Cemetery.

Duke, Harry b Battle 1892, s of James, domestic gardener. Primary school teacher. Yew Tree Cottage, Hollington. e Dover. Pte 10209, 2 Gordon Highlanders. d Germany 01.10.15. Valenciennes (St Roch) Communal Cemetery.

Dyer, William b Battle 1882. Farm labourer. Battle workhouse. e Herstmonceux. Pte SD/585, 11 RSR. d Somme 30.08.16. Engelbelmer Communal Cemetery Extension.

Eldridge, Basil Richard b Battle A1888, s of David, general labourer. Confectioner. Parks Yard. m Annie Irish 1917. 104 Londesborough Road, Portsmouth. e Hounslow. Pte 33834, 7 Bn Norfolk Regt. d France 05.09.18. Peronne Communal Cemetery Extension. BC BM

Eldridge, Ernest John b Battle Nov 1879, s of Elijah, bricklayer. Bricklayer. Caldbec Hill. Married Ruth Amy Wood 1909. Child. 9 Camperdown Street, Sidley. e Chatham. Pte 46721, 11 Bn Leicestershire Regt. d 12.10.17. The Huts Cemetery, Dickebusch. Bexhill Memorial.

Eldridge, William b Battle A1883, s of Elijah, bricklayer. House painter. Caldbec Hill. 9 Camperdown Street, Sidley. Pte TF 202102 2/6 Bn N Staffs Regt. d France 03.18. Arras Memorial. Bexhill Memorial.

Eldridge, William Herbert b Battle C1894. Farm labourer. Phillips Buildings, Mount Street. m Ida Pocock Mitchell 1918. e St Leonards. Driver 534340, 491 Field Coy, RE. Wounded April 1916. d Gommecourt 22.08.18. Gommecourt British Cemetery No 2, Hebuterne. BC BM

Fletcher, Frederick Nelson b Battle A1888, s of Henry, tailor. Mount Street. e Hastings. Pte 25356, 6 Bn Northants Regt. d near Croisilles 20.03.17. Croisilles British Cemetery. BC BM

Flint, Henry Frederic b Battle C1896, s of Henry, coach painter. Cowman on farm. Little Park. Gunner 905999, 222 Bde, RFA. d Mesopotamia 28.05.17. Basra Memorial.

Foster, Alfred Henniker b Battle B1884, s of Henry, builder's labourer. General labourer. 50 Church Street, Ore. Married Elizabeth Charlotte Puxty 1909. e Hastings. Pte L7596, 7 RSR. d France 08.04.16. Vermelles British Cemetery.

Franks, Robert b Battle C1883, s of Robert, gardener. Potman. 61 Eastwood Street, Streatham. e Lewisham. Pte 31377 Royal Fusiliers, then 60356 Labour Corps. Death reported by CWGC as Royal Fusiliers. d of wounds 14.05.18. St Sever Cemetery Extension, Rouen.

French, John Henry b Battle C1893, s of Herbert, carter. Milkman. Lower Lake. e Battle 31.01.10. Gunner 60773, 66 Battery, RFA, d Mesopotamia 23.02.16. Basra memorial. BC BM

Fuller, Charles Andrew b Warbleton D1893, s of Frank, engine driver (jam factory). Apprentice saddler. Newbery's Cottages. e Tonbridge 1914. L/C 113862, Machine Gun Corps, 30 Coy. Formerly Royal West Kent Regt. d France 09.11.18 (pneumonia). Terlincthun British Cemetery, Wimille. BC BM

Fuller, Philip Ernest b Netherfield 1886, s of William, stoker. Soldier. 5 Caves Road, St Leonards. e Hastings. Pte 7659, 1 Royal Munster Fusiliers. d Gallipoli 07.05.15 (wounds). Helles Memorial.

Fuller, Thomas John b Mountfield B1881, s of Stephen gypsum miner. Storekeeper, gypsum mine. Netherfield. Children. e Hastings. Gunner 154692, 6 Reserve Battery, RFA. d at sea east of Malta 15.04.17. Chatby Memorial, Egypt. N

Fuller, William George b Netherfield C1893, s of Thomas, agricultural labourer. Cowman on farm. Battle workhouse 1911. e Eastbourne. Rifleman 4724, 2 Bn, Rifle Brigade (Prince Consort's Own). d 14.03.15. Le Touret Memorial. N

Goodsell, Charles Lewis b Battle 11.12.1875, s of Samuel, farmer, wood merchant. Wood merchant. Netherfield Road, Netherfield. The Downs, Netherfield. Married Caroline Selmes 1900. Children. 41 Southwater Road, St Leonards. e Gillingham. 12.05.15. Sapper 2084, 1/3 Kent Fortress Coy, RE. Active service 12.10.15. d at sea at Cape Helles 28.10.15. Helles Memorial. N

Gower, Arthur b Battle A1891, s of Henry, engine driver (tannery). Gardener. Watch Oak. Pte 29615, NZ Machine Gun Corps, d Passchendaele 12.10.17. Tyne Cot memorial. BC BM

Hale, Stuart Anthony b Westfield 03.07.1898, s of Charles, hotel coachman. Railway Hotel Cottage. e Hastings 02.04.17. Pte G26424, 7 Bn, Royal West Kent. To France 15.08.17. Wounded at Poelcappelle 12.10.17, d Poelcappelle: 61 Casualty Clearing Stn 13.10.17. Dozinghem Military Cemetery, Belgium. BC BM

Harris, George b Battle B1884, s of Thomas, shoemaker. Jobbing gardener. 12 Avenue Road, Kearsney, Dover. m Mary Jane Bushell 1909. Child. e Canterbury. Pte 22907, 8 East Surrey Regt. d 03.05.17. Arras Memorial. Temple Ewell memorial.

Hayler, Ernest John Edgar b Battle 18.10.1884, s of Alfred, cowman on farm. Farm labourer. Stone Bridge Cottage, Crowhurst. e St Leonards 09.11.14. Driver 1082 1 Sussex Battery 3/2 Home Counties Bde RFA, with Indian Army. Home then to India 25.02.16. d India 13.08.16 (disease). Kirkee 1914–18 Memorial, Poona. Crowhurst Memorial.

Highwood, William b Battle B1894, s of James, assurance agent (Pru). Cycle maker's apprentice. 6 then 11 St Mary's Villas. m Annie Reed 1913. e Hastings 09.14. Pte 2570 11 Bn RSR. Wounded on Somme 1916. Trsfr Lincs Regt 44969 March 18. Reported missing 16.04.18, presumed d 08.03.19. Tyne Cot Memorial. BC BM

Hoad, Frank Albert b Battle C1889, s of Nelson, farmer. Farmer. Warbleton. e Eastbourne 08.09.14. Pte 429, 11 RSR. Cpl 23.12.14. L/Sgt 03.07.16, A/Sgt 10.07.16, Sgt 14.07.16. To France 03.03.16.d Somme 03.09.16. Commemorated in Edmund Blunden's poem. Thiepval Memorial.

Hobday, George Henry b Penhurst A1896, s of William, estate worker. Farm worker. Battle Lodge. e Hastings.Pte SD/5159, 11 RSR. d Somme 21.10.16. Grandcourt Road Cemetery. N

Holden, Frederick b Battle C1896, s of Thomas, domestic gardener. Phillips Buildings, Mount Street. Whole family to Canada after 1911. Pte 1063046, 4 Bn CEF Infantry. Name but no record held by CEF. d France 03.1918. Wanquetin Communal cemetery.

Holland, Albert b Netherfield 15.07.81, s of Walter, agricultural labourer. 3 Council Cottages, Netherfield Hill. e Hastings. Pte G/6696, 9 Bn RSR att 73 Light Trench Mortar Battery. d Méharicault 03.18. Pozières memorial. N

Holland, Franklin Gilbert b Netherfield 16.03.94, s of William, domestic gardener. General labourer. Sea View, Netherfield. e Hastings. Acting CSM.SD/806 11 Bn RSR. MM. Médaille Militaire. d Ypres area 24.09.17. Tyne Cot Memorial. N

Holland, George David b Battle B1881. Netherfield. e Hastings. Pte SD/2103, D Coy, 12 Bn RSR. d Richebourg 30.06.16. Loos memorial. N

Holland, Harry [George Henry] b Battle 03.01.94, s of Walter, agricultural labourer. General labourer. Stoney Wood Cottage, Netherfield. m Florence Martin, Battle 15.05.15. Pte 9089, 2 Bn Wiltshire Regiment. d 15.06.15. Le Touret Memorial. N

Holt, Frederick George Bradley b Battle B1888, s of John, grocer. Grocer's assistant. 82–83 High Street. e 01.01.16. 2 Lt 1/20 Bn, London Regt. Church memorial says Queen's West Surrey Regt. d Aveluy Wood 05.04.18. Arras Memorial. BC BM

Jempson, Charles Stapley b Battle C1893, s of Charles, wood sawyer. General labourer. 21 Adelaide Street, St Leonards. e Hastings. Pte then L/C SD/3611, 13 RSR. d 30.06.16. Cabaret Rouge British Cemetery, Souchez.

Jenner, John Henry b Battle B1890. Farm carter. 2 Chapel Cottages. e Battle. Pte G13381, 1 Bn Royal West Surrey Regt. d Somme front 11.02.17. Bray Military Cemetery. BC BM

Jesson, Thomas John b Battle C1869, s of Frederick, drill instructor. Harness maker. Drill Hall then 8 Ashton Street, Brighton. Married Mary Jane Fry. 97836 RHA/RFA. d at home 24.03.15. Brighton (Lewes Road) Cemetery.

Kendall, Robert b Clapham C1892, s of Alfred, chemist. Shipping clerk. Uncle George at 69–70 High Street, Battle. Mother at 5 High St 1911. e Battle. Sgt STK/1031, 10 Bn, Royal Fusiliers. d (wounds) 08.09.16. Loos British Cemetery. BC BM

Lambert, Henry McLaren b Sevenoaks 25.07.1879, s of Edward, civil engineer, JP, landowner. Soldier ret 1908. Telham Court. Harrow and Trinity College, Cambridge. 1 Royal Dragoons. 2Lt 06.12.99, Lt 03.10.00, Capt 04.12.07. d near Ypres 13.05.15. Hop Store Cemetery, Vlamertinghe. Muthaiga Club War Memorial, Kenya. Harrow School memorial. BC BM

Lamborn, Charles Douglas J N b Battle 24.09.86, s of William, teacher. Possibly tailor; then letter carrier. Grammar School, High Street. 1915: 850, Phoenix Street, Victoria, BC. e Victoria BC 14.09.15. L/C 154100, 1 Bn Canadian Pioneers (1 Bn, W Ontario Regiment). d near Ypres 30.06.16, probably near Ploegsteert Wood. Lijssenthoek Military Cemetery.

Ling, Edward b Buckland, Berkshire D1898, s of George, hotel manager. Star Hotel then Abbey Hotel. L/C 11892 Royal Berkshire. d 26.06.16. Cabaret Rouge British Cemetery, Souchez.

Ling, Frank Richard b Buckland, Berkshire D1897, s of George, hotel manager. Auctioneer's clerk; barman in Australia. Star Hotel then Abbey Hotel. e Melbourne 24.02.15. Pte 587, 23 Bn (Infantry), Aust Army. Gallipoli 30.08.15; severe wound to shoulder 03.12.15; to Alexandria etc.

Rejoined unit 05.05.16. Embarked HMS *Scotian* Alexandria 09/10.05.16, arr Marseille 18.05.16. d Somme 23.08.16. Villers Bretonneux Memorial.

Lovell, George b Netherfield Apr 1884, s of William Lovell. Farm labourer. Darwell Hill. e 05.04.16. Gunner 73989, RGA. d Chelmsford 18.12.18 (accident). Netherfield churchyard.

McQuillan, Leonard Ernest b Battle D1893, s of James, surveyor and inspector of nuisances, Battle UDC. Starrs Green. e Marylebone. Cpl 7445, 20 Bn Royal Fusiliers, 2 Divn. To France 15.11.15. d Somme 30.07.16. Caterpillar Valley Cemetery, Longueval. BC BM

Marchant, William E b Battle D1886, s of Henry. Farm labourer, builder's labourer. 3 Beechwood Cottages, Netherfield Lane. e Hastings, 28.08.1914. Pte SR/898, 2 Bn RSR. Prev 3 RSR. d Vadencourt 18.09.18. Jeancourt Communal Cemetery Extension. BC BM

Markwick, Sydney b Ninfield D1899, s of George, gardener. Entrance Lodge, Normanhurst. 1 Lower Lake. e Chichester. Rifleman 45742, 2 Bn, Rifle Brigade. d Rouen base hospital 28.04.18 (wounds). St Sever Cemetery Extension, Rouen. Catsfield Memorial. BC BM

Marsh, Tom b Battle D1894, s of Tom, publican. Gamekeeper. Squirrel Inn. e Hastings. Pte G18130, 7 Bn RSR. d near Senlis Mill 05.04.18. Bouzincourt Ridge Cemetery, Albert. BC BM

Martin, George Johnston b St Austell C1894, s of Constantine, workhouse master. Workhouse master's clerk. Battle workhouse then Eastbourne workhouse. Pte 4350, 19 Royal Fusiliers. 2 Lt RFC, 2 Lt 13 RSR. To France 14.11.15. d Ypres 26.09.17. Tyne Cot Cemetery.

Meppem, Ormond Edwin b Battle A1882, s of Ormond, estate bailiff. Butcher's assistant. Rose Cottage, Imberhorne Lane, East Grinstead. Pte 225100 London Regt (Royal Fusiliers), 1 Bn att 2 Bn. d Ypres area 15.06.17. Menin Gate Memorial.

Meppem, Sydney Clarence b Battle C1895, s of Ormond, estate bailiff. Clerk. Rose Cottage, Imberhorne Lane, East Grinstead. Pte 6192 London Regt. d Somme 08.10.16. Warlencourt British Cemetery.

Miller, Arthur John b Pevensey March 1880, s of postman. Postman. 3 Castle Terrace, Pevensey. e 05.02.15. Pte 7 Bn RSR. Wounded twice 30.06.16. Trench fever + home Oct 1917. d Morlancourt 13.08.1918 ('Friendly fire'). Two brothers died in war. Pevensey memorial. Vis-en-Artois Memorial.

Morley, William Charles b Battle 1878, s of Frederick, farm labourer. Grocers's porter. m Louisa Gertrude Burns 1901. 3 Little Common Road, Bexhill. e St Leonards. Spr 909, 2nd Home Counties Field Coy RE. d 06.05.15 (wounds). Boulogne Eastern Cemetery. Bexhill Memorial.

Murdock, Archibald James b Hastings A1881, s of Archibald. Rural postman. 1911: Rodmell. Married Beatrice Maude, Hastings 03.07.05. Children. e 30.12.99. 2 Bn East Kent Regt, S African war. Reserve 1902. L/6174, 3 Bn East Kent Regt A/Cpl 25.09.16, Cpl + L/Sgt 26.09.16, A/Sgt 28.03.17, Sgt 09.04.17. Wounded 24.06.16. d 12.09.17. Philosophe British Cemetery, Mazingarbe.

Neeves, Samuel b Battle B1895, s of Samuel, wood dealer. Porter in stores. Whatlington Road. e Hastings 11.12.15. Pte F/3118, 27 then 23 Bn Middlesex Regiment (Duke of Cambridge's Own). To France 04.05.16. d Somme 01.10.16. Thiepval Memorial. BM

Newbery, Charles Joseph b Battle B1888, s of Joseph, manufacturing confectioner. Architectural assistant. Forest View, Mount Street. Pte 2201, 3 Bn Royal Fusiliers. d near Ypres 08.05.15 (wounds). Tyne Cot Cemetery. BC BM

Newman, Frederic Charles b Battle D1882, s of William, groom, gardener. Chauffeur. 1 Upper Lake; 5 St Mary's Cottages. 1911: W Hampstead. Army records: Hackney. m Kate Amy Hodgson, Battle 13.04.04. Children. e London. Gnr 191289, RGA. AA Battery. d France 22.03.18. Pozières Memorial.

Noad, Charles Stephen Gaisford b Hamsterley, Durham D1877, s of Charles, coachman. Domestic gardener. The Lodge, Telham Court. Later Sidley. m Florence Buck 1910. Children. e Chichester. Pte G/3/21409, East Surrey Regt then G/18906 Middlesex Regt. d Fulham 26.06.17. Kensal Green Cemetery.

Noakes, Frederic b Battle A1877, s of Frederic, farmer. 1911: Crippenden Manor, Edenbridge. Paternal: 4 St Mary's Villas. m Margaret Jardine Carruthers, East Grinstead C1914. Children. Lt Staffs Yeomanry. d Palestine 25.08.17. Church memorial gives death as 26.08.17. Ramleh War Cemetery. BC BM

Oliver, Percy John b Erith C1893, s of Henry, railway official (mother widow baker + confectioner). Baker. 49 High Street. e Hastings. Pte SD956, 11 Bn RSR. d near Béthune 21.05.16 (wounds). Bethune Town Cemetery. BC BM

Orford, Lancelot Edwin b Little Eaton, Derbyshire C1887, s of Edwin, teacher. Merchant's clerk. Church Lane, Marsham, Norfolk. G/5176 Pte 2 Bn RSR. d Loos 13.10.15. Loos Memorial.

Parks, Jabez Juina b Battle 1881, s of Robert, agricultural labourer. Mineral water carman. Virgins Croft. e Bexhill. Pte 267435 Herts Regt. d Ypres 06.05.15. Menin Gate Memorial.

Partington, John Bertram b Netherfield 07.05.1884, s of Thomas, Vicar. Educated Radley and Pembroke, Oxford. Teacher. e Aug 1914. 28.11.14 Capt, 4 Bn (Territorial) Devonshire Regiment. Mesopotamia. India Dec 1914–Jan 1915; Australia Jan–Autumn1915; India Aut 1915–Oct 1916. d Mesopotamia 03.02.17. Amara war cemetery, Oakham School Memorial. N

Pook, Richard Thomas b Battle 15.04.83, s of James, carter. Coal carman. Beanford, Ashburnham, Tunbridge Wells. Married Florence Edith Gardener 1907. Children. Driver 2268, 1/3 Kent Fortress Coy, RE. d at sea at Cape Helles 28.10.15. Helles Memorial.

Raper, Robert George b Battle B1877, s of William, solicitor. Solicitor. Richards Hill. Married Ida Macadam-Smith. Children. Temp Maj

31.05.15. Maj, 8 Bn S Staffs Regt. d near Fricourt 2.07.16. Fricourt British Cemetery. BC BM

Relf, Percy Edward b Battle A1898, s of Charles, woodman dealer. Squirrel Hill. e Hastings. Pte G42731, 23 Bn Middlesex Regt. d near Arras 03.18. Arras Memorial. BC BM

Ripley, Percy b Smarden B1878, s of James, blacksmith. Butcher's assistant. 9A Lower Lake. e Hastings 23.04.15. Pte ASC then G/92545, 1/7 Middlesex Regt. Pte L/7866, 2 Bn RSR. d 26.05.18. Wanquetin Communal Cemetery Extension.

Rooke, Ernest John b Brighton D1884. Policeman. Lewes Police Barracks. e Chichester 01.09.1914. PC at Battle 28.03.11–1913. Joined Reserve 1911. d Aubers Ridge 09.05.15. Le Touret Memorial. Police memorial, West St, Lewes.

Sadler, Stanley Victor b Mortlake B1897, s of James, coachman. Journeyman baker. Virgins Croft, Battle. e Hastings. L/C SD2335, 7 Bn RSR. Formerly 12 Bn. Wounded near Hardecourt. d Rouen military hospital 28.08.18. St Sever Cemetery. BC BM

Santer, William Aubrey b Battle B1888, s of William, carpenter. Confectioner's assistant. 9 Upper Lake, 2 Carriers Yard, High Street. m Annie Bean C1909. Child. e Hastings. Pte G12141, 9 Bn RSR. d near St Quentin 03.18. Pozières Memorial. BC BM

Saunders, Alfred b Netherfield c1887, s of Harry, gypsum mine labourer. General labourer. Soan's Cottages, French's Farm, Mountfield. e Hastings. Driver 38882, No 6 Pack Wireless Section RE. Egypt 13.08.17 (appendicitis). Cairo War Memorial Cemetery. N

Saunders, Nelson b Netherfield D1898, s of Harry, gypsum mine labourer. Ivyland Green, Netherfield. e Hastings. Pte 50765, 9 (Glasgow Highland) Bn (Territorial), HLI. Was 2121 RSR. d Etaples hospital 19.04.18 (wounds on 14.04.18). Etaples Military Cemetery. N

Scotton, Donald Victor b Claybrooke, Leics D1892, s of William, farmer. On farm, Netherfield. Pte 63679, 2 Bn N Auckland Regiment, NZEF. d between Albert and Bapaume 24.08.18. Adanac Military Cemetery, Miraumont. N

Sellens, James Walter b Battle B1885, s of James, stoker. Soldier. 5 Edward Terrace, Hollington. e New Cross. Pte L/6596, 2 Royal W Kent Regt. d Mesopotamia 14.09.16. Baghdad (North Gate) Cemetery.

Sellman, Sidney Alfred b Crowhurst C1891, s of James, foreman on farm. Butcher's assistant. Spital Hill. e St Leonards. Sapper 534541, 258 Tunnelling Coy, RE. d near Amiens 03.18. Hangard Communal Cemetery Extension.

Sharp, John b Battle 21.04.83, s of Edward, farm servant. Sailor. m Emily Hutchings 1909. Child. 1916: 28 Spring Garden View, Landport. Stoker First Class 307371 (Po), RN, HMS Scourge. d at sea 19.11.15. Buried at sea. Portsmouth Naval Memorial.

Skilton, Frederick b Battle B1894, s of Caleb, UDC roadman. Poultryman. 8 Jubilee Cottages. e Bedford 13.10.13. Pte 21024, 2 Bn Border Regt. Formerly 10314 Bedfordshire Regt, trsfr Jan 1914. d Somme 01.07.16. Dantzig Alley British Cemetery, Mametz. BC BM

Smissen, George Franklin b Mountfield C1893, s of Franklin. Darwell Road, Netherfield. e Hastings. Pte G/76, 7 Bn RSR. d Arras 31.03.17. Faubourg d'Amiens Cemetery, Arras. Brightling Memorial. N

Smith, Arthur Neville b Battle A1897, s of Walter, railway signalman. Apprentice grocer. Railway Crossing, Marley Lane. e Hastings 23.03.1916. Pte 27728, 9 Bn Royal Fusiliers. d Somme 07.10.16. Thiepval Memorial. BC BM

Smith, William Hiram b Brede C1885, s of William, agricultural labourer. Miller's carman. King's Head Mill. m Minnie Eliza Pope, Battle B1913. e Hastings. Pte SD/12911, 12 Bn RSR. (Medal card says Sgt.). d Hastings 27.09.16 (wounds). Hastings cemetery and Memorial.

Spray, William b Battle 26.07.88, s of Aaron, wood cutter/dealer. Sailor. 3 Osborne Cottages, Hollington Old Lane. 235034 (Po), RN. HMS Mersey. d 03.01.19 (disease). Conotan Lane Protestant Cemetery, Braila, Romania. Now in Bucharest War Cemetery, Romania.

Stapley, Percy Edward b St Leonards C1887, s of Charles, bricklayer. General gardener. The Cottage, Old Roar, Silverhill Park, St Leonards. m Louisa Freeman, Battle B1908. e Hastings. Pte G31392, 6 Bn Royal West Kent Regt. d Amiens 09.08.18. Dernancourt Communal Cemetery Extension. BC BM

Stemp, Albert William b Staplehurst B1890, s of William, wood hoop maker. Market gardener. Mill Cottages, Hastings Road. e Fremantle, WA. Pte 2728, 51st (W Aust) Bn, Aust Infantry. d near Villers Bretonneux 05.04.18. Villers Bretonneux memorial. Australian War Memorial, Canberra. BC BM

Stephens, Alfred William Holman b Battle 1883. Tailor (maker). 18 Bavant Road, Norbury. e Kingston. G/41318, 2 Middlesex Regt. d 27.03.18. Pozières Memorial.

Stevenson, Leonard Percival b Battle B1897, s of Walter, warehouseman. Ironmonger's assistant. 4 Leopold Road, Bexhill. Pte G/3774 East Kent Regt (The Buffs). d Somme 18.08.16. Thiepval Memorial.

Strevens, William Henry Noel b Chelsea B1888, s of William. Manservant. Battle Abbey. Wife at 45 Sulgrave Road, Hammersmith. e Hastings 11.12.15. Gunner 82866 RGA, 203 AA Section. To France 06.11.16. d General Hospital, Calais 14.10.18 (broncho-pneumonia etc). Les Baraques Military Cemetery, Sangatte.

Thomas, Arthur Cecil b Battle c1882, s of John, builder. Carpenter. The Briars, Caldbec Hill. Pte 40306, 10 Bn S Wales Borderers. Formerly with RSR. d at home 15.08.17 (trench foot). Battle Cemetery. BC BM

Turner, Percival John Henry b Battle B1882, s of Arthur, saddler, collar & harness maker. Plumber. Cruttenden's Yard. 1911: 15 Beech Lane,

Shrewsbury. 1915: 29 Duke St, Lower Broughton, Manchester. e Manchester 27.03.15. Pte 11166, 18 Bn Manchester Regt. d (scarlet fever) at Monsall Fever Hospital, Prestwich 19.05.15. Manchester (Philips Park) Cemetery. BC BM

Vitler, Henry James b Battle B1898, s of Henry, farm labourer. 9 Harold Terrace then Spital Hill. e Maidstone. Pte G/21137, Royal W Kent. d near St Quentin 03.18. Pozières Memorial.

Vitler, Thomas W b Battle C1891, s of Henry, farm labourer. Soldier. 9 Harold Terrace. e Hastings. Pte 5022, 7 Hussars, Household Cavalry. d Mesopotamia 28.10.18.

Wait, William b Battle B1879, s of William, carpenter. Bricklayer's labourer. 17 Lower Lake. e Hastings. Pte G50601, 2 Middlesex Regt. d Somme front 22.04.17. Thiepval memorial. BC BM

Webster, Godfrey Vassall George Augustus b London 1897, s of Sir Augustus, landowner and soldier. Soldier. Heir to Battle Abbey estate. Eton, Sandhurst. Powdermill House. Lt 3 Bn, Grenadier Guards. To France 02.03.17. d near Ypres 04.08.17. Buried on battlefield. Menin Gate memorial. BC BM

Weller, John Lourine Tavinor b Battle D1874, s of Walter, gamekeeper. Sailor. 3 Langleigh Terrace. Ilfracombe. m Emma Willoughby Linton, Liverpool 1909. Son Jack Lourine b 1909. AB 181557 (RFRChB 2414)(Ch), RN. HMS Aboukir. d North Sea 22.09.14. Chatham Naval Memorial.

Whistler, Ralfe Allen Fuller b Glasgow 24.07.1895, s of Fuller, soldier. Soldier. King's School Canterbury, Sandhurst. Caldbec House. e 24.03.14. 2 Bn, HLI. 2 Lt 24.03.14; temp/Capt Feb 1916; Cpn Aug 1916. To France August 1914. Mons; wounded on Aisne 12.09.14; wounded at Festubert May 1915; wounded at Kut Apr 1916; invalided to India with typhoid. France Mar 1917. Wounded at Oppy 26.04.17, d 27.04.17. Aubigny Communal Cemetery Extension. Memorial at St Mary's; window at Worcester Cathedral. BC BM

White, Frederick Joseph b Hastings C1888, s of Henry, butcher. Tramcar conductor. Driver T/23281 ASC. Married Elizabeth Kate Fuller 1915. d (suicide) 08.05.15. Samer Communal Cemetery.

Whiteman, James b Warbleton A1881, s of George, farmer. Newlands Farm, Dallington. m Annie Bessie Mepham 1900. Children. e Hastings. L/C G/1112, 7 Bn RSR. France 04.01.15. Wounded Spring 1915. d Somme 07.07.1916 (wounds). Albert Communal Cemetery Extension. Brightling Memorial. N

Willats, Harry Ashley b Margate B1889, s of Henry, hotel manager. Rochester GS. Stock exchange trader. Hemingfold Farm. e 09.1914. 2 Lt RFA, previously ASC. d Salisbury Plain 12/13.02.17 (chill). Abney Park Cemetery, Stoke Newington.

ANALYSIS OF DEATHS

Date of birth

Pre-1870:1	1870–74: 2	1875–79: 11	1880–84: 24
1885–89: 24	1890–94: 30	1895–99: 20	**TOTAL: 112**

Battle residence

Hastings Road includes all premises from the Powdermill junction to the Black Horse area, excluding St Mary's Terrace and Villas. High Street includes Watch Oak and the lower end of Netherfield Lane.

Caldbec Hill: 6	High Street + yards: 16	Upper/Lower Lake: 6
Hastings Road: 8	Whatlington Road etc: 4	Marley Lane etc: 1
Netherfield: 20	Mount St: 7	St Mary's: 6
Farms etc: 16	**TOTAL 90**	

Regiment (i. e. final regiment, including attachment)
*includes all branches

ASC	3	Labour Corps	1	Royal Engineers	8
Australian	3	Leics	1	Royal Fusiliers	9
Border Regt	1	Lincolnshire	1	Royal Munster F	1
Canadian	3	Manchester	1	Royal Navy	4
Devonshire	1	Middlesex	6	Royal Sussex	25
E Kent (Buffs)	2	New Zealand	1	Royal W Kent	6
Grenadier G'ds	1	Norfolk	1	Royal W Surrey	1
Herts	1	North Staffs	2	S Staffs	1
HLI	2	Northants	1	S Wales Bord's	1
E Surrey	1	Rifle Brigade	2	South African	1
Household Bde	2	Royal Artillery*	10	Staffs Yeomanry	1
Gordon High'rs	1	Royal Berkshire	2	Suffolk	1
KOYLI	1	Royal Dragoons	1	Wiltshire	1
				TOTAL	**112**

Year and place of death

	1914	1915	1916	1917	1918*	Total
Belgium		3	1	8	1	13
France		6	24	11	31	72
Gallipoli		1				1
Near/Middle East			2	5	1	8
Africa			1			1
India			1			1
At sea	2	**3	1	1	1	8
Germany		1				1
In UK		2	1	3	1	7
Total	2	16	31	28	35	**112**

*including one 1919 death in the UK from wounds received in France in 1918.
**all three were at Gallipoli.

Appendix B
Those who Survived

The following abbreviations are used in addition to those used generally in this account:

A, B, C and D (each upper case) refer to the quarters of the years, starting with A meaning 1 January to 31 March. In all cases these are civil registrations not actual events. Birth/marriage data drawn from public sources generally refers to registration districts and not to places. This means that unless determined by other means an event in Netherfield is recorded as Battle and (later) one in Battle is recorded as in Hastings. It also means that an event taking place late in one quarter might be registered, and therefore recorded here, in the next following quarter, or sometimes even later.

b	born
BC	on the churchyard memorial in Battle
BM	on the plaque in the Memorial Halls in Battle
c	(lower case) about
d	died
e	enlisted
m	married
N	on the churchyard memorial in Netherfield
S	on School List, December 1915.
s	son

Other abbreviations are either obvious or are those given in the list at the beginning of the account.

Abrey, Arthur Reginald b Hollington 04.10.95, s of William, butler. Footman. Beauport Park then 30 York Road, Silverhill. e Hastings 26.02.15. Pte SD/2293, 12 RSR. To France 02.03.16. Missing 30.06.16; unknown how returned. Wounded 04.01.17. Discharged as unfit 14.11.17. d Hastings B1972.

Abrey, William Charles b Hollington 11.06.89, s of William, butler. Manservant. South Cliffe House, Eastbourne; then 30 York Road, Silverhill. e Redhill 29.02.16. 23035 Northants Regiment. France 18.04.17–25.11.18. Wounded 10.10.18. Discharged physically unfit 25.09.19; 40 % disabled. d Eastbourne C1978.

Archer, Alfred Edward Harry b Battle 20.01.89, s of Harry, bootmaker. Boot trade. 4 Upper Lake. e Hastings 10.08.14. 7 RSR. L/C 05.09.14, Cpl 02.12.14, L/Sgt 27.09.15, Sgt 06.01.16. To France 31.05.15. To Royal W Surrey (9283) 01.12.15. Gunshot wounds to l arm and l foot 29.12.15. Discharged 'no longer physically fit' 25.12.17. S. d Weston-super-Mare C1977.

Arnold, Thomas Archibald Douglas b Polegate 15.11.91, s of John, dentist. Electrician. 3 St Mary's Villas. e Valestier, Ontario 23.09.14, Shorncliffe 10.12.15. CEF: 225107, 12 Reserve. Lt 3 RSR. m Lilian M A Parker, Croydon A1916.

Ashby, Albert Clement b Netherfield A1895, s of William, farmer. Farm labourer. High House, Ebony, Ashford. e Canterbury 09.04.14. Pte E Kent then RAMC then 88844 RFA 16.01.15. France 30.05.15. Discharged 20.02.19. m Kathleen Edith Emily Phillips, Gloucester B1927. d Ashford 02.09.55.

Austin, Edwy b Hastings 27.04.90, s of Edward, solicitor's clerk. Seaman. 5 St Mary's Terrace. Joined before 1906. AB RN 235901. m Adelaide E Wright, Maidstone B1914. Children. S. d Maidstone A1977.

Ayres, George Edward b Staplehurst c1881, s of Gideon, blacksmith. Blacksmith. Rose Cottage, Blackhorse Road (53 Heaver Road, Battersea at death). m Alice Kate Hipgrave, Hastings C1903. Children. d Westminster 01.04.1948.

Barnes, Albert b Netherfield 15.10.95, grandson of Matthew. Bavin maker. Netherfield Road. Driver 7 Field Coy RE. S. d Hastings B1974.

Barnes, William H b Netherfield 1898, grandson of Matthew. Bavin maker. Netherfield Road. Pte 2/5 RSR. m Annie Sargent, Battle A1925. Child. S. d Hastings A1967.

Barrett, Frederick b Dorset 1880. Butler. 48 Ebury Buildings, London SW. Machine Gun Section. m Florence Holman of Battle.

Bateman, Harry b Thame D1880, s of James, domestic groom. Police constable. Police Station, Battle then 9 Ticehurst Cottages. e Hastings 14.12.15. Joined police 25.11.02, resigned 17,05,17. Gunner/Signaller 160443, RGA. France 01.10.17. Hospital with trench fever 08.06.18. Discharged 19.02.19. Reappointed PC 18.02.19; resigned 08.01.28. m Florence Eleanor French, Mark Cross 28.06.05. Child. d High Wycombe

28.04.53.

Batten, Percy Woodruff b Tranmere 18.06.93, s of John. Journalist. The Hammonds; later London, Australia. RAMC; commissioned 2 Lt, 5 Manchester Regt 17.04.15; later Capt, 24 Tank Battalion. Gallipoli 07.15. MC. m Gladys M Daniels, London 11.10.26. Children. d Belle Vue, NSW, 28.09.58.

Beale, David b Warbleton 1892, s of Henry, farmer. Bodle Street. L/C. m Dorothy F Stubberfield, Battle C1920. Children. d Battle A1927.

Beney, Arthur George b Hastings B1891. Baker's vanman. Mount Street e Brighton 23.02.16. Pte Sussex Yeomanry; transferred to 29 Middlesex Regt 19.10.16; to 133864, 2 Labour Corps 28.04.17; discharged 11.09.19. No overseas service. d Hastings 08.04.60.

Beney, Jack b Battle 1898, s of Charles, rural postman. Lower Lake. Pte 41369 R West Surrey; L/C 68419 Labour Corps. d C1961 Warwick.

Bennett, Henry C b Southborough c1890, s of Herbert, cricket ball maker. Draper's assistant c/o Miss Sylvester, High Street. Pte 16 Dragoon Guards.

Blackman, Charlie b Battle A1896, s of Thomas, thatcher. Baker. Newington Cottages, Level Road, then Virgin's Croft. e Hastings 10.03.15. Pte 2334, 12 RSR. To France 04.03.16. Wounded 'in 15 places' 02.07.16, discharged physically unfit 21.02.17. S. Uncle of Stanley Sadler KIA. d Battle 26.01.1959.

Blackman, Harry b Battle 24.04.89, s of William, gardener. Tailor. St Mary's Terrace. e Winnipeg, 17.02.16. CEF 187350. 90 Bn; to 190 Bn 16.05.16. m Kate.

Blackman, James Henry b Netherfield B1895, s of Thomas, wood merchant. General labourer. Netherfield Road. e Hastings 08.12.14. Pte 13 RSR, 14 RSR (01.03.16), 11 RSR (01.04.16), 1 Worcs Regt 58007 (18.06.18). To France 02.04.16–22.01.19. L/C unpaid 10.08.18. Wounded 30.04.18 (gas?). Re enlisted in Reserve 29.07.19; demob 31.03.1920. m Minnie Kiley, Battle. B1919. Children. d Battle 25.07.1965.

Blackman, Thomas Charles b Battle 1900, s of Thomas, coal merchant. 66 High Street. Aircraftman 2 Cl 282656 RAF. S. d in air accident, Paris, 17.09.19. Buried City of Paris Cemetery, Pantin.

Blackman, William b Battle 26.05.91, s of Thomas, coal merchant. 30 Mount Street. 5 RSR: Cpl, A/Sgt 5/1164, CSM 2400037, CQMS 6392773. With Sniper Section KRRC 12.06.15. m May Creese, Battle D1919. Children. d Hastings D1969.

Blain, Leslie Charlton b Southborough D1895, s of Frederick, manager to baker/corn merchant. Cycle trade. Fern Cottage, Starrs Green. Pte M2/032198, ASC. To France 18.01.15. m Kate F Giebler, Hackney B1920. Children. d Battle B1967.

Bodle, Alfred b Hastings B1879. Quarryman, miner. Thatch Cottage, Netherfield Hill. e St Leonards 22.10.14. Pte 2 HC Coy RE. No overseas service. Discharged as permanently unfit 28.01.16. m Louisa Jane Isted, Battle A1902. d Hastings A1940.

Bodle, Charles b Battle 1877, s of Stephen, domestic gardener. Railway platelayer. Cottage at Telham Court; later Crowhurst. Pte 5 Bn RSR. m Frances Mary Hayward, Battle, B1900. Children. S. d Hastings D1937.

Bodle, Walter James Ernest b Battle B1896, s of William, horsekeeper, stockman on farm. Gardener. Tollgates, later 2 St Marys Gardens. Cpl 5 Bn RSR. m Alice Maud Dillon, Lambeth 20.07.20. S. Walter + Alice left Southampton for Wellington, NZ, 02.12.20; SS *Ruahine.*

Bones, Joseph William b Battle D1871, s of William, general labourer. Labourer then soldier and postman. Breadsell Farm. e Chichester 11.03.90, 19.02.00. Service in S Africa and elsewhere. Recalled 27.11.14. Gunner 340795, 13 Coy RGA. Shore defences, Felixstowe. m Elizabeth Stainforth, Watton at Stone 25.12.93. d Ipswich 06.06.19.

Bothwell, Horace E b Kingston c1898, s of Charles, upholsterer. 6 St Mary's Terrace. Pte RE. S. d Hailsham D1968.

Bourner, Llewelyn b Battle 28.12.89, s of William, agricultural labourer. Railway coalman. Hemingfold Farm. e Hastings 13.08.14. Sapper 537915 RE. France 12.08.16. Discharged 12.03.19. m Florence Brann, Hastings A1910. d Chatham D1958.

Bowers, Charles Richard b Battle c1896, s of Richard, soldier, shoemaker. Lower Lake (at death 8 Chandos Crescent, Edgware). Pte ASC. S. d Westminster 15.03.1940.

Bowers, Ernest b St Leonards 1896, s of Oscar, boot repairer. 19 Aldborough Road, St Leonards. Pte RSR. MM Nov 1916. m Beatrice Baker, Hastings D1925. Children. d Hastings A1969.

Bowers, Oscar b Battle c1894. Lower Lake. e 12.08.14. Pte 9659 2 RSR, then Acting L/C 2/9 HLI 52085, then RAMC 13111. m Clara M Honeyball, Fulham A1925. Child.

Boxall, Percy b Battle 1889, s of Albert. Motor fitter. 11 Mount Street. e 24.06.16, Brighton 02.05.18. Driver 401720 ASC. France 29.06.18–04.12.19. Demob 03.01.20. m Ruth Goodsell, Battle 09.05.14. Children.

Boxall, Sidney H Battle 23.09.93, s of Harry, baker. Fishmonger. 6 Upper Lake. m Emily Roberts, Battle B1922. Pte Home Counties RFA then Cpl then Sgt. S. d Battle A1972.

Breeds, Thomas Walter b Hastings B1879, s of Thomas, brewer. Brewing director. Telham Hill. m Gertrude Frances Woodd, Battle C1907. Child. RNVR: Lt 1905. RN 2 Lt (temp) 1914, Lt (temp) 1915. Capt 8 Welsh Regt. To Mesopotamia 04.17. d Hastings B1957.

Brett, Harry b Sedlescombe B1882, s of Alfred, farm bailiff. Shepherd. Spilstead, Sedlescombe. Glebe Cottages, Hooe. m Caroline M Bray, Battle B1928. Driver 261499, 51 Bde RFA. S. d Battle D1967.

Brett, Percy Raymond b Battle 14.08.90, s of Harry, policeman. Butcher. m Lilly Best, Hailsham A1922. Child. e Eastbourne 03.09.14. Pte 304310, 8 RSR then 17.12.17 Cpl. 58814 Tank Corps. France 24.07.15–19.12.17, 09.09.18– . Wounded 14.10.16. d Uckfield D1969.

Brodie, Ivor de Haga d Farnham 1888, s of William, surgeon. 2 Upper

Lake. m Winifred Kathrine Fidgeon, Paddington 24.07.16. Children. Lt then Capt RASC. To France 22.11.16. d Worthing 06.07.51.

Brough, Daniel b Dunbar c1872. GP. 2 Upper Lake or 3? Marlow, Marley Lane at death. m Barbara Wicksteed, Chelsea 04.01.06 [divorced July 1916]. e Jan 1915. RAMC. Was medical super of workhouse till enlisted Jan 1915. MB (Edin) CM (Edin) MRCS (Eng) LRCP DPH (Camb). MOH. d Battle 01.04.1942.

Broxup, Percy b Abingdon B1882. Elementary schoolmaster. m Clarissa Tucker Larkin, Sandwich 13.04.09. Children. e Hastings 08.02.15. Gunner 164439, RGA. France. Discharged 10.02.19. d Hailsham 23.03.51.

Buckwell, Charles W b Brighton c1885, s of John, solicitor. Solicitor. 12 Wellington Road, Brighton. Later 34/35 High Street. 1945 The Guildhall, Battle. m Dora Beatrice Pierce, Brighton 1911. Child: John Ade b Battle 1921 KIA Italy 06.07.1944. e Jan 1915. Maj RE. France April 1915 (signal coys). Invalided out (shell shock) 1918. Mentioned in Despatches. Member of Guardians 1923–, also Battle UDC, RDC. d Battle 05.01.45.

Burton, Arthur Cecil b Torquay C1876. Veterinary surgeon. Old Almonry Farm. m Jean Letitia Foster, London 24.06.1913. Lt Army Vet Corps 27.02.1915. MRCVS. Left Battle – leaving party reported 1.11.19. d 130 High Street Epsom 19.11.1928.

Buss, Albert Sampson b Burwash 1882, s of Charles, agricultural labourer. Gypsum labourer. Netherfield Place. 1951: Hill Crest, Netherfield Road. m Edith M Efferney, Battle B1920. Child. Sapper 105 Field Coy RE. France. d Hastings 01.06.51.

Buss, Charles Edward Frank b Netherfield D1895, s of Charles, general labourer. Plumber's mate. m Lydia Pallister, Knaresborough A1917. e Hastings 10.10.12.Pte 4845, 1 Rifle Bde. A/Cpl 30.08.14, Cpl 02.07.16, L/Sgt 28.10.16. 19.05.17 reversion to Cpl. France 07.10.14–04.12.14, 16.02.16–27.10.16, 18.03.17–11.10.18. Frostbite Nov 1914. Shell shock then wounded (gas) 09.02.17. MM 17.12.17. Discharged as no longer physically fit 11.10.18. d Hull A1919.

Buss, Ernest Arthur b Reigate c1898, s of George, grocer's assistant. Coach painter. 7 St Mary's Villas. Pte 14 Bn RSR. d Battle 26.06.1921.

Buss, George Henry b Reigate 21.11.1893, s of George, grocer's assistant. Market gardener. 7 St Mary's Villas. m Dorothy Hann, Eastbourne C1918. Child. e Hastings 20.09.14. Pte 2082, 8 Bn RSR. Discharged (medically unfit) 23.11.14. d Battle D1972.

Buss, James H b Netherfield 1889, s of Charles, agricultural labourer. Waggoner's mate. Netherfield Place. Pte 13 RSR. L/C 09.17. Wounded at Zillebeke 26.02.17. d Hastings A1964.

Buss, Percy Leonard b Reigate B1896, s of George, grocer's assistant. Baker's assistant. 7 St Mary's Villas. 1928: Elfords Cottage, The Moor, Hawkhurst. m Beatrice Mary Rich, Ampthill, B1921. Child. e St Leonards 10.07.14. Pte 905389, 2 HC, RFA. Pte, actg Bdr 13.01.17, briefly Bdr 19.07.17. Signaller. Discharged medically unfit (30% disabled) 26.04.19. Service in

India (Jullundur, Multan, Poona), Mesopotamia. Seriously ill at Baghdad 1918. d Battle 01.05.28.

Buss, Walter John b Burwash D1878, s of Charles, agricultural labourer. Gypsum miner. 1891: Netherfield Place Farm. 1936: Hillcrest, Wattles Wish. m Kate Daines, Netherfield 01.01.17. e Hastings 12.02.16. Earlier service with RSR ending 11.12.00. Pte then Acting L/C 10.05.16, L/C 31.10.18; 13 Royal Fusiliers then 23568, 1 Royal West Kent. To France 16.11.16, Italy 14.11.17, France 02.03.18. Discharged 01.05.19. d Battle 23.06.36.

Butchers, William Joshua b Battle D1883, s of George, brickfield foreman. General labourer. 1919: Pillgreen Cottages, Wadhurst. Later 1 Newbury Lane, Cousley Wood, Wadhurst. e Hastings 07.09.14. Pte 14057 RFA, then Cpl 18.05.16. France 08.09.15, Mediterranean 05.11.15–22.11.18, Salonica 14.01.19–30.03.19. Discharged 12.05.19. d Pembury 06.07.60.

Button, Frederick Richard b Battle 1879, s of Charles, butcher then agricultural labourer. Butcher. High Street then Battle Road, Whatlington. 1966: 33 Buckhurst Road, Bexhill.. e Hastings 17.07.17. Pte 9 RSR then 32 Royal Fusiliers 65512. France 08.05.17–25.08.17. Discharged as physically unfit 07.11.17. d Battle 06.02.66.

Carter, Albert Edward b Battle c1894, s of Edward, gypsum miner. Grinder. Netherfield. Gunner 17778, RFA. RE 01.01.18. France. Wounded 22.03.18 (right arm). Came from Sydney to enlist (SS *Otway*, left 26.09.14, arr Tilbury 07.11.14). Returned 23.06.1922 SS *Euripides*.

Carter, Arthur Victor b Netherfield c1880, s of William, gypsum labourer. Kiln filler, gypsum works. Netherfield Road. 1948: the Post Office, Netherfield. m Nellie Rebekah Whybourn, Battle C1906. Men's Detachment, Battle VAD. Orderly No 2 Brit Red X Hosp, Rouen. d Battle 28.09.48.

Carter, Charles Gilbert James b Battle c1893, s of Charles, jam packer. Baker, jam factory. 7a Mount Street. Cpl 5 Bn RSR.

Carter, Charles Richard b Netherfield 28.03.70, s of Edward, general labourer. Jam packer. 7a Mount Street. RAMC. S. d Battle 12.04.1929.

Carter, Edward b Battle c1894, s of Charles, jam packer. Barber's assistant. 7a Mount Street. RE. S.

Carter, (John) Thomas b Netherfield 03.01.74, s of Edward, general labourer. Butler. m Emma Bellward, Knightsbridge, 23.05.03. Children. Pte, Royal West Surrey.

Carter, Percy b Netherfield 14.09.77, s of Edward, domestic gardener. Baker's carter. Netherfield Road; 3 Western Avenue. m Annie Elizabeth Beney, Battle B1907. Child. ASC. France.

Carter, Sydney b Battle c1898, s of Charles, jam packer. 7a Mount Street. Pte 13 RSR. Wounded in r leg seriously, hosp London 18.05.18. S.

Carter, Tom b Battle 26.06.70, s of William, gypsum labourer. Council Roadman. Hillside, Netherfield Hill. m Alice Maud Squire, Netherfield 28.04.06. Children. e Hastings 13.01.17. Previously in RHA 17 years.

Pte 233960 later WR/21279, RE (Road Construction Corps). To France 10.02.17. Discharged 12.02.19. d Battle D1940.

Catt, Herbert Walter b Battle B1882, s of James, hotel keeper then confectioner. Painter, photographer. Temperance hotel, Bulverhythe then 606 Fulham Road, Hammersmith. m Kathleen Dora Bolton, Brixton 02.09.04. Children. e Hammersmith 02.09.14. Pte 18433, 12 Hussars. Discharged 13.01.15 as unlikely to be efficient soldier. d Fulham A1930.

Chacksfield, Charles Thomas b Battle A1886, s of Charles, odd man (domestic). Motor mechanic. Little Park; 19 Mount Street; 7 Chapel Cottages. Later 6 Chapel Cottages. 1944: 5 Wellington Gardens. m Alice May Evans, Eastry D1912. Child. e Hastings 10.12.16. Driver 193073 ASC (MT). To France 21.09.16. Various hospital times (debility). Disch 14.11.19. d Battle 29.01.44.

Champion, Percy William b Crowhurst c1898, s of William, farm labourer. Pepper in Eye Farm. m Elsie M Croft, Battle B1924. Children. Notts and Derby Regt. Wounded (2nd) 18.04.18 at Beaumont Hamel. POW, returned Nov 1918. d Battle D1960.

Chrismas, Alan B W b Battle c1888, s of Benjamin, cash dealer, formerly farmer. Butcher's assistant. 6 Caldbec Hill; Almonry House. m Marguerite Fox, Hastings D1925. Child. RE 534589, RE (T) 1963.

Chrismas, Edgar Gerald Russell b Alfriston 30.06.89, s of Benjamin, cash dealer formerly butcher, farmer. Butcher's assistant. 6 Caldbec Hill; Almonry House. RE. S. To Australia 1911. Died Brisbane 26.12.50.

Chrismas, Frederick Thomas Russell b Battle c1891, s of Benjamin, cash dealer formerly butcher, farmer. Soldier. Almonry House; 1911 at Combermere Barracks, Windsor. Trooper, Royal Horse Guards. d Hastings D1961.

Chrismas, Henry Charles b Ashburnham c1888, s of Trayton, carter. m Agnes M Stentiford, Battle C1920. Pte RSR 8902, MGC 124666. d Battle C1956.

Chrismas, Thomas Leonard b Battle 27.06.1892, s of Thomas, butcher then boarding house keeper. Butcher. 1911: Station Road, Hastings; later 4 St James Block, Portage and Beverley, m Nina. Winnipeg. e Winnipeg 23.07.16. Pte 1250063, 76 Bty CEF. Previously 1 year with Sussex Yeomanry.

Christian, Charles Edward b Battle 1870, s of John, groom. Shoeing smith, soldier. Hastings then 12 Parade Road, Ipswich. m Mary Campbell, Aldershot 19.09.05. Children. e Dublin. 18.01.98, Aldershot 09.11.09. 1898: 1 Dragoon Guards. 4139 Pte; L/C 18.04.00; Pte 17.09.01; L/C 05.11.01; Cpl 15.09.02; L/Sgt 30.05.03; Sgt 05.11.04; SSM 07.08.14. South Africa 08.01.01 to 14.11.03, 26.10.05 to 29.12.08. 10.05.16: D20234, 2/1 Royal Gloucestershire Hussars. 5294, 4 Dragoon Guards 17.09.18; 18.09.18: 314546, Tank Corps. France 14.04.19–17.05.20. Occupation army at Cologne 1920. Discharged 05.07.20. d Ipswich A1963.

Christian, William Dann b Hurst Green c1880, s of John, groom. Town postman. Lidcox Cottage, Marley Lane. m Ellenor Clara Bowers, Battle B1903. Children. Pte 1758, P12994 RSR Military Foot Police. d Hastings A1960.

Church, James Edward Albert b Battle 1878, s of Francis, shoemaker. Sawyer. 1919: 43 High Street, Robertsbridge. m Harriet Cheetham, Brighton 27.07.96. 7 children 1904–20. e Gillingham 17.03.15. Sapper 1898, RE. France 22.09.17–10.02.19. Discharged 10.03.19. d Battle A1939.

Clements, Sydney Charles b Rye 29.08.87, s of George, auctioneer, valuer, estate agent. Auctioneer. The Hammonds, Caldbec Hill; High Street; Squirrel Farm. Later Kingsnorth, Ashford. m Madeline A Baily, Battle B1913. e Hastings 09.12.15. Inns of Court OTC. Discharged 18.02.19. d Ashford A1979.

Clifton, Alfred b Battle c1896, s of Stephen, hotel waiter. Cycle shop assistant. Caldbec Hill; 1 Harold Terrace. Pte 5 RSR. S. NB record of whole family v unclear (12 siblings).

Clifton, Frank or Frederick b Battle c1890 or c1894, s of Stephen, hotel waiter. Caldbec Hill; 1 Harold Terrace. Pte 5 RSR. S. NB record of whole family v unclear (12 siblings).

Clifton, Stephen or Stanley b Battle c1879, s of Stephen, hotel waiter. Caldbec Hill; 1 Harold Terrace. e Battle c1900. 1 Harold Terrace. Pte. NB record of whole family v unclear (12 siblings).

Coad, Leslie Herbert b Hastings 1895, s of Charles, auctioneer's clerk. House furnisher and antique dealer. 8 Harold Terrace. e Hastings 11.12.15. Gunner then Signaller 22.10.18, 951688, 6 Res Bde RFA. France 01.10.16–06.02.17, 06.02.18–. Discharged 06.03.19. d Westminster A1943.

Cockett, William George b Battle 09.07.95. Baker. 119 Battle Road, St Leonards. e St Leonards 14.04.14. Gnr 312 then 905178 2 HC Bde RFA.France 29.10.14, then India, France 08.06.18–07.07.18. Discharged 28.02.19. d Hastings D1974.

Collins, Albert b Mountfield 25.07.79, s of John, gypsum miner. Gypsum miner. Netherfield then Mountfield. m Elizabeth Jane Harris, Mountfield 06.07.07. Children. Driver 534284, RE. Commendation. d Mountfield 28.03.38.

Cook, George b Hooe 1885, s of William, farm bailiff then baker, grocer. Domestic gardener. Lower Lake. Pte 6 Bedfordshire Regt. Lost leg in war but unknown where, when. S. d Battle 23.03.36.

Coomber, William Lindsey b Merstham 1871, s of James, shoemaker. Painter then coach builder. Lansdels Cottages, Mount Street; Upper Lake; Mount St. Later 4 Mount Terrace, Hailsham. m Rose Ellen Leeves, Hailsham 29.08.03. Children. e Brighton 04.07.18. Pte WR/43513, RE. 342 Road Construction Coy. To France 12.08.18. Discharged 08.03.19. d Hailsham C1944.

Cooper, Charles Augustus b Battle 19.11.99, s of Charles, labourer. Painter then grocer's porter. 37 Lower Lake. m Lilian V Ray, Battle D1925. e Hastings 14.03.17. Pte 156310, 51 Royal W Surrey then 14313, 1 East

Kent then 2278, 6 Royal W Kent. France 01.06.18–10.10.19. Discharged 10.10.19. Re-enlisted in 5 RSR at Battle 23.02.23 to 22.02.27. L/C 12.03.23, Cpl 03.08.23. d Hastings A1965.

Coppard, Ernest William b Netherfield 07.08.93, s of William, gypsum miner. Seaman. The Hollies, Mount Street. m Ada Sophia Leverett, Southwark D1920. Children. RN J6364. d Hackney A1942.

Coppard, Sydney b Battle 19.10.79, s of Martin, solicitor's clerk. Railway clerk. Uckham Lane. 1918: 200 Vine Street, San Antonio, Texas. e Toronto 29.08.18. CEF 3312138. Previously 3.5 years US army, Corporal.

Cornford, Frederick Frank b Battle C1884, s of Frederick, blacksmith. Blacksmith. m Frances Ellen Wickens, Crowborough 07.10.11. Children. m Elizabeth Wickens, Uckfield D1919. m Lilian May SImons, Tonbridge C1959. e Tunbridge Wells 06.01.03. Pte 25393 ASC (farrier/driver). Malta 18.06.04–28.05.05, Crete 29.05.05–10.03.07, France 20.08.14–24.12.15. Discharged (termination) 11.01.16. Recalled 20.01.17. Salonica 19.09.18–13.03.19. Discharged 07.06.19. d Tunbridge Wells 15.01.66 (address: 69 Auckland Road).

Cowley, Arthur b Cosgrove, Northants 15.03.96, s of James, publican. Chauffeur. 66 High Street. e Towcester 07.12.15. Pte 2222 Northants Yeomanry; transferred to ASC 27.04.17 as Pte M2/28102. Acting L/C 27.07.17, reverted 21.09.17. To Basra 21.09.17. Egypt 18.06.18–28.09.19. Discharged 24.11.19. Re-enlisted in 5 RSR at Battle 23.02.23 to 22.02.27. L/C 12.03.23, Cpl 03.08.23. d Overstone 27.09.58. Nephew of Clarke, tobacconist.

Cox, John Edward b Battle 19.04.87, s of Edward, contractor. Farmer. Black Horse Road. 1918: Keatley, Saskatoon. e Regina, Saskatchewan 05.01.18. CEF 256660.

Cramp, Walter George b Ewhurst c1896, s of George, waggoner on farm. Cowman. Fullers Farm. m Constance Eldridge, Hastings D1927. Children. Pte RSR. Wounded Jul 1916. By 1918 Cpl in Trench Mortar Bn. MM 1919 (Italy). d Newport Mon 1978.

Crouch, Albert John b Battle C1892, s of William, stockman on farm. Farm labourer. Olive's Farm, Hooe; Walter's Farm Cottages, Ticehurst. e 04.04.12. Pte 5 RSR. To France 24.07.15. Discharged 08.05.18. d Worthing D1939.

Crouch, Charles J b Brightling 1873, s of Stephen, quarryman. Gypsum labourer. Windy Cottage, Netherfield. m Sarah Elizabeth Jennings, Battle 1895. Children. Pte 18 RSR. Wounded at Givenchy 03.03.16, Yser Canal near Ypres, 10.10.17. d Battle A1956.

Crouch, Henry Ernest b Netherfield 04.04.96, s of Charles, gypsum labourer. Farm labourer. Windy Cottage, Netherfield. m Evelyn Jessie Mitchell, Hastings B1917. Pte 240209 RSR, Pte Labour Corps 483396. To France 18.02.15. Wounded. d Hastings C1969. Known locally as 'Kruger'.

Crouch, Samuel Walter b Battle 1864, s of James, millwright. Coachman, groom. Hastings Road; Wroxall Post Office, IOW. m Emily Charlotte

Jenkin, Hastings 25.06.84. Children. e Pall Mall 09.03.01. Imperial Yeomanry, Cpl 11.01.02. South African war. Discharged (medical) at East London 23.07.02. Pte 2 Hampshire Regt. No overseas service. Discharged (medical) 29.05.16. d IOW C1949.

Crowhurst, Ebenezar b Battle D1882, s of John, agricultural labourer. General labourer. Wattles Wish; Watch Oak. m Hannah Vigar, Uckfield C1919. Sgt ASC. To France 18.02.15. S. d C1927 Hastings.

Crowhurst, Harry Alfred b Battle D1886, s of George, carpenter, ex agricultural labourer. Carpenter, ex general labourer. Beech Hill farm; 68 Albion St, Hastings. m Annie E Turk, Battle B1913. Children. Driver RFA. d Braintree B1955.

Crowhurst, Tom b Netherfield C1882, s of Samuel, firewood merchant. Ironmonger's labourer. Netherfield. m Beatrice Ellen Blackman, Netherfield 24.11.09. Child. e Hastings 11.12.15. Gnr 179290 RGA. Wounded nr Amiens in head and lost eye, 06.08.18; invalided to London. Discharged as unfit 18.02.19. d Battle C1939.

Cruttenden, Frederick Edward Samuel b Battle A1885, s of Frederick, plumber. House decorator. 21 Upper Lake; 9 Lower Lake. m Alice May Neller, Brentford 14.04.06. Children. e Battle 26.11.15. Gunner (signals) 156906, RGA. To France 18.11.17. Discharged 12.03.17. d Tonbridge C1959.

Cruttenden, Harold Lancelot b Battle c1886, s of Frederick, plumber. Housepainter. 21 Upper Lake. m Agnes Shaw, Hastings A1919. Pte T2/14019 ASC Motor Transport, GS/96957 Royal Fusiliers. d Battle D1942.

Curry, Frank Raymond b Quetta, India 03.04.1889, s of Thomas, engineer in chief, Frontier Rlys. Farmer, soldier, PT instructor. Breadsell Farm. m Dorothy Holmes Blundell, St Albans C1921. Children. 2 Lt 2 Dublin Fusiliers then Maj 4 Dublin Fusiliers. To France 04.01.1915. Wounded April 1915. India 1916–21 with 1 Garrison Bn Bedfordshire Regt. d Tiverton A1978.

Curry, Frederick Roland Pope b Quetta, India 1894, s of Thomas, engineer in chief, Frontier Rlys. Farmer. Breadsell Farm. m Sybil Woods, Hastings A1917. Children. 2 Lt then Capt then 2 Lt RFA. Maj on retirement. d Fordingbridge 18.06.55.

Curtis, Robert William b Battle 1873, s of Robert, agricultural labourer. Tanner. 20 Lower Lake. m Edith Emily Coleman, Battle A1896. Child. e Battle 12.11.11. Pte 1483, 1 RSR; mobilised 05.08.14. 202035, Pte 4 RSR 01.09.16. Mobilised 05.08.14. No overseas service. Discharged 14.08.17. d Battle A1930.

Davison, Kaye Farquhar Rashell b Battle 1884, s of Rashell, GP. Medic. m Ethel Mary Murray, Bayswater 26.07.17. Capt then Major RAMC. Salonica 1916–18. Westminster Hospital Medical School. MRCS, LRCP. GP at New Malden. d Plymouth D1946.

Dawson, Robert Charles b Battle 12.04.80, s of William, painter. Boy tailor then soldier. 7 Winchester Street, Pimlico. e London 12.10.06. Boy then Pte 4445, Welsh Regiment. S Africa 04.11.99 to 08.08.04. Pte 12911, 2 Grenadier Guards. France 30.01.14 to 12.09.18. Discharged 06.08.19 (defective vision).

Dengate, Arthur Archibald b Crowhurst 1892, s of James, navvy. Under-housekeeper then farm labourer. Telham Farm; 3 Gray Street, Malvern, Victoria. m Caroline A Blackford, Battle, D1913. Child. e Australia 1916. Pte 6495, 14 Australian Infantry; later L/C 59 Bn. Embarked at Melbourne 02.10.16, HMAT *Nestor*. Awarded MSM 03.03.18.Left for Melbourne on SS *Indrapura* 14.10.13. d Melbourne 1959.

Donald, Stuart Burton b Hutton, Cumberland 1879, s of Joseph, land agent. Saffron Walden. m Zine Solonvitz, St Pancras D1915. Capt Kent Cyclist Bn, E Kent Regt (The Buffs). To France 1916. d Hendon 15.03.1937.

Douch, Charles b Battle 1892, s of Charles, tailor (maker). Grocer's assistant. 16 Mount Street. m Winifred Stead, Hastings B1922. Child. e Hastings 15.11.14. Pte 240757 1/5 RSR. To France 10.07.15; to rest camp 09–26.06.17; UK leave 09–22.06.18; then Italy. Demob 05.05.19. S. d Battle C1967.

Douch, Frank b Battle c1890, s of Charles, tailor (maker). Grocer's assistant. 16 Mount Street. m Naomi Taylor, Battle D1918. Pte 14 RSR. d Hastings B1958.

Douch, Frederick b Battle D1894, s of Napthali, basket maker. Basket maker. Mount Street. m Mabel G Broadhurst, Battle C1927. Child. e Hastings 09.09.14. Pte 11 RSR. Acting L/C 06.05.16, L/C 05.07.16. Transferred to 11 Bedfordshire Regt 15.03.17. France 04.03.16–04.07.17. Bullet wound to chest (?) 24.06.17, invalided out. Discharged 18.03.19. d Battle D1974.

Duke, (James Henry) Guy b Battle 05.11.1892, s of James, domestic gardener. Cowman on farm. 3 Ticehurst Cottages, Mount Street; Level Road. m Elizabeth R M Maynard, Battle D1931. Pte 7 RSR then L/C 1914, Cpl 1917, Sgt 1917. MM 1917. In hospital 15.01.18 to discharge as unfit 10.09.18. Orderly at Normanhurst VAD 1918. S. d Battle D1975.

Duke, John b Battle D1891, s of Thomas, domestic gardener. Domestic gardener. 1 High Street. m Ada Hutchinson, Battle A1918. Children. 5 RSR. S. d Battle D1945.

Duke, William John b Battle 1880, s of James, domestic gardener. Blacksmith's striker then scaffolder, bricklayer's labourer. 3 Ticehurst Cottages, Mount Street. e St Leonards 15.07.15. Sapper 534698, 5/2 HC Field Coy RE. To France 02.04.17. Hospital 12.07.17–23.07.17. d Battle B1939.

Edwards, Thomas b Etchingham 1896, grands of Thomas, farm labourer. Farm labourer. Cherry Tree Cottage, Black Horse. m Ethel Mizon D1923. e Hastings 28.08.14. Pte/Gunner/Driver 94021 RFA. To France 01.06.15. Wounded 22.10.18, to UK 27.10.18. Hospital discharge 31.01.19, demob 05.03.19. S. d Hastings A1966.

Eldridge, Albert John b Battle c1897, s of John, general labourer. Farm labourer. Spital Hill. m Gladys Jennings, Battle D1925. Pte ASC Motor Transport. d Battle A1939.

Eldridge, Bertram James P b Battle 23.03.92, s of J R, commercial traveller. Farm labourer. 18 Mount Street. m Ida Bean, Hailsham A1922. Children. Gunner 5 RSR. S. d Uckfield B1988.

Eldridge, Charles Elijah b Battle 1885, s of Elijah, bricklayer. Plumber. 2 Forge Cottages, Sidley then 15 North Road, Bexhill. m Sarah Louise Bristow, Bexhill 06.11.15. Children. e Hastings 07.10.14. Sapper 534163, 84 Field Coy RE. L/C 21.04.15, Sapper 21.11.16. Gunshot wound to right foot 02.07.15. Hospital Aug/Sept 1916. Discharged 28.02.19. d Battle C1944.

Eldridge, Harry b Battle 1878, s of Elijah, bricklayer. Watchman. 24 Camperdown Street, Sidley. m Alice Deeprose, Battle 28.06.02. Child. e Bishop Auckland 06.07.16. Pte 326577, 2/9 Durham Light Infantry. To Salonica 06.11.16. Malaria. Discharged 27.02.19. d Southampton C1962.

Eldridge, Harry Lionel b Battle 20.07.88, s of Edmund, baker. Law clerk. Lower Lake. m Gladys Burke, Cranbrook C1919. e Hastings 03.09.14. Pte 2316, 5 RSR: then L/C 25.02.15–12.07.15, A/Cpl 13.07.15–17.09.15, A/Sgt 18.09.15–03.12.15, Pte 04.12.15, L/Sgt 07.12.15–15.04.16, Sgt 16.04.16. Demob 09.04.19. To duty with PoW repatriaton camp. Dover, 25.11.18. d Brighton A1976.

Eldridge, Percy b Battle C1884, s of Elijah, bricklayer. Bricklayer. 2 Forge Cottages, Sidley. e Hastings 29.02.16. Pte G18343, 11 Royal West Kent Regiment. In France 06.09.16–16.10.16. Gunshot wound to right wrist 07.10.16. Discharged unfit 03.12.17. d Battle 18.09.63.

Eldridge, Robert Victor b Battle 19.05.97, s of James, commercial traveller. Jam factory. 18 Mount Street. m Dora Abbott, Battle, D1942. Pte. To France July 1916. POW from Jan 1918. d Hastings C1977.

Eldridge, William b Catsfield 1876, s of David, general labourer. Stableman. Parks Yard; 54 Western Road, Bexhill. e Hastings 07.07.15. Pte 10595 Army Vet Corps. Mediterranean 17.10.15–19.12.15. Serious rib injuries when fell into ship's coal bunker at Alexandria, 1915, followed by pneumonia. Discharged unfit 12.04.16. d Hastings C1958.

Elliott, Frank C b Battle 1896, s of William, hoopmaker. Butcher. 3 St Mary's Terrace. m Flora J Saunders, Battle C1919. e Battle 18.05.14. Pte 5 RSR then S/441803 ASC. 1918 399 (HC) Coy. Demob 11.07.19. S. d Battle A1941.

Elphick, Archibald b Battle 14.05.90, s of Alfred, insurance agent. Gardener. e Bexhill 30.12.07. Middlesex Regt: Pte 12112, L/C 20.05.13, Bandsman 19.07.13, Cpl 14.10.14, L/Sgt 10.05.15, Sgt 10.06.15. Malta 12.09.13 to 25.09.14. France 05.11.14 to 23.03.19. Discharged 22.04.19. d Hastings A1976.

Fieldwick, Edward William b Battle 16.05.95, s of Edward, bricklayer's labourer. Painter. Crouch Cottage, East Street, Mayfield. e London 07.09.14. Pte 1995 7 East Kent Regt. France 07.10.15–22.10.15. Shot in hand 26.10.15, UK hospital. France 20.04.16–26.07.16. Shot in left thigh at Hardelot 15.07.16, UK hospital. India. Transferred to Pte 134362 RAMC 13.12.17. Discharged (wounds) 12.05.21. Joined 5 RSR Defence Unit as Pte 5RSX151, discharged 02.07.21; service in Sussex. d Tonbridge B1946

Fleet, William Henri b Hawkhurst c1890, s of Edmund, grocer's assistant. Tailor (maker). 8 St Mary's Terrace. 1963: 1 Mount Road New Malden. m Olive G G Fathers, Kingston C1925. e Clapham 05.05.15. Pte 45775, 1/1 Surrey Yeomanry. To Egypt 21.01.16 then Salonica. Considerable illness during service. S. d New Malden 07.04.1963.

Fletcher, Clifford Victor b Battle 12.05.1895, s of Henry, tailor (maker) Mount Street. m Daisy Prodger, Battle, C1925. Children. Gnr TF821486 then 163492 RFA. d Eastbourne C1979.

Forbes, Allan Hall b Hamilton, Ontario 01.04.88. Painter. 194 Locke Road N, Hamilton. 1918: c/o George Peters, Caldbec Hill. m Kate Emily Ponsford, Battle 17.12.18. e Kingston, Ontario 08.11.1914. Pte 59330, 21 Bn Canadian Infantry, Cpl 13.09.16, L/Sgt 30.10.16, Sgt 13.10.17. Hospital at Shorncliffe June 1915. Dangerously ill from gunshot to chest 19.06.18; did not return to front. Demobilised 15.05.19, then to Canada. d Oshawa, Ontario, 07.05.1946.

Foster, John b Battle 1885, s of Alfred, labourer, soldier. 59 Percy Road, Ore. m Florence Annie Shoesmith, Hastings 15.07.12. e Hastings 12.01.03. Pte 7346, 2 RSR; 25.07.16 Pte 450347 Labour Corps. Malta 18.06.04 to 12.09.05. Mobilised 06.08.14. France 08.14 to 22.10.14, 24.03.15 to 01.10.15, 31.08.16 to 21.09.19. Discharged (termination) 11.01.16, recalled. Discharged 27.02.19.

Freaks, Charles b Battle 1869, s of Charles, marine store dealer. General labourer. 5 Weymouth Road, Poole, later Birmingham. m Battle A1889. e Poole 07.09.14. Gunner 16265 RFA. France 24.07.15. Discharged 06.06.20. d Christchurch A1948.

Freeland, Clarence Edward b Whatlington 1884. Grocer's assistant. Windgrove Cottage, Caldbec Hill. m Charlotte Edith Beale, Battle D1909. Children. Gunner 906161 RFA then 225570 RGA. d Hastings C1956.

Freeman, Alfred b Battle 10.01.87, s of Harry, roadman. Seaman. Starr's Green. AB 220830, HMS *Minotaur*. Pacific 1914. Jutland 1916, then remained in North Sea. S. d Battle A1961.

Freeman, Frederick b Battle 1868, s of Joseph. Quarryman. St Mary's Road, Hastings; 6 Kent Road, West Wickham. m Emma Fuller, West Wickham 11.12.97. Children. e Erith 21.01.89, Hastings 08.08.14. Pte 3076, RSR. Transferred to RA 31.08.92. India 12.11.90–02.01.97, S Africa 13.11.99–21.01.02. 1914: 4 HC Bde, RFA, 358718: Gunner, A/Bdr 13.05.16. France 07.09.17–28.11.17. Discharged 07.03.19. d Lewisham C1941.

Freeman, Sidney b Battle 09.03.98, s of Harry, roadman. Starr's Green. Stoker HMS *Grafton*. S. d Battle C1971.

Freeman, William b Battle 2.09.95, s of Harry, roadman. Baker (grocer's). Starr's Green. 1943: 2 Duly's Cottages, Langney. m Ellen Ray, Eastbourne C1923. Stoker K21052, HMS *Maidstone* (submarine depot ship based at Harwich throughout war). S. d Eastbourne 12.06.43 (injured on Home Guard duty 04.06.43).

French, Caleb b Battle, c1896, s of Reuben, agricultural labourer. Labourer. Netherfield. m Isabel E Pellett, Battle A1933. Pte S/26667, Royal Highlanders. Netherfield List says Argyll+S H, Scottish Horse, 9 Black Watch. France.

French, Horace b Battle c1891, s of Herbert, carter. Lower Lake. m Mabel Jones, Ticehurst B1922. e 23.11.14. Pte 2 RSR. Later Labour Corps 635475. d Tonbridge A1961.

French, John Arthur b Battle c1887, s of Reuben, agricultural labourer. Netherfield. 1949: 16 Hoath Hill, Mountfield. m Edith Kate Pennells, Battle D1906. Pte RE. S. d Mountfield 25.04.1949.

Fry, Arthur William Blakerough b Battle 28.12.75, s of William, miller. Carpenter. 10 Pemberton Road, Ashford; Mill House, Smarden; 42 Cornwall Road, Bexhill; Galanogue, Ontario. m Lizzie Minnie Pitchess, Battle C1903. e Galanogue, Ontario 13.03.16. CEF 156 Bn, 639852.

Fuller, Charlie b Battle, c1900, s of Thomas, gypsum mine worker. Farm worker. Darwell Hill, Netherfield. AB HMS *Minotaur.*

Fuller, Frank William b Warbleton 13.02.88, s of Frank, stoker, jam factory. Assistant, jam factory; later nightwatchman. Newbery's Yard. m Hilda Hunt, Hastings D1930. AB RN 230470, Torpedo Bn, HMS *Crane*, before 1905. S. d Battle A1943.

Fuller, Ernest Edward b Netherfield 01.04.97, s of Stephen, gypsum miner. Netherfield. m Matilda C A Stonestreet, Battle D1926. Children. Pte 19 Middlesex. Wounded near Ypres 08.17. d Hastings C1978.

Fuller, Eric Gilbert b Netherfield B1882, s of William, stoker at mine. Vanman, labourer. e Hastings 05.02.02. Pte 48622 then Cpl 6 Dragoon Guards. India. Attested 10.11.14. Pte 2678 RSR. Discharged 09.06.16.

Fuller, Henry Albert b Netherfield 27.12.89, s of Stephen, gypsum miner. Gypsum miner. Soan's Cottages, Netherfield. m Mary Ellen Hodgskin, Battle A1926. Child. e Hastings 12.02.16. Gnr 132399 RFA. France 06.10.16–19.08.17. Gunshot wound to left hand nr Ypres 16.08.17, to UK; in hospital to 20.03.18. Discharged 23.03.19. d Hastings A1972.

Fuller, Stephen F b Netherfield c1886, s of Stephen, gypsum miner. Assistant engine driver, mine. Netherfield. m Annie Ballard, Battle C1911. Children. Pte 6 Duke of Cornwall's Light Inf. Wounded nr Ypres 22.08.17. Disch 08.18. d Battle B1944.

Fuller, Victor b Netherfield c1892. Pte 12278, 16 Lancers. To France 14.09.14. Discharged 04.05.16.

Fuller, William Everest b Battle C1898, s of Frank, private coachman. 138a St James's Street, Liverpool; 35 Enid Street, Liverpool. m Ethel Murdoch, Liverpool C1923. Pte King's Liverpool Regt. MM 1919, France. d Enfield

B1968.

Gilbert, Harry Cecil b Battle 30.06.93, s of Charles, smart hoopmaker. Labourer, hoopmaking. Netherfield. Pte 14 RSR. d Battle C1972.

Gilbert, Thomas W b Battle 1887, s of Charles, smart hoopmaker. Grocer's assistant. Netherfield. Pte Royal Fusiliers.

Gilbert, William b Battle 1889, s of Charles, smart hoopmaker. Netherfield. Pte AOC.

Goldie-Taubman, Reginald b Brighton 1888, s of Alexander. Farmer. Blackfriars Farm. m Jane C Peirce, Battle D1912. Child. Pte 205552, Tank Corps. d Horsham B1952.

Goodsell, Henry b Netherfield, 1884, s of Samuel, farmer, wood merchant. Working on farm. Netherfield Road, Netherfield. 1963: Shooting Box, Netherfield. m Mary Smale, Hastings D1924. Child. e 20.05.16. Pte ASC 428278. MM 1919, France. Discharged 12.11.19. d Hastings 17.03.63.

Gower, Charles b Battle c1879, s of Harry, tanner/engine driver. Butcher's assistant. Watch Oak. m Elizabeth Susan Peacock, Sevenoaks, C1910. Children. d Sevenoaks 13.06.49.

Gower, Frank b Battle 26.06.82, s of Harry, tanner/engine driver. House painter. Watch Oak; 2 Florence Cottages. m Esther Crowhurst, Battle D1909. Children. RN F19143. d Battle C1932.

Gower, Percy b Battle 08.09.92, s of Harry, tanner/engine driver. Baker's clerk. Watch Oak; Black Horse Road. m Ada Oliver, Battle May 1915. d Weymouth Aug 1985.

Gower, William J b Battle c1878, s of Harry, tanner/engine driver. Grocer. Watch Oak; 118 Wood Vale, Forest Hill. m Rosa Annie Olney, Hertford 1907. Child. d Lewisham D1967.

Green, Frank Evelyn Millington b Guildford 25.10.1893, s of Arthur, watchmaker. Jeweller. 169 High Street, Clapham; 89 Hambalt Road, Clapham. e Battle 31.08.14. L/C G2080, 2 RSR. Seriously wounded Givenchy 27.01.15. At home 27.02.15 to 20.03.16. Disch as physically unfit 20.03.16. d Brent D1971.

Gurr, Edwin Charles b Battle c1891, s of Henry, draper's porter. Hairdresser. 2 Burgess Cottages, High Street. m Amy Levett, Battle A1918. L/C 5 RSR G/2148. To France 24.07.15. Demob 11.06.19. Says Pte on medals card. S. d Andover D1960.

Haines, A Netherfield. e 14.08.15. Sapper 1 HC RE.

Hannay, Kenneth b Ulverston c1889, s of George, iron master. Co director [1933]. St Mary's Farm. 26 Bedford Place WC. m Bessie Tompsett, Tonbridge B1919. Children. Cpl 109707 RGA. Commissioned 2 Lt 18.08.18. To North Russia 12.07.19. Wounded report 08.09.17. d Harrow Weald 06.05.42.

Harris, Albert b Battle 1893, s of Thomas, gypsum worker. Agricultural labourer. Netherfield; Watch Oak.. Sapper RE.

Harris, Harold b Battle 1899, s of Harry, gypsum worker. Mineshaft, Mountfield. Pte RASC MT, 39 Siege Battery.

Harris, James b Battle 1882, s of Thomas, gypsum worker. Bavin maker. Netherfield. Cpl 13 RSR. Wounded 10.03.18 nr Heudicourt.

Harris, Thomas b Battle 1890, s of Thomas, gypsum worker. Netherfield. Pte 8 RSR. Wounded at Thiepval. d Battle A1969.

Harris, William b B1892, s of Henry. Policeman. 1 St Mary's Terrace then 2 Park Lane. e Lewes 18.11.15. L/C P2709, Military Mounted Police. France 14.02.16, Italy 07.11.17. Discharged 03.05.19.

Hawkins, Herbert James b Mar 1900. Groom, gardener. Battle Hill. e Brighton 05.04.18. Pte 136812, 51 Royal Fusiliers. Discharged physically unfit (TB) 25.07.18. No overseas service.

Hayler, George Arthur Charles b Battle 04.05.97, s of Alfred, cowman on farm. Hollington. m Emma Eldridge, C1925. Pte Rifleman GS/42756 Royal Fusiliers. d Bromley A1972.

Hesmer, John b Hastings 1889. Cowman on farm. 1 Liberty Hall Cottages. Later Chichester. m Henrietta Crouch, Hastings 25.10.12. Children. e Chichester. Pte 3 RSR then 2 RSR 01.05.15 then 3 RSR 08.11.15. Previous service as territorial with 5 RSR. Discharged unfit 18.01.16. d Ashford B1967.

Hewett, L Pte Hussars. S.

Hibbs, Henry George b Poole 1874, s of Edward, gardener etc. Farmer. Park Dale Farm. 1952: Hawthorn, London Road, Addington, West Malling. e Maidstone 27.08.14. 1053 W Kent Regt: Cpl 26.09.14, L/Sgt 01.10.14. To France. MM (Somme). Transferred 11.12.16 as Pte 270665 to 10 East Kent Regt. Serbian Silver Medal. d Dartford 20.04.1952.

Hickmott, Richard b Battle C1884. Labourer. 1943: 258 Spring Road, Ipswich. m Gertrude Florence Last, Ipswich 04.07.09. Children. Driver RH/RFA 34916, to reserve 15.10.07. Recalled 06.08.14, Gunner; France 14.09.14 to 04.10.17. Wounded Sept 1917 (gsw hip). Discharged 18.02.19. d Ipswich 22.11.43.

Highwood, Frank b Battle 11.12.95, s of James, assurance agent. Telegraph messenger. 11 St Mary's Terrace. m Annie Santer, Battle C1921. Child. Pte F7979, RNAS. S.

Highwood, Harold b Battle 1900, s of James, assurance agent. Gardener. 11 St Mary's Terrace; 6 St Mary's Villas. m Florence Dean, Battle A1925. Children. e Brighton 05.04.18. Pte 35190, RAVC. Discharged 29.08.19. d Croydon A1968.

Hoad, Thomas Henry b Hastings c1893, s of John Hoad, carman's carter. Fruit gardener. Spital Hill. m Ellen Swabey, Battle D1917. Child. Cpl 5 RSR. Wounded Jul 1916. S d Hastings C1961.

Hobday, Godfrey b Ashburnham c1896, s of Henry, plaster works labourer. Farm labourer. 1 Beechwood Cottages, Netherfield Lane. e 12.09.14. L/C then A/Sgt 8076, 2 RSR then attached King's African Rifles. MM then DCM 1919.

Hobday, Harold b Ashburnham 1894, s of Henry, plaster works labourer. Farm labourer. 1 Beechwood Cottages, Netherfield Lane. m Adelaide E

Braban, Battle C1919. Child. e Hastings 12.02.16. Pte G/15826, 11 RSR. France 07.09.16–03.11.16. Wounded 21.10.16. Discharged 22.05.17.

Hobday, Robert French b Ashburnham 06.12.91, s of Henry, plaster works labourer. Gypsum labourer. 1 Beechwood Cottages, Netherfield Lane. Pte G/4073, RSR. France 12.08.15. d Battle D1975.

Holland, Alfred Joshua Methuen b Netherfield 28.08.00, s of William, domestic gardener. Sea View, Netherfield. m Annie Paddon, Battle D1920. Children. e Brighton 07.09.18. Pte 62467, 20 KRRC. Pleurisy July 1919, hospital October 1919. Discharged 31.03.20. In occupied Cologne. Re-enlisted at Battle 15.04.21; A/LCpl. Discharged 05.07.21. d Hereford Jan 1996.

Holland, Charles b Netherfield 28.01.72, s of Walter, agricultural labourer. Agricultural labourer. Netherfield; Ivyland Green. Pte 17 Middlesex Regt. Wounded at Messines Ridge. [but identity unclear: see next entry]. d 04.03.55.

Holland, Charles b Netherfield 1876, s of James, railway carter. Netherfield Orderly, 2 British Red Cross Hospital, Rouen. Cpl May 1918. [but identity unclear: see preceding entry]

Holland, Ernest William b Netherfield c1885, s of William, domestic gardener. Netherfield. 1948: 29 Church Road, Privett, Alton. Pte ASC MT. In training 1917. d Petersfield 12.02.1948.

Holland, Harry b Netherfield 03.05.78, s of James Holland. Labourer. Netherfield. m Annie Maria Saunders, Battle D1911. Child. Pte SD/5159, 11 RSR. d Battle 1933.

Holland, Herbert Augustus b Netherfield c1892, s of William, domestic gardener. Domestic gardener. Netherfield. 1962: Seaview, Netherfield. m Margaret Hislop, Battle B1931. Pte RSR. d Battle 26.09.62.

Holland, Stephen Claude b Netherfield c1891, s of William, domestic gardener. Police constable (London). Motor driver (domestic). Netherfield Pte M2/074036, ASC MT. Wounded 19.09.17, to hospital in Birmingham. d Bristol A1930.

Holland, Walter b Battle A1884, s of Josh, butcher. Slaughterman, butcher. 17 Upper Lake. 1919: 22 Sabine Road, Brixton. m Ethel Louise Harris, Streatham 10.11.12. Child. e St Leonards 17.05.16. Gunner 906298, 3/2 HC Bde RFA. India 1916, Mesopotamia 1917, Egypt 1918, home 19.06.18. Discharged 23.08.19.

Hollands, Tom b Battle c1894, s of Tom Hollands, gypsum miner. General labourer. Netherfield Road. Pte 11 RSR. Wounded at Trônes Wood, 15.08.16. Discharged July 1918. S.

Hollands, Walter James b Netherfield 22.04.1896, s of Tom, gypsum miner. Footman. Fir Tree House, Netherfield. m Ellen D Draper, Battle D1921. e Hastings 29.04.15. Pte 3822, 11 RSR; to 239348 Labour Corps, 21.07.17. Gunshot wounds in left arm and buttock 30.06.16. Discharged as medically unfit 22.11.17. d Bromley A1972.

Honeysett, Walter Thomas b Brightling 1886, s of George Honeysett, farmer. Carter on farm. Staceys, Dallington; The Laurels, Netherfield. m Nellie Beatrice Bishopp, Reigate B1908. Children. Pte 5 Royal W Kent. d Battle 03.10.58.

Honeysett, Walter b Brightling B1875, s of William, agricultural labourer. Baker's vanman. Blackhorse Road; 200 Old Lane, Hollington. m Elizabeth Hutchinson, Sedlescombe 26.12.03. Children. e Hastings 25.06.18. Pte 154585 RAMC. Discharged 28.08.19. d Battle A1953.

Hook, Cecil b Battle 1892, s of Henry, domestic coachman. Wattles Wish. m Edith M Crowhurst, Battle, B1919. Driver ASC. Egypt, Salonica. d Battle C1963.

Hopkins, Neville Douglas b Battle C1899, s of Russell, ostler. Kenwards Yard. e Hastings 11.09.15. Pte 14 RSR. To France 20.09.15. Discharged (no longer physically fit) 04.07.16. S. d Battle A1936.

Hopkins, Russell John b Battle c1895, s of Russell. Ostler. Kenward's Yard. 1965: 10 Lincoln Avenue, Whitton, Twickenham. m Ethel M Histon, Hastings A1921. Child. e 09.09.14. Lichfield 17.04.17. Pte 1056, 12 RSR then Sgt. Appears to have been 60610 2 S Staffs Regt 1917, with temp trsfr to 12 Royal Irish Rifles. Temp Sgt 18.04.20, Sgt 01.05.20, discharged 04.06.20. MM 21.11.17. S. d Caterham 22.09.65.

Hutchison, Charles Thomas b B1878. Police constable. Ladysmith Cottage, Western Road, Jarvis Brook. m Ada J Wickham, Uckfield 1910. Children. e 1917. Resigned from police to join up 16.05.17; returned to police 29.01.19. d Hastings B1948.

Hyland, Reginald Ernest b Battle c1894, s of Charles, wheelwright. Mount Street. 1966: 170 Old Tovil Road, Maidstone. m Jessie Florence Short, Maidstone B1924. Children. Pte 90 Bn RFA. S d Maidstone 28.10.66.

Hyland, Victor Stuart b Battle 1899, s of Charles, wheelwright. Mount Street. m Ethel F Baker, Maidstone D1923. Gunner 200642, RGA. d Hastings D1925.

Jenner, Alexander Robert b Battle 05.03.88, s of Thomas, agricultural labourer. Netherfield. 19 Mount Street. m Emily Beatrice Chacksfield, Battle C1913. Child. e Hastings 07.11.14. L/C 20272, 5 RSR. Discharged 18.02.15 (not likely to become an efficient soldier). d Battle B1975.

Jenner, Benjamin James b Netherfield C1880, s of Samuel, general labourer. Gypsum miner Netherfield Hill. 4 Spray's Cottage, Netherfield Hill. m Emma Louisa Smale, Battle 02.06.06. Children. e Hastings 03.06.16. Pte G/26929, 1 Royal W Surrey; to 29 Middlesex 17.11.16; to 158795 Labour Corps 18.05.17; to T/419874 ASC 23.03.18. Discharged 01.03.19. No overseas service. d Battle 20.07.50.

Jenner, Charles Herbert b Battle c1886, s of Charles, agricultural labourer. 5 Council Cottages, Netherfield Hill. Pte 5 RSR. S. d Hastings 28.05.48..

Jenner, Percy Augustus b Netherfield 21.06.91, s of William, farm labourer. Sawyer. Netherfield. m Florence Holland, Battle D1920. Children. e Gillingham 21.01.15. Sapper 6 Coy Kent RE, L/C 23.03.17. No overseas service. Discharged (medical) 04.03.19. d Hastings A1950.

Jenner, Walter Robert b Battle A1878, s of Tom, agricultural labourer. Baker. 12 Gladstone Terrace, Hastings. Weston Road, St Leonards. e St Leonards 07.04.08. Volunteer Cinque Ports 09.03.97 to 20.12.01; 29.01.06 to 31.03.08. 299 HC RFA: Gunner, Bombardier 21.11.12. Mobilised 05.08.14. France 21.12.14 to 24.02.15. Termination of duty 24.04.16. Hospital: effects of cold 22.02.15. d Reading C1969.

Jennings, Arthur E b Netherfield 1882, s of Owen, gypsum miner. Blacksmith. Council Cottages, Netherfield. m Grace Taylor, Battle B1909. Children. Pte R Irish Rifles, R Irish Fusiliers 1918. d Battle C1967.

Jennings, Reginald b Netherfield 1896, s of William, gypsum miner. Farm worker. Netherfield; 1940: Wattles Wish. m Gertrude Grace Ollive, Battle B1925. Driver 12 RSR, 16 Transport Section, Sussex Yeomanry. d Hastings 26.05.40.

Jennings, William J b Battle C1870, s of Owen, agricultural labourer. Miner. Council Cottages, Netherfield. m Kate Fellowes, Battle D1912. e Sandwich 01.02.17. Gunner 234029 RE. France; hospital 17.09.–12.10.17. To England 29.10.17. Discharged (physically unfit) 24.08.18. d Battle C1947.

Jesson, Clement Victor b Battle B1875, s of Frederick, army pensioner. Grocer's assistant then labourer. 1891: 5 St George's Road, Hastings. e 11.01.94. Pte RSR; served on Malta, in India (Tirah campaign 1897–98), Crete. Discharged at own request 16.03.12. Mobilised 09.09.14. Pte 11 then 14 RSR; transferred to Royal West Surrey Regt 12.09.16, to 57840 Labour Corps 09.05.17. Discharged 27.03.19. d Chelsea A1935.

Jones, Frederick b Playden 25.04.85, s of William, coachsmith. Housepainter. Virgins Croft; 44 Lower Lake. m Alice Emily Curtis, Battle D1908. Children. Sapper RE. Lost leg in war. S. d Battle C1973.

Kane, Frank L b Battle c1885, s of Frank, brewer's clerk. Ironmonger's assistant. Florence Cottages, Mount Street; 39 High Street. Pte 6 Bn E Kent Regt. Wounded St Julien May 1915. S d Battle D1965.

Keable, Louis John b Ticehurst B1882. Confectioner's carman. 9 Mount Street. m Lilian Playford, Battle C1909. Child. Pte 6551 East Kent Regt, later 120903 Labour Corps. To France 07.09.14, also Egypt, Salonica. Shrapnel wound in thigh, home leave 05.12.14. d Chelsea D1964.

Kenward, Jesse b Ore A1886, s of Jesse Kenward, mine store dealer. Bricklayer's labourer. Whatlington Road; London Road. 1963: 3 Meadowside Cottages, Sedlescombe. m Catherine Ellen Winchester, Hastings A1920. Children. e Hastings 19.08.14. Pte 2255, 5 Bn RSR, 47830, 389th Labour Corps. To France 14.02.15–04.10.17 (gunshot wounds in thigh that day). 1915 German measles. Flu 10.04.15. Hospital 1919. Discharged 01.03.19. 60% disabled – bronchitis, debility. d Hastings 23.12.63.

Kiley, John Patrick b Haggerston 17.03.84, s of John, plasterer. Gypsum works labourer then miller. 1 or 2 Beechwood Cottages, Netherfield Road. m Lilian Backshall, Hastings C1913. Children. e 14.12.15. Pte G/33282, 4 Middlesex. Wounded in France 11.04.17. Discharged 21.06.18. d Battle

15.02.71.

Lambert, Reginald Everitt b Battle D1882, s of Edward, engineer and landowner. Telham Court. m Evelyn Dick-Cunyngham, St George's Hanover Square July 1907. Children. Lt RHA later Captain. Educated at Harrow and Trinity, Cambridge. Cricketer. d Shaftesbury 23.01.1968.

Langridge, James Alexander b Polegate D1892, s of Noah, wheelwright. Fuller's Farm. m Mary E Parks, Hailsham 02.10.11. Children. e Battle 07.03.10. Pte, drummer. 1147, 5 RSR. L/C 05.08.14; reverted to Pte at own request 11.09.14. L/c 09.01.15. A/Cpl 08.04.15. Sgt 18.09.15. France 12.11.15–17.12.15. To 286007 Labour Corps 30.01.18. To 21088, 12 Bedfords Regt 16.04.18. Demobilised 04.07.19: shell shock, debility. Re-enlisted Hastings 29.08.19: S/10402 Pte RAOC, later A/L/C, reverted to Pte 18.09.20. Egypt 27.10.19. Discharged 18.10.20. d Hastings A1955.

Larkin, Charles Amos b Battle D1862. Soldier. 1956: Vendome, Colvill Avenue, Shoreham by Sea. m Edith Minnie Ward, Great Yarmouth 03.08.90. Child. e Canterbury 06.03.82. Gunner 20509 RA; Bdr 15.07.85; Cpl 15.04.87; Sgt 02.06.87; Sgt Maj 01.03.00. Ceylon 19.12.83–17.12.85; Hong Kong 19.12.85–28.02.89. Long service and Good Conduct medal. Discharged 05.03.07 because of reduction in establishment. Recalled 05.08.14. Discharged due to age 20.01.19. d Shoreham 15.01.56.

Lavington, George b Battle c1886, s of George, publican. Black Horse. m Gertrude A Briggs, C1918.Pte then Sgt ASC motor transport. Wounded 11.04.17, in hosp in France May 1917. Meritorious Service Medal June 1919. S d Petersfield D1957.

Lee, Walter Samuel b Battle D1870. Labourer; later tube worker. m Elizabeth Lambrick, Swansea 22.10.08. e Swansea 11.09.14. Pte Royal W Kent, to Essex Regt 31.07.15, attached Garrison Bn Suffolk Regt 26.09.16. France 09.12.14–21.02.15. India 28.04.15–29.8.16; invalided out. Discharged no longer physically fit 29.06.17. d Swansea B1943.

Levitt, Ernest Ralph b Icklesham 01.01.86, s of John, domestic gardener. Seaman. AB RN 213891. S d Hastings C1961.

Ling, George Richard b Battle 1891, s of George, hotel manager. Motor mechanic. Abbey Hotel. 1959: 56 Hugh Road, Stoke, Coventry. m Mabel Evelyn Wood, Coventry D1917. Child. e Hastings 04.12.16. Driver M/273784, ASC MT. Physically unfit for service and discharged 19.02.18. d Coventry 26.04.59.

Longley, Charles W b Battle c1896, s of William, hairdresser. 58 High Street, 3 Mount Street. m Cissy D Douch, Battle A1921. Children. L/C 5 Bn RSR. S. d Hastings C1964.

Lovell, William Henry b Netherfield 1883, s of William, gypsum miner (above ground). Agricultural labourer. Darwell Hill. 1965: 1 Barley Grattens, Netherfield. m Edith Rose Parfitt, Reigate A1925. Children. e Hastings 22.02.16. Gunner 130275, RH+RFA. France 23.07.17; GS wound to left leg 03.08.17. Back to France 14.08.18; GS wound to left arm 13.10.18. Discharged 28.01.19. d Hastings 10.05.65.

Lowson, George b Forfar 1875. Domestic gardener. Netherfield Court Lodge. m Elizabeth 1903. Child. Pte 8 RSR. India.

Luck, John b Baldslow 1886, s of George, gamekeeper. Metal machinist. 4 Lower Lake. m Amelia Hardy, Chelsea A1916. Children. e Uxbridge 27.01.16. Pte 7 RSR. Attacks of trench fever requiring home treatment. Wounded in foot when cleaning rifle at Bouzincourt 23.06.18; toe amputated. Discharged unfit 28.02.19. d Lambeth C1963.

Lusted, Alfred Frank b Battle B1873. Coal merchant's manager, army pensioner. 1911: barracks at Chichester; 1918: 100 Western Road, Lewes. m Annie Towner, Hastings B1904. e Chichester 04.03.91, 01.09.14. Volunteer to 1891 then Pte 3665, 2 RSR, Colour Sgt 04.09, SgtMaj 07.09.14, WO Class 1 29.01.15, CSM 26.07.16. Ireland 1891, India 1893–28.01.02, Malta 13.10.04–03.04.05, Ireland 1911. France 1918. DCM 1918. Discharged (termination of service) 18.08.18. d Lewes D1936.

McQuillan, Archibald Arthur John b Battle c1890, s of James, surveyor etc UDC. Starr's Green; 1958: 37 Ditton Road, Surbiton. m Mabel Lavinia Phillips, Battle B1917. e 14.10.14. Pte 51474 later Actg Cpl 9 Bde RFA. S d Surbiton 29.05.1958.

McQuillan, Reginald George b Battle 09.08.1896, s of James, surveyor etc UDC. Fitter's mate. Starr's Green. m Mabel Russell, Hampstead A1929. Children. e Wimbledon 14.06.17. Pte 394571, Labour Corps. No sign of overseas service. Selected for retention 1919. Discharged 31.01.1920: polio, 30% disability. d Stratford on Avon B1983

McQuillan, William James b Battle 1885, s of James, surveyor etc UDC. Auctioneer. Starr's Green. 1915: 8 St Peter's Street, Winchester. 1917: May Cottages, Lane Street, Reading. 1940: 11 Kingsgate Street, Winchester. m Emily Dart, Sidcup 02.09.09. e Winchester 02.12.15. Pte. Earlier 3 yrs Royal West Surrey. Discharged (asthma) 22.03.17.

Maplesden, George James b Battle 1892, s of James, housepainter. Housepainter. Mount Street. 1911 boarder in Kenward's Yard (Smale). m Edith A Dengate, Hastings D1916. Child. Pte 1814, 5 RSR then 367352 Northumberland Fusiliers. To France 18.02.15. S d Hastings A1941.

Marchant, Edward Henry James b Catsfield 1876, s of Henry, farm labourer. Mount Street. Pte 315402, RSR, 041045 AOC. To France 25.07.15. d Hastings C1955.

Marchant, Frederick William b Catsfield 1882. Gardener. 1917: 8 Church Street, Old Town, Bexhill. 1919: Two Houses, Haddocks Hill, Bexhill. m Edith Vinall, Reigate 04.11.11. Children. e Hastings 14.12.17. Pte 12441 RSR (Labour Coy).; in hospital 7 weeks; discharged 24.07.16. Re-enlisted 139021 Labour Corps.

Marchant, Robert b Catsfield, 23.11.99, s of James, brickmaker. Pit prop sawyer. Starrs Green. e Brighton 07.09.17. Pte 14345 51 Bn Royal West Surrey. Wounded in shoulder 17.10.18; Sefton Park Hospital 23.10.18–13.11.18. Discharged 24.01.19. d Hastings B1975.

Marchant, John Thomas b Battle 1888, s of Henry, general labourer. General labourer. 3 Council Cottages, Netherfield Road. m Mary Breeds, Battle C1910. Children. Pte 21240, 2 Hants then 52843 Devonshire then 139021 Labour Corps (agric). d Hastings C1961.

Marchant, Victor George b Battle c1898, s of Edward, coal carman. Parks Yard. Pte 2364 RSR then 446187 Labour Corps. To France 18.02.15. Wounded in leg Aug 1916. d Bexhill 11.11.65.

Marchant, William b Battle 1889, s of Henry, general labourer. General labourer. Netherfield Road. e Hastings 28.08.14. RFA 94020. Discharged 29.09.14 as not likely to become an efficient soldier. S.

Martin, Frederick Charles b Battle 05.1890, s of Charles , cowman on farm. Grocer's van man. Tollgates. d Hastings D1969.

Martin, Peter b Burwash Common c1895, s of Jesse, farmer. Farm worker. Beech Farm. NZ Infantry. S.

Martin, Wilfred b Heathfield 26.07.98, s of Jesse, farmer. Beech Farm. 5 RSR. S. d Hastings C1983.

Matthews, Frederick Arthur b Eastbourne c1878, s of James, brickmaker. House furnisher. 8 High Street. m Eva Nellie Clarke, St Pancras D1900. Child. Retd from Egypt Feb 1919; there since Aug 1917. d Hastings A1947.

Mepham, Albert b Battle A1884, s of Alfred, general labourer. Plate layer. Battle Hill. 1959: 236 Holtye Road, East Grinstead. m Margaret Ellen Bell, Battle 04.04.01. e Hastings 07.01.02 and 04.04.14. Pte 1798, 5 RSR. Malta 18.06.04–05.01.06. India 06.01.06–20.01.10. Malaria. Discharged (termination) 06.01.14. Enlisted RSR 1914; discharged as not likely to become efficient soldier 13.10.14. d East Grinstead 22.02.59.

Mepham, Frederick J b Battle 11.01.1879, s of James, milkman's labourer. UDC labourer. The Warren, Mount Street. Netherfield. m Elizabeth Eldridge, Battle C1900. Children. e Hastings 10.12.15. Pte S71790, 1 Middlesex. Then Labour Corps. To France 25.10.16–26.11.17. On re-enlistment, Pte 205890 RAMC (home service). Final discharge 28.08.20.

Mepham, George b Netherfield 23.09.72, s of Moses, agricultural labourer. Labourer. 1881: Ivy House Lane, Hastings. 1939: 253 Harold Road, Hastings. m Nellie Louise Knight, Hastings D1916. Children. e Hastings 28.01.90 and 25.04.16. Pte 3372, 4 RSR then 31.05.93 Gnr 97804 RFA. Ireland 1891; India 28.11.91–12.12.96; S Africa 15.05.97–30.12.00. Discharged as physically unfit 14.08.01. Pte 16935, AVC 1916. Discharged as physically unfit 20.11.16. d Hastings 24.04.39.

Mepham, George Lewis b Battle 13.06.80, s of Lewis, jam packer. Jam packer. Newbery's Court; 9 Western Avenue; Whatlington Road. m Bertha M Geer, Hastings A1900. Children. e St Leonards 06.01.15. Driver 534352 RE 2 HC (R) Field Coy. To France 11.05.18–24.08.18. Trsfr to training depots 02.04.18. 15.8.18 heart problem: hospital in Boulogne, then Chelmsford. Disch as physically unfit 31.01.19. General debility. Disability 70%. S. d Battle 28.11.1930.

Mepham, James b Battle 1878, s of Alfred, agricultural labourer. General labourer. Netherfield Road. m Mabel Wrenn, Battle D1914. Children. Pte

12 RSR. S. d Battle A1933.

Mepham, Thomas Frederick b Battle 1875, s of Alfred, agricultural labourer. Soldier, labourer. Marley Lane. 1953: 32 Zealand Road, Bow, E. m Alice Clara Wood, Poplar A1901. e Dover 22.10.97. Gunner 23414 RGA. India 08.10.01–15.04.09, 09.10.11–20.12.15. Mesopotamia 21.12,15–14.04.18. Egypt 06.05.18–10.02.19. Disch 04.04.19. Reenlisted as Pte 205891 RAMC. Discharged 29.08.20. S. d Bethnal Green 13.08.53.

Meppem, Samuel Edgar b Ewhurst 1884, s of Ormond, woodman. Domestic coachman. Maresfield; 1 King's Parade, Lower Coombe Road, Croydon. m Albertine Isabel Burton, Godstone C1908. Children. Pte Army Vet Corps. Invalided out. S. d Hastings A1972.

Mercer, George b Battle 21.12.92, s of William, gamekeeper. Farmer. Netherfield Place Farm. e Canada 02.09.14. Pte 8573, 2 Canadian Infantry. Previously four years with Durham Regiment.

Mercer, Thomas b Netherfield A1892, s of William, gamekeeper. Gamekeeper. Netherfield Place Farm. e 27.02.11. Gnr 24722, RGA; L/Bdr 17.02.18. Singapore (mutineers Feb/Mch 1915), France 02.10.15–07.04.18. GSW to thigh ?19.03.18. Discharged no longer fit 03.11.19.

Metcalf, Alfred Douglas b Battle 15.04.91, s of Henry, domestic gardener. Gardener. Watch Oak; 23 Perth Road, St Leonards. m Lilian A Dalmon, Battle C1917. Children. Pte AA Section. S. d Petersfield C1972.

Metcalf, Percy George b Battle 03.11.93, s of Henry, domestic gardener. Journeyman baker. Watch Oak; Mount Street. m Bertha Pook, Battle C1917. Children. Pte L8299, 5 Lancers. To France 18.10.15. S. d Eastbourne D1969.

Mewett, Albert b Battle D1896, s of Arthur Mewett, domestic gardener. Gardener, Powdermill. Park Dale. m Ethel M Spurling, Hastings D1926. Child. Pte G/19663, 8 Bn RSR (Pioneers). Wounded 29.07.16. S? d Ipswich C1957.

Mewett, Arthur b Willingdon B1891, s of Arthur, domestic gardener. Chauffeur. 114 Langney Road, Eastbourne. m Ada Brettell, Battle C1915. Children. S? d Eastbourne 14.12.58.

Mewett, George b Battle 1894, s of Arthur, domestic gardener. Sailor. 1911: RN Barracks, Chatham. m Alice Edwards, Eastbourne C1920. Child. RAMC.

Morris, Frederick Charles b Battle 07.02.00, s of George, laundryman. Whatlington Road. AB RN F53652. S. d Battle C1961.

Morris, George b Battle D1870, s of Edward. Labourer. 1916: Shooter's Hill, Greenwich. e Hastings 20.10.91. Gunner 87047, RA. France 23.08.15–28.06.16. Discharged 19.10.16.

Morris, Griffith John b Battle 22.04.91, s of Samuel, evangelist. Little Park Farm. 1915: 31 Wetheril Street, Leichhardt, Sydney. e Australia 27.10.15. Gunner 11587, 2 Div Ammunition Column. Embarked RMS *Osterley* 15.01.16. Wounded 31.07.16 and July 1917. Disch 11.01.18. d with Canadian forces 24.12.1943.

Morris, Harold Frederick b Battle c1894, s of James, horse feeder for miller/ baker. Milk cart driver. Hastings Road (Hemingfold). 1956: 9 Offa Road, Ore. m Emily Feist, Hastings B1920. Children. Pte RSR. S. d Hastings 24.01.56.

Moulton, Havelock Adrian b St Leonards B1891, s of George, manager, wine merchant. Clerk. 1914: Church House. Pte 1777, 5 RSR. Then 240206, L/11655, 6391042 RSR. d Croydon B1923.

Nash, John b Battle c1888, s of George, builder's labourer. Tailor's apprentice. 7 Upper Lake. Pte ASC. S.

Neeves, Edmund James b Peasmarsh B1875, s of John, agricultural labourer. Baker's vanman. Blackhorse Road. 1919: 29 Manor Road, Hastings. m Margaret Mona Horne, Hastings 28.10.07. e Hastings 25.10.15. Pte 145006, ASC. France 06.05.17–24.02.18. Discharged 01.10.19. d Hastings D1943.

Newbery, Benjamin b Battle 08.12.90, s of George, confectioner. Chartered accountant. 71 High Street. m Florence M Davies, Brentford C1918. e 25.09.16. Pte G14341 RSR; transferred to Pte 8819 Army Pay Corps 29.06.16. On Reserve 28.09.17, discharged 14.12.18 (asthma etc). d Hastings Dec 1984

Newman, William J P b Hastings C1876, s of William, gardener. Butcher's assistant. In a shed, Uckham Farm. Pte ASC. S. d Battle B1927.

Noakes, Walter b Battle C1893, s of Frank, farm labourer. Seaman. 1893: Pepper-in-Eye. Later, Bardoc, Western Australia. m Gladys Victoria Martin, Bermondsey A1918. Child. e 03.07.15. Pte 51 Aust Infantry. MM for gallantry 1916. d Claremont, WA, 23.07.69.

Notley, Ralph Ambrose b Egham C1884, s of Richard, surveyor. Fruit farmer. The Whitelands; Black Firs. 1964: The Old Place Manor, Pulborough. m Phyllis E Jenkins, Windsor B1923. Children. 2 Lt then Lt, RFA. To India 29.05.17. d Worthing 23.04.64.

Oliver, Arthur b Battle 14.08.1892, s of Harry, carter (tannery). Groom (domestic). 4 Clive Villas; New Cottage, Battle Hill. Pte RE. S. d Hastings C1973.

Oliver, Charles Herbert b Burwash 1875. Assistant grocer. Sunnyside, Dallington. m Emily Brook, Ticehurst D1898. Children. Pte 5 East Kent Regt. S. d Hastings D1939.

Oliver, Frank b Battle 05.02.1899, s of Joseph, labourer. 9 Chapel Cottages. m Winifred Jalfron, Battle B1929. Children. Gunner RGA. S. d Battle D1975.

Oliver, Frederick Joseph b Battle 1893, s of Joseph, labourer. Grocer's assistant, then tanner. New Cottages, Battle Hill. 1918: 183 High Street, Cheriton. e Dover 14.10.15. Gunner 59458, RGA. Bombardier 04.07.16, A/Cpl 04.07.16, Cpl 04.07.16. France 15.09.16–29.04.17. Discharged 14.08.17: nephritis. S. d Battle B1966.

Oliver, Harry b Battle A1886, s of Harry, carter (tannery). Jam factory labourer. 4 Clive Villas. Pte RE. S. d Battle 17.03.48.

Oliver, Percy b Battle 08.02.1895, s of Harry, carter (tannery). Domestic gardener. 4 Clive Villas. Pte 8 RSR. S. d Battle A1977.

Oliver, Stanley b Erith 17.07.97, s of H J, baker. 49 High Street. m Dorothy G Matthis, Battle C1922. Pte 14 RSR. S. d Battle A1970.

Oliver, William John b Battle c1893, s of Harry, carter (tannery). Railway clerk. 4 Clive Villas Pte 2 Bn RSR. S. Injured (frostbite) winter 1914–15. d Battle 14.02.1923.

Orford, Charles Edward b Battle 1895, s of Edwin, teacher. 1941: Church Cottage, Marsham, Norfolk. m Gertrude Hannant, Wayland D1920. Children. e 13.09.15. Pte 2610 RAMC, 3/1 Field Ambulance. Illness; discharged 29.05.16. d Norwich 28.06.41.

Osborn, Arthur b Battle A1896, s of Arthur, police constable. East Dean. e Eastbourne 04.09.14. Pte 11 RSR then 14 RSR then G/18493, E Kent Regt. France 07.10.16–04.05.17. Gunshot wound to left leg 09.04.17. Discharged as no longer physically fit 20.11.17: shell shock. d Winchester C1959.

Owen, Herbert b Bowdon, Cheshire Jan 1878, s of John, hatter. Boot, shoe repairer. 49 High Street. m Amelia E Wellstead, Hastings D1924. Child. e Hastings 15.02.16. Gnr 68865, 6 Res Bn, 32 Res Coy (Motor) Machine Gun Corps. France 29.03.18–20.10.18. POW, repatriated 03.12.18. d Hastings A1956.

Pantry, George Edward b Battle 17.07.97, s of Caroline, domestic servant. Farmer. Ashburnham and Battle Workhouse. 1914: Goodwood, Ontario. e Uxbridge, Ontario 27.12.15. CEF 74516.

Parker, Ernest b Battle B1883. Clerk. 39 Hillier Street, Wandsworth. e London 22.05.16. Ex Cape Mounted Rifles. Gunner 85780 RGA. France 04.12.16–28.12.16. Discharged 22.09.19.

Parks, Harry b Battle A1879, s of Richard, hay trusser. Miller's carman. Wattles Wish, 2 Mill Cottages, Whatlington; Fairlight Mill Cottage, Guestling. 1957: 152 Ashburnham Road, Hastings. m Ellen Mary Barton, Battle 22.02.02. Children. e Hastings 18.03.18. Pte 128437 RAMC. No overseas service. Discharged 28.02.19. d Hastings 10.05.57.

Partridge, James b Hatherleigh, Devon 1890, s of William, farmer. Farmer's son. Pepper in Eye Farm. m Edith M Quaife, Battle B1925. Child. d Uckfield A1949.

Pepper, Reginald Arthur b Battle 12.06.94, s of James, baker. Motion picture operator. Mount Street. 1915: 271 Lizzie Street, Winnipeg. e Winnipeg 31.12.15. CEF 700534, 101 Overseas Bn.

Peto, Arthur John b Farncombe C1890, s of Edward, bricklayer. Insurance agent. Starrs Green. m Sarah Jane Dickern, Hastings 08.04.01. Children. Guardsman 18428 Coldstream Guards. Overseas 14.03.17–01.01.18. d Winchester A1959.

Pettitt, Ernest Edward b Fairlight 12.02.92. Cowman on farm. Netherfield Place. m Florence Weller, Battle D1933. Child. Pte 35 Labour Corps.d Battle A1976.

Picknell, James Arthur b Bexhill c1896, s of Albert, painter. Milkman on farm. New Cottages, Battle Hill. 1949: 61 Bedwell Gardens, Hayes. m Dorothy Elizabeth Spicer, Battle A1927. Children. Pte 7 Bn RSR. To France 08.02.15. Discharged 12.03.19. d Hillingdon 03.02.1949.

Pierce, R Pte S/1563 then 240113, 13 RSR. S.

Ponsford, George Henry b Brighton 20.08.96. Market garden labourer. Blackfriars Cottage; 1919: 3 Prospect Cottages, Caldbec Hill. m Mary Bertha Spray, Battle 1922. Children. e Hastings 30.08.15. Rifleman then L/C P16171, 16 KRR. France 26.01.16–19.07.16, 20.10.16–16.04.17, 06.09.17–31.12.17. Acting L/C 26.01.17, then Pte then L/C 04.09.18. Wounded: shell shock 20.06.16–14.04.17, GSW 17.07.16, wounds + shell shock 01.12.17. Discharged as not physically fit 08.02.19. Military police duties, Birmingham late 1918. d Hastings A1953.

Pook, Charles b Battle 09.04.1886, s of Caleb Pook, agricultural labourer, Ironmonger. Virgin's Croft. Later 32 Norman Road, St Leonards; Watch Oak. Then The Croft, Battle. m Lydia Jane Gower, Battle 04.08.13. e Hastings 11.12.15. Served 4 yrs with RSR before war. Active from 21.03.16. Gunner 906163, 336 Bde RFA. Arrived Basra 19.11.17. Bombardier 30.06.18. Acting Cpl 12.09.19. Discharged 31.03.20. d Battle D1973.

Pook, Thomas Charles Jesse b Battle B1889, s of Jesse, warehouseman. Bootshop assistant and clerk. Tanyard Cottages. m Belinda Hobden, Hastings 15.07.12. e Hastings 24.11.16. Pte 98815 RAMC, Acting L/C 24.04.17. Discharged 09.07.19. d Battle C1968.

Potter, Arthur Sidney b Battle A1892, s of David, domestic gardener then gate custodian. e Hastings. Pte S/4/093849 ASC then L/C then Cpl; Sgt 18.05.18. To France 07.07.16. d Battle D1967.

Potter, Albert Edward b Battle c1881, s of David, domestic gardener then gate custodian. Carpenter. Blackhorse Road. 86 Denbigh Street, Pimlico.

Potter, Charles Frederick b Battle 1882, s of David, domestic gardener then gate custodian. Postman. Blackhorse Road. 1916: 94 Flaxton Road, Plumstead. m Ethel May Balderson, Woolwich, 16.01.08. Child. e Woolwich 04.12.15. Gnr 358546 RGA. To France 26.09.17–23.10.18, 07.11.18–19.04.19. Carrickfergus 28.07.19–23.08.19. Discharged 27.09.19. d Hastings C1968.

Potter, David John b Battle c1872, s of David, domestic gardener then gate custodian. Groom (domestic) then policeman. Blackhorse Road. 1911: police station, Hailsham. 1931: 72 Rutland Road, Hove. m Fanny Beatrice, Lewes C1896. Children. d Kingston by Sea 22.03.31.

Potter, Edwin E b Battle c1885, s of David, domestic gardener then gate custodian. Groom (domestic). Blackhorse Road.

Potter, Henry W b Battle c1878, s of David, domestic gardener then gate custodian. Policeman. Blackhorse Road. 1901: police barracks, Devonport. 1911: 7 Rosebery Gardens, Sutton. m Florence Rebecca, Lambeth A1907. Child.

Radford, George Anthony b Peckham 18.10.93, s of Alfred, furniture salesman. Bootshop assistant. Kenward's Yard (lodger with Smales). 1968: 41 Clewer Hill Road, Windsor. Pte 5 RSR. (Own report) wounded and gassed at Cambrai late 1917, also shell-shock. S. d Eastbourne C1973. Name changed to Radford-Twyman.

Ransom, Thomas b Sidley B1893, s of Frederick, bricklayer. Brickmaker. 1911: 9 North Road, Sidley. 1919: 13 Sidley Street, Sidley. m Edith May Carter, Battle A1914. Child. e Bexhill 12.10.14. 534216 then I/1550 2 HC Coy RE (Signals). Driver. Discharged 16.05.19. d Bexhill C1966.

Raper, Godfrey Curzon b Battle D1881, s of William, solicitor. 1951: The Mill House, Roadwater, Somerset. m Stella Hartcup, St Faith's, Norfolk C1921. Children. 2 Lt Horse Trspt ASC; 07.05.15, Major. d Cleeve, Exmoor 09.02.51.

Relf, Charles Henry b Battle 1882, s of Charles, woodman dealer. Wood merchant. Squirrel Cottages. e Hastings 12.02.16. Gunner 640687 then 660077 RFA. To Mesopotamia 22.06.17. d Hastings A1949.

Relf, John William b Brightling 1883. General labourer. Workhouse. e Hastings 20.04.15. Pte 5677, 3 RSR. Discharged as unlikely to make an efficient soldier, 16.06.15. d Battle D1936.

Rice, William Darby b Battle B1875, s of Henry, harness maker. Saddler. 1891: High Street, Uckfield. m Alice Mary Toogood, Uckfield 04.12.02. Children. e Brighton 29.08.14. Pte 7362, 6 Dragoons, then Cpl 01.12.14. Transferred to 37189 S Lancs Regt 30.11.16, Royal Fusiliers 02.05.18. Discharged 20.05.19. d Hailsham A1925.

Rich, Alan b Silverhill 12.03.82. Seaman then miner. 1901: HMS *Vindictive*, Malta. 1923: 3 Beechwood Cottages. m Gertrude Ellen Freeland, Battle A1905. Children. AB 206531 RN. HMS *Royal Arthur, Swiftsure, Basilisk.* North Sea, Atlantic. d Hastings A1929.

Rich, Frederick Charles b Battle A1858. Carpenter. 20 Bruce Road, S Norwood. m Mary Ann Repton, Charlton 26.02.82. e Kingston 25.09.14. Ex 2 Bn Sussex Artillery. Pte G1010, 3 E Surrey Regt. Discharged as no longer physically fit 09.06.16. No overseas service. d Croydon D1916.

Richardson, Ernest Dudley b Bournemouth A1876, s of George, wine merchant. Medic at workhouse. 1911: Camberwell. 1918: Cressex Lodge, St Leonards. Later Bexhill, St Leonards. m Elizabeth M G van Sandau, Kensington C1899; Margaret Emily Thomas, Hastings B1958. e Aug 1916. Capt RAMC. Invalided out 1918. LMSSA Lond. d St Leonards, 23.06.1964.

Richardson, William b Battle 20.03.1866, s of Charles, harness maker. Baker. 1939: 42 Mayfield Avenue, Dover. e Hastings 25.11.85 and 03.12.14. Gunner 51907 RA, temp A/Bdr (reverted at own request "not to escape trial by court martial" (29.04.89). Gibraltar 03.03.86–23.11.86. Discharged 24.01.07. d Dover 12.04.39.

Rideout, Albert George b Shaftesbury A1876, s of Isaac, woodman. Dean's coachman. 87 High Street. m Emma Maude Cheshire, Bromley A1898. Children. Sgt (Medal card says Pte) 18111 Dorsetshire Regt. d Salisbury

D1961.

Rose, J L/C Aust Army Medical Corps. France. Official records appear to have no information on this man. Source: Netherfield List.

Rose, Samuel b Sturminster Newton B1890, s of John, railway signalman. Gypsum miner. Shooting Box, Netherfield Place. m Emily Harriet Whiteman, Netherfield 04.11.03. Children. e Hastings 28.11.15. Pte G/24914, 10 Royal W Kent. To France 18.06.17. Also Italy.

Rose, Sydney Roland b Brightling B1895, s of John, farmer. 1911: Homestead Farm, Brightling. m Bessie W Tozer, Battle D1924. Children. Sgt 2119, 12 RSR. Belgium. MM 04.06.17. d Battle B1967.

Rose, Thomas Whateley b Westminster c1877, s of Frederick, partner in Broadwood, piano manufacturer. Ex-clerk to Raper. Solicitor. 1920: Main Street, Katoomba, NSW. 2Lt then Lt then Capt 5 Bn RSR. MC 27.11.16. [citation] MBE (Military) Italian Silver Medal for Valour. Ment in desps in Italy 08.06.18. Returned from Australia to enlist 1914. Died Sydney 20.12.27.

Rushman, Harry Charles b Warbleton 27.09.97, s of Harry, cowman on farm. Gypsum labourer. Shooting Box, Netherfield Place. m Sybil M J Pullen, Isle of Wight D1937. Child. e Hastings 03.11.15.Pte 136942, RE. Acting L/C then L/C, reverted to Pte (neglect of duty) 14.05.18. Discharged 17.07.19. d Horsham D1973.

Salusbury, Roger Wingfield b Llangibby, Mon 1890, s of Folliott, Rector. Dairy farmer. King's Well Farm. 1964: Wingfield, Earl's Colne, Essex. Lt RE. d Earl's Colne 09.02.64.

Saunders, Albert b Netherfield 1894, s of Henry, general labourer. Gypsum labourer. Netherfield Road. Pte 2211, 12 RSR. Wounded on Somme front 09.05.18. Died in industrial accident on railway at mine, Oct 1951.

Saunders, Arthur b Battle 1892, s of Henry, agricultural labourer. New Council Cottages, Netherfield Hill. Netherfield Toll. Later French's Farm. Bombardier RGA. MM.

Saunders, Frederick J b Battle D1889, s of Henry, agricultural labourer. Carter then farmer. New Council Cottages, Netherfield Hill. 1914: 2a Grove Villas, Horsell Moor, Woking. 1919: Southwick. m Edith Oliver, Battle D1919. Child. e 03.10.07. Bugler, drummer. Ireland 1908. Pte 8829, 2 Bn RSR. Wounded and disabled by bullet through right elbow 30.10.14. 30.04.15 unfit for active service. Tfr to Labour Corps 07.12.17: Pte 490533, home duties only. d Battle B1965.

Saunders, Jim b Netherfield 11.08.97, s of Robert, gypsum burner. Netherfield Hill. m Kathleen D Jenner, Battle D1924. Pte 11 RSR. Wounded on Somme 16.09.16. d Hastings C1990.

Saunders, Richard b Netherfield 1886, s of Henry, gypsum mine labourer. Soldier. French's Farm, Mountfield. Then Ivyland Green. 1919: 28 Gordon Road, Aldershot. e Hastings 03.02.05. Pte L8174, 1/7 RSR, L/C 02.03.10, Cpl 03.04.12. Put on reserve 02.02.14; mobilised 06.04.14. L/Sgt 23.05.16, A/Sgt 15.06.16, Sgt 18.09.16, A/CQMS 0309.16; reverted to Sgt 26.10.16 after incorrect return. Malta 27.09.05–01.04.06, Crete 02.04.06–18.03.07. France 21.08.14–28.01.18. Wounded (shell?, thigh and foot) 10.09.14, slight 17.08.16. 1918: varicose, both legs. Discharged 02.03.19.

Saunders, William b Netherfield 1876, s of Thomas, gypsum miner. Bricklayer's labourer. 3 St John's Cottages, Netherfield Road. e Hastings 10.01.16. Pte Royal Fusiliers, then East Kent Regiment 04.09.16, then Royal Defence Corps 49414, 17.08.17. Demobilised 13.09.19. d Battle D1974.

Saunders, William b Battle D1892, s of Henry, agricultural labourer. General labourer. New Council Cottages, Netherfield Hill. Bugler. L/C 8 Bn RSR 2307. Appeal for mags 04.09.15. Badly wounded badly wounded in right shoulder 18 Aug 1917. S.

Saxby, Robert Frederick b Battle c1885, s of John (own means). Coal borer (1911). Caldbec Hill. 1911: Bobbing, by Sittingbourne. 1918: Cross Keys, Marlow. 1945: The Stores, Hambleden, Buckinghamshire. m Mary Barksfield, Wycombe 01.01.17. Child. e St Leonards 14.06.15. 2048, later 534662 RE: A/Cpl then Cpl RE. 495 Kent Field Co. France 20.01.18–20.04.18; Egypt? Demobilised 02.02.19. S. d Wycombe 12.01.45.

Saxby, Thomas Fred b Battle c1874, s of John (carpenter, then own means). Motor driver. Level Road 1891. 1911: 153 Station Road, Portsmouth. 1916: 8 King Edward's Crescent, North End, Portsmouth. m Jennie Martha Glazier Buss, Battle 25.01.97. Children. e Portsmouth 23.06.16. M2/191686 ASC. Pte, unpaid L/C 12.09.16-24.02.17. Embarked Devonport 13.03.17, arrived Margil (Basra) 22.05.17. In field from 10.09.17. Hospital at Amara 30.09.18. Discharged 27.04.19. d Horndean 05.02.54.

Schaper, Reginald Henry b Battle 14.08.89, s of Ann, laundress. RN, sailor. 1911: HMS *Triumph*, Med. AB RN 235398. Joined by 1905. S. Recorded as leaving Liverpool for USA 15.02.13. Likely to have emigrated there after 1918 and to have died there 1964.

Schlienger, Albert Victor b St Pancras C1887, s of Victor, wool warehouseman. Farmer. 1911: Burnt Chimney Farm. 1916: Bildeston Manor, Suffolk. m Agnes Ruby Martin, 28.09.16. Child. e Sudbury, Suffolk 25.11.15. Pte 53667, 58 Machine Gun Corps. France 13.01.17–10.02.19. Discharged 10.02.19. d Hackney 18.01.51.

Schnorr, Alfred James b Battle 1885, s of John, domestic coachman. Grocer's assistant. 1915: insurance agent. Croft Cottage, Whatlington Road. 1960: 88 High Street. m Sally Crowhurst, Netherfield 18.10.09. Child. e Hastings 06.06.15. Pte Pay Corps. No overseas service. Took over Pilgrim's Rest. d Battle 25.10.60.

Scotton, Harold Douglas b Claybrooke, Leics 1891, s of William, farmer. Netherfield. m Helen E Ayres, Thanet, D1926. Cadet, RAF. d Canterbury C1963.

Sellens, Arthur b Battle c1888, s of Charles, farm bailiff. Domestic gardener, Spital Hill. 1959: 12 Waldegrave Street, Hastings. m Ellen Barrett,

Hastings D1912. Pte 5 RSR. S. d Hastings 04.07.59.

Sellens, Harry Robert b Battle c1884, s of Charles, farm bailiff. General labourer (jam factory). Spital Hill. m Lilian Emma Pont, Battle D1932. Pte G/2079, 8 RSR. To France 24.07.15. S. d Stepney 22.03.1938.

Selmes, Stephen Edward b Battle A1884, s of Stephen, bricklayer. Navvy. 1919: 46 Duke Street, Silverhill. 1945: Sampson's Farm, Crowhurst. e Hastings 10.08.14. Ex RSR Reserve. Pte 2247 RSR Reserve. Transferred to 1 Garrison Bn East Kent Regt 15.07.16, 230418 Labour Corps 30.07.17. France 29.11.14–16.02.15. Discharged 21.02.19. d Hastings 10.06.44.

Seward, William Thomas b Whitestone, Devon 1875, s of Tom, cattle man on farm. Farmer. 1893: Underdown, Upottery. 1911: Stream Farm. 1915: Maudlin Farm, Steyning. 1919: Warren's Farm Upottery. e Brighton 01.10.15. Gunner 900895, 1/1 HC Bde RFA. India 08.02.16–14.05.16, Mesopotamia 22.05.16–09.10.18. Discharged 15.03.19. d Exeter 04.10.66.

Sheather, Edward Henry b St Leonards c1889 **OR George William** b St Leonards c1892, ss of George, farmer. Working on farm. Horsman's farm. Edward m Mary C Bishop, Battle, D1918. d Hastings A1960. G died Battle D1969.

Sheppard, Frederic Charles b Battle c1882, s of Charles, solicitor. Solicitor. 1 St Mary's Villas. Later Loxbeech. m Edith Gladys Dickins, Warwick 1906. e Jan 1918. Lt RNAS. d Hastings A1960.

Shipp, Arthur Jack b Battle C1888, s of Arthur, insurance agent. Grocer's porter. Virgin's Croft. 1919: 12 New Road, Eastbourne. m Nancy Standen, Eastbourne 29.10.13. Child. e Eastbourne 23.07.07. Gunner 47063, 4 Bde RFA. A/Bdr 16.08.11, Bdr 14.04.13, Cpl 03.09.15.Reverted Bdr 09.03.16, A/Cpl 17.10.17, A/Sgt 25.11.17, Sgt 25.11.17. Captured 21.03.18. Discharged 25.03.19.

Sitch, Albert James b Ingatestone B1885, s of Edward, domestic gardener. Chauffeur. Netherfield Court. m Alice Medcalf, Tendring C1914. Children. Pte ASC MT. Salonica 1915. d Battle C1967.

Skilton, Harry b Battle 03.03.97, s of Caleb, UDC roadman. 8 Jubilee Cottages. Pte 905831 RFA. S. d Hailsham A1972.

Smale, Arthur Overy b Battle A1891, s of Thomas, rural letter carrier. 5 Market Green. Pte L/2431, 21 Lancers. Served in India. S. d Hastings A1968.

Smale, Charles E H b Sutton, Surrey 1878, s of Thomas, rural letter carrier. Chauffeur. 1 Kenwards Yard. 2 Scots Guards. Served in France. d West Ham B1931.

Smale, Frank William b Battle 01.09.82, s of Thomas, postman. Seaman. 1911: Royal Navy Barracks, Portsmouth. 198906 RN PO First Class. Joined in or before 1898. S. d Hastings D1968.

Smale, Herbert George b Battle c1894, s of Thomas, rural letter carrier. Stable groom at Burton's. Old Almonry Farm. m Edith Chapman, Cranbrook C1918. Children. Tpr then L/C 1631, 1 Sx Yeomanry, then L/Sgt RSR. To Balkans 07.10.15. Discharged 19.02.19. S. d Hastings A1962.

Smale, John Reginald Pocock b Battle B1898, s of Thomas, rural letter carrier. Kenwards Yard. 1956: 96 Dale View, Hove. m Edith Highwood, Battle C1921. Children. Gunner 374710 RGA, later Driver RE. Discharged 22.01.19. d Brighton 09.05.56.

Smale, Thomas A b Battle 1886, s of Thomas, rural letter carrier. Chauffeur. 5 Market Green. 1919: Newnham Hill, Henley on Thames. m Ethel Beatrice Herwood, Henley on Thames A1918. e Portsmouth 08.08.14. Motor driver MT/3206 ASC. In France 12.08.14–20.01.18, 13.02.18–15.03.19. Discharged 18.04.19. S. d Brighton D1964.

Smissen, Edwin b Mountfield 1895, s of Franklin, farmer. Darwell Road, Netherfield. 1955: Peter Pan, North Trade Road. m Margaret Harrison, Battle B1928. Children. Pte 1 Garrison Seaforth Highlanders. France, Salonica. d Battle 01.04.55.

Smissen, Ernest b Mountfield 26.10.96, s of Franklin, farmer. Darwell Road, Netherfield. Pte AVC, ASC. d Battle A1981.

Smith, George Graham b Netherfield 17.07.00, steps of George Wood. Bricklayer's labourer. Marley Cottages. Pte 14 RSR. d Battle D1974.

Smith, Henry Tilden b Netherfield D1879, s of Tilden Smith, farmer. Carter. Stream Cottage, Netherfield. m Harriet Elizabeth Schnorr, Battle 18.10.05. Children. e Hastings 12.12.15. Pte 2284 Household Battalion. Then 2296 Coldstream Guards 12.02.18; then 8095 Guards Machine Gun Regt 14.06.18. France 06.05.17–18.10.17, 06.10.18–15.03.19. Gunshot wound in left arm 09.10.17. Discharged 19.04.19. d Hastings B1959.

Smith, Sidney C b Battle 1897, s of William, fishmonger hawker. Fish hawker. Gate Farm Cottage. e Codford S Mary, Wilts 13.12.15. Pte 14 RSR then Pte 28231, 1 East Surrey 20.09.16. In France 1916/17. GSW wrist 01.11.16, face 05.05.17. Discharged as physically unfit 11.06.17. S.

Sperling, Eric Stephen Astle b Earls Court 1878, s of Henry, landowner, JP. Stockbroker. Netherfield Court. Also 28 Clarges Street, W1. 1962: 16 The Avenue, Summersdale, Chichester. m Olive Grace Sassoon. Child. 2 Lt 33 London Regiment then Lt 4 Gloucestershire. d Chichester 07.12.62.

Spray, Charles b Battle 1892, s of William, farm labourer. Agricultural labourer/stockman. Then baker with Pepper & King. Caldbec Hill; Watch Oak; The Level, Mount Street.' Later 1 Stone Cottage, Watch Oak.. e Hastings 21.01.16. Gunner 35967 Royal Fusiliers, Machine Gun Coy. Wounded (gas) 05.08.18. MM 25.04.1918. A/LC 1918. To Rhine Army 23.04.19. Overstayed leave June 1919 and returned to ranks. Discharged 10.11.19. d Battle C1923.

Spray, Frank Charles b Battle 21.03.99, s of Edward, carpenter. Motor mechanic. Netherfield Stream. m Gladys Vaughan, Tenterden A1928. Children. RNAS F28055. d Battle D1974.

Spray, Henry b Battle C1889, s of William, farm labourer. Baker (nights). Whatlington Road. Moved away; married and died in Middlesex. Pte 4 Middx. Wounded at Loos. S. d S Middx D1962.

Spray, James b Battle B1878, s of James, agricultural labourer. Bricklayer, gypsum mine. Netherfield Road. Later 10 Virgin's Croft. m Bertha Smith, Battle B1899. Children. e Eastbourne 18.10.15. Sapper 4233 later 536218, RE. France 25.09.17–14.04.19. Discharged 05.05.19. d Battle D1950.

Spray, William Caleb b Battle 26.07.87, s of William, farm labourer. Groom, gardener. Whatlington Road. RN 235034. d Battle 20.03.67.

Stapley, Frederick Charles b Battle 23.08.95, s of Frederick, journeyman baker then railway shunter. Checker. Crowhurst. 1911: 1 Quarry Cottages, Sevenoaks. e Winnipeg 11.09.15. CEF 132421.

Stokes, Kenneth Henry b Highbury D1883, s of Henry, GP. Physician/surgeon at workhouse. 16 Parkhurst Road, Bexhill. 1921: The Laurels, Sutherland Avenue, Bexhill. m Mary Fisher, Barrow in Furness B1911. Children. e Aug 1916. Lt then Capt RAMC. To India 24.09.16, France Sept 1917. d Battle 30.12.1962.

Suggitt, Robert b Hastings A1878, s of Robert, carpenter. Bricklayer. Phillips Buildings, Mount Street; 1 Holts Yard. m Elizabeth Soan, Hastings 19.04.99. Children. e Eastbourne 14.06.08. Pte RSR 15.01.01, in S African war; medals. St Helena 15.06.02–11.09.12. Pte 8487, 3 RSR, L/C 18.05.14. France 29.11.14–05.01.15, 25.11.15–21.09.18. Wounded 21.09.18: gunshot to left thigh. Discharged 07.03.19. d Hastings D1962.

Thomas, Charles Edward b Battle c1876, s of John, builder. Bricklayer. Virgins Croft. m Ellen Crowhurst, Battle B1895. CSM RSR. DCM 1918. S. d Battle 12.11.1953.

Thomas, Charles John Albert b Battle B1888, s of Nelson, farm labourer. Farm labourer. Pont's Farm, Burwash. e 20.04.07. Ex-volunteer RGA. Pte RSR. India 05.08.14–03.08.16. Transferred as Pte 31571 to 7 Gloucestershire Regt. Mesopotamia 4.08.16–01.01.19. Discharged 31.03.20. d Hammersmith A1956.

Thomas, John b Battle c1890, s of John, builder. Carpenter. The Briars, Caldbec Hill. Pte 35 Coy RAMC. S.

Thomas, James Dennis Nelson b Battle D1886, s of Nelson, publican. Labourer. e 03.09.14. Pte 2280, 8 RSR. Discharged as not likely to become efficient soldier 21.10.14 (goitre). d Winchester D1964.

Thompson, Samuel Arnold b Ore c1896, s of George, army pensioner, gardener. Domestic gardener, Deanery. Market Green. Cpl 5 RSR (prom 04.04.15) Commissioned 2 Lt 11.12.15. S.

Thornhill, William Upton b Maidstone 1883, s of James, schoolmaster. Journalist. 1915: 22 Colehill Gardens, Fulham. m Ida Annie Rayner, Battle C1910. Child. e Wimbledon 12.12.15. Pte 765743, 2/28 London Regt (Artists Rifles). Transferred to Honourable Artillery Coy, Tower of London 09.10.17.To USA on training duty Nov 1917. Discharged 17.02.19. d Hastings D1958.

Ticehurst, Arthur Cecil b Battle A1880, s of Frederick, RDC Clerk etc. Assistant electrical engineer. Langton House, High Street. m Dorothy Jerrard Thurman, Hove A1918. Maj 2 HC Field Coy RE. France Dec 1914. Wounded July 1915, home 5 days. MC Jan 1917. d Battle 04.01.68.

Ticehurst, Frederic Gorham b Battle 02.02.80, s of Frederick, Clerk to Battle Union etc. Electrician.81 High Street. e Regina, Saskatchewan 27.12.14. CEF 426166. Previously Territorial. Spr 34036, RE. To France 02.08.15. CEF records give birthdate as 02.02.81 but birthplace and next of kin are as above.

Ticehurst, John William b Battle C1885, s of Frederick, RDC Clerk etc. Mechanical engineer. Langton House, High Street. m Muriel A Kilby, Maidenhead B1916. Child. Maj RE prom Jul 1917. d Wycombe A1964.

Tickner, Sydney Walter b Bromley 1895, s of George, farm bailiff. Grocer's apprentice, later newsagent. 1911: Swaffenden Cottages, Cranbrook. m Gladys Sargent, Battle, A1926. Child. Pte L/7975, Lancers then D/19945 Royal Dragoons. France 15.06.15. d Robertsbridge 31.05.35.

Turner, Albert Edward b Hastings A1891, s of Edward, odd man at hotel. General dealer's assistant; upholsterer. Caldbec Hill; Park Lane. Driver ASC. S. d Hastings 27.06.1926.

Turner, Charles Edward b Battle c1894, s of Robert, bricklayer. Domestic gardener. Thorpe's Plot; Spital Hill. m May W Nelson, Battle D1922. Child. Pte. d Battle 22.09.1981.

Turner, Sidney Ernest b Loose, Kent 17.09.95, s of William, roadman: daughter at Battle B1922. d Battle D 1983.

Turner, Thomas J b Hastings C1889, s of Edward, odd man at hotel. 20 Mount Street. Caldbec Hill. m Clarice Blanche Whitting, Faringdon A1919. Child. Driver ASC. S. d Battle C1952.

Veness, George b Battle D1873. Labourer.17 Salisbury Road, Bexhill. m Clara Wait, Battle 04.02.05. Children. Driver 905349 RFA. India, Mesopotamia 13.10.17–17.07.18. Discharged 01.03.19.

Vidler, Major Frank b Battle 28.10.89, s of Tom, house painter. House painter. 6 Walden Terrace, Lower Lake. m Annie Winchester, Battle 19.07.14. Children. e Hastings 11.12.15. Gunner 74064, RGA. To France 06.08.16. Wounded in chest late April 1917; sent home. Discharged 11.12.19. Later Subscriptions Sec, Battle British Legion. d Hastings B1971.

Vidler, Tom b Battle C1885, s of Tom, house painter. House painter. 4 High Street. m Florence Foord, Hastings C1923. Sapper 534671, 2 HC Field Coy RE; L/C Oct 1917. d Battle A1927.

Vine, Carlos Frederick b Sedlescombe B1891, s of George, carter with UDC. 1915: 5 Chapel Cottages. 1919: 2 Newbery's Cottages. m(1) Annie Carter, Battle, 25.12.16. Children. m(2) Emily Spray, Battle, 23.03.18. e 09.12.15. ASC M/286750. Discharged 12.09.19. d Hastings A1965.

Vitler, Frederick b Bexhill 1879, s of James, agricultural labourer. Housekeeper for borough council. 20 Preston Road, Sidley. m Margaret Ann Dolman, Battle B1907. Children. Pte 5 RSR. d Battle A1959.

Wait, Joseph b Battle B1881, s of William, joiner. Tanner's labourer. Park's Yard. Lower Lake. m Elizabeth Beale Bodle, Battle C1900. Children. Pte 2009 then 315158, 14 RSR. To France 18.02.15. Demobilised 24.02.19. S.

Wait, Leonard b Battle D1887, s of William, joiner. Groom. Park's Yard.

Lower Lake. Later Compass Cottage, Ashburnham. m Beatrice Douch, Battle A1928. e Hastings 24.08.14. Pte G187, 7 RSR. France 31.05.15–13.03.19. Discharged 10.04.19. d Battle 22.02.1967.

Wait, Pelham b Battle C1890, s of William, joiner. Sub-postman. Park's Yard. m Christina Rose Wood, Battle A1922 Battle. Children. RE. S. d Battle 24.08.1970.

Wait, Percy b Battle B1883, s of William, joiner. Tanyard assistant. c/o Mr Keep, High Street. 1937: 39 Wellington Gardens. m Ellen Crouch, Battle B1904. Pte 13 RSR L/C Wounded 22.09.17, right arm and chin. To England 01.10.17, VAD hospital Walmer. S. d Battle 11.04.1937. (gunpowder for fireworks, explosion).

Warren, Basil Abbotts b Wooburn, Buckinghamshire C1880. Bank clerk. 9 St Mary's Villas, then 36 Dartmouth Road London N6. 1936: Hawkersbury, Tilsmore Road, Heathfield. e Hastings 20.10.16. Non Combatant Corps. Exempted from combatant service on conscientious grounds. Discharged 07.05.19. d Heathfield 05.12.36.

Watts, Bernhard Oscar b Icomb, Glos. C1889, s of Owen, farmer. Grocer's assistant. Upper Almonry Farm. 1911: Canterbury. 1964: 29 Winchester Road, Walton on Thames. m Kate Holmes, Wandsworth, B1928. e Aug 1914. 2 Lt. Wireless Op RFC. S. Mentioned in despatches. Commissioned RFC Jan 1917. d Walton on Thames 04.06.1964.

Webster, Sir Augustus Frederick Walpole Edward b 10.02.1864. Landowner, soldier. Powdermill House. m Mabel Crossley 12.11.95. Grenadier Guards 1884–94; Lt then Capt. General Staff in WW1. Eton. d Hove 13.08.1923.

Welsford, Aleck E Meadows b St Olave Southwark C1897, s of Arthur Gerald Welsford, medic. Sandhurst Soldier. Hemingfold House. 2 Lt May 1917 then Capt Wilts Regt. To France 29.05.17. d Hastings 19.08.24.

Welsford, Arthur Gerald b USA 1865. Medic. Hemingfold House. m Frances Adelaide Cross, Battle D1892. Temp Lt 14.05.15, Capt RAMC. France 19.04.15. 1916 Egypt. d Rome 20.04.31. Author, contributor to medical press. 1891: asst head Cleveland St Asylum, London.

Wenham, Henry Albert b Lewes A1872. Bricklayer's labourer. 1911: Blackfriars Cottage. m Ada Alice Bowers, Battle D1902. Children. Pte 3172 Somerset Light Inf. Gibraltar 10.11.91–18.12.93. E Indies 19.12.93–14.02.99. To Reserve 17.02.99; recalled 09.10.99. S Africa 14.11.99–23.06.00, 08.01.01–06.09.02; medals. Cape, Transvaal, Tugela Heights, relief of Ladysmith. Disch 12.06.03. Re-enlisted 04.07.03. Disch 03.07.07. Pte RE 598810: engagements unclear. Re-enlisted Whitehall 22.05.19 as Pte 3876 RE: Cpl 22.05.19, A/Sgt 12.08.19. France 15.06.19–26.01.20. Discharged 19.05.20. d Surrey Mid-E C1956.

West, Albert b Battle 22.09.75, s of Robert, shoemaker. Farmer. Ticehurst Court, Mount Street. e Halifax, Nova Scotia 26.11.14.3 yr + 87 days in East Kent Regt; 4 yrs + 2 mo in RSR. CEF 67533. May have emigrated from Southampton to New York 9.02.13.

Whibley, Robert b Sedlescombe 1889, s of Walter, agricultural labourer.

Cpl SD 1921, 12 RSR. Wounded Oct 16, Schwaben Redoubt; Nov 17, Cambrai. d Hastings A1957.

Whibley, William Fred b Battle 1897. Stockman. Little Homestead Farm, Netherfield. e Hastings 09.02.16. Pte 33087, 36 Royal Fusiliers. Discharged on medical grounds. 23.06.16. Probably d Chatham D1983.

Whistler, Fuller b Hollington C1859, s of Rose, clergyman. Soldier. Caldbec Hill. m Gwenllian Robinson, India. Children. Maj HLI. Lt 08.09.92, Capt 03.02.92. Retired pay 1908. On general staff. Active service in France 28 Bde First Army Dec 1914 then commander of small arms training at Hythe. Sutton Valence School. d 25 Dorset Sq 16.03.1922.

Whistler, Hugh b Mablethorpe 28.09.1889, s of Fuller, soldier. Soldier. m Margaret Joan Ashton, 02.10.1925. Children. 2 Lt Indian Army Reserve Officers. Aldenham School. Ornithologist, author. Later JP. d Battle 07.07.1943. FZS and MBOV.

Whistler, Webster William b Battle 1870, s of Rose, Clergyman. Clergyman. Essex, Norfolk, Sussex. Finally Elsted. 1939: 18 West Drive, Brighton. m Lilian Meade, St Neots B1898. Children. E Anglian Territorial Force. 2nd Class Army Chaplain 04.08.14–1919; 1st Class 1919. TD. d Brighton 18.11.39.

White, Herbert Percy b Battle 30.10.1888, s of Mark, farmer. Kenwards Yard. 1916: 1 Parks Bldgs, High Street. m Ida Emma Jones, Canada April 1917. e Hamilton, Ontario 03.05.16. Pte, 86 Machine Gun Bn, CEF.

White, Reginald Arthur Horace b Battle 29.07.1899, grands of Henry, agricultural labourer. Blacksmith's mate. Caldbec Hill; Great Wood Cottage. e 17.03.17. Pte Labour Corps. Served at Ripon. Discharged as physically unfit 26.01.18. d Brighton B1982.

White, Reginald Walter Wallace b Battle 1896, s of Walter, jobbing gardener. Solicitor's clerk. Park Dale. 1966: 8 Effingham Road, Lee, SE. m Hylda Susie Cole, Wandsworth C1926. Child. e 26.04.17. Pte 20177 Labour Corps. d Lewisham 30.09.1966.

Whiteman, Charles Edwin b Brightling 1896, s of George, farmer. Working on farm. Netherfield Place Farm. e Hastings 30.07.15. Pte, G/9313, 3 Royal West Kent. France 08.12.15–11.03.16; returned 1916, wounded (gunshot) to hand 1918. Discharged before end of war. d S W Surrey B1966.

Whiteman, Stanley b Brightling 1895, s of George, farmer. Working on farm. Newlands Farm, Dallington. m Marguerite M Dench, Battle C1945. Pte 5/1980, 202412, L12916, 5 RSR. France, Italy.

Whitton, Harry Percival L b Willesden D1896. High Street. m Winifred Jay, Battle, B1923. Children. Pte 27435, East Surrey Regt.

Willsher, Henry Robert b Battle 10.04.98, s of Hugh, grocer. Grocer's assistant. 8 Lower Lake. 1916: High Street, Tenterden. m Lillie Care, Tenterden B1929. Child. Driver MT/284461, ASC. L/C 06.04.19. Discharged 01.12.19. d Ashford B1976.

Wilmshurst, George b Battle B1886, s of Stephen. Labourer. 1915: Bay Villas, Mount Pleasant, Hildenborough. m Emma Ponsford, Hildenborough

01.05.15. Child. e Maidstone 18.02.02. Pte 1 Royal W Kent Regt. Malta 06.04.04–01.06.05, France 14.08.14–19.02.15, 12.05.15–31.12.15. Discharged (termination) 31.12.15. Re-enlisted Maidstone 21.11.16. France 06.01.17–08.17. S. DCM 1918.

Wilmshurst, James b Battle A1893, s of James, railway platelayer. Butcher. Thorpe's Cottages; Station Yard. m Alice M Carlton, Hastings B1921. Children. e St Leonards 28.09.14. Gunner 905422, 2 HC Bde RFA. Bdr 14.05.16, reverted at own request 06.10.16. India (Peshawar) 23.05.16–18.11.19. Disch 16.12.19. Injured at No 4 Artillery Training School, High Wycombe, March 1916; 20% disabled. S. d Battle 06.09.1932.

Winchester, James b Penhurst 1875, s of Mark, agricultural labourer. Gypsum labourer. 2 Beechwood Cottages. m Sarah Wilson Pack, Battle C1900. Children. Sapper RE. France. d Battle C1947.

Woodhams, James Percy b Hastings A1883, s of James Woodhams, auctioneer. Auctioneer. 29 High Street. 1953: 27 High Street. m Muriel Lavinia Abbott, Battle A1910. Child. 2 Lt 8 RSR then Capt 5 RSR. To France 09.17. Wounded Mar/Apr 1918. Later Chairman, Battle, British Legion; JP. d Hastings 31.05.53.

Wrenn, Frederick James b Battle 01.01.84, s of Walter, auxiliary postman. Coachman (domestic). 2 High Street. Parks Yard. 1919: 67 High Street. m Frances Hayward, Battle, D1913. Child. e St Leonards 31.05.15. Driver, L/C 534604, 3/2 HC Field Coy RE. To Greece October 1917. Discharged 05.05.19. S. Hastings C1972.

Young, Reginald Harry b Battle D1895, s of William, carpenter. Ironmonger's shop assistant. 10 St Mary's Terrace. e Hastings 13.01.15. Pte 13 RSR, to Pte 353226 ASC MT 16.11.17. No foreign service. Discharged 17.12.19 unfit physically – 100% disabled with dysentery. S. d Hastings D1983.

Young, William Harry b Bewdley 1874, s of station master. Carpenter. Spital Hill. m Martha Matilda Turner, Battle C1894. Children. Sgt London Scottish. d Battle 26.07.1944.

Analysis of Survivals

Date of birth

Pre 1870: 8	1870–74: 23	1875–79: 50	1880–84: 54
1885–89: 77	1890–94: 86	1895–99: 81	1900– : 7
Unknown: 4	**TOTAL: 393**		

Battle residence (where known)

Hastings Road includes all premises from the Powdermill junction to the Black Horse area, excluding St Mary's Terrace and Villas. High Street includes Watch Oak and the lower end of Netherfield Lane.

Caldbec Hill: 15	High Street + yards: 53	Upper/Lower Lake: 27
Hastings Road: 45	Whatlington Road etc: 11	Marley Lane etc: 3
Netherfield: 90	Mount St: 28	St Mary's: 18
Farms etc: 42	North Trade Road: 7	**TOTAL: 333**

Regiment (i. e. final regiment, including attachment) *includes all branches

Army Ordnance Corps	2	New Zealand forces	1
Army Pay Corps	1	Non-Combatant Corps	1
Army Service Corps	30	Northants	2
Army Veterinary Corps	5	Notts + Derbys	1
Australian forces	4	RAF*	6
Bedfordshire	2	Rifle Brigade	1
Canadian forces	13	Royal Army Medical Corps	13
Chaplaincy	1	Royal Artillery*	51
Coldstream Guards	1	Royal Defence Corps	1
Dorset	1	Royal Dragoons	1
Dragoon Guards		Royal Engineers	37
Dublin Fusiliers	1	Royal Fusiliers	6
Durham Light Infantry	1	Royal Highlanders	1

Duke of Cornwall's Light Inf'ry	1
East Kent (The Buffs)	6
East Surrey	3
Gloucesters	2
Grenadier Guards	2
Hampshire	1
Highland Light Infantry	1
Hussars	2
Indian Army	1
Inns of Court OTC	1
King's Afghan Rifles	1
King's Liverpool	1
King's Royal Rifle Corps	2
Labour Corps	12
Lancers	3
London Scottish	1
Machine Gun Corps*	5
Middlesex	7
Military Mounted Police	1
Royal Horse Guards	1
Royal Irish Fusiliers	2
Royal Navy*	13
Royal Scots Guards	1
Royal Sussex	95
Royal West Kent	7
Royal West Surrey	4
Seaforth Highlanders	1
South Staffs	1
Suffolk	1
Surrey Yeomanry	1
Tank Corps	3
VAD	2
Welsh	1
Wiltshire	1
Worcestershire	1
Unknown	22
TOTAL	**393**

Index

NB vpp.nIic.s v anI B list th. nam.s anI, bri.fly, th. p.rsonal I.tails of thos. who s.rv.I. Information giv.n th.r. is from th. main t.xt.